PRACTICE
YOUR ENGLISH

PRACTIQUE
SU INGLES

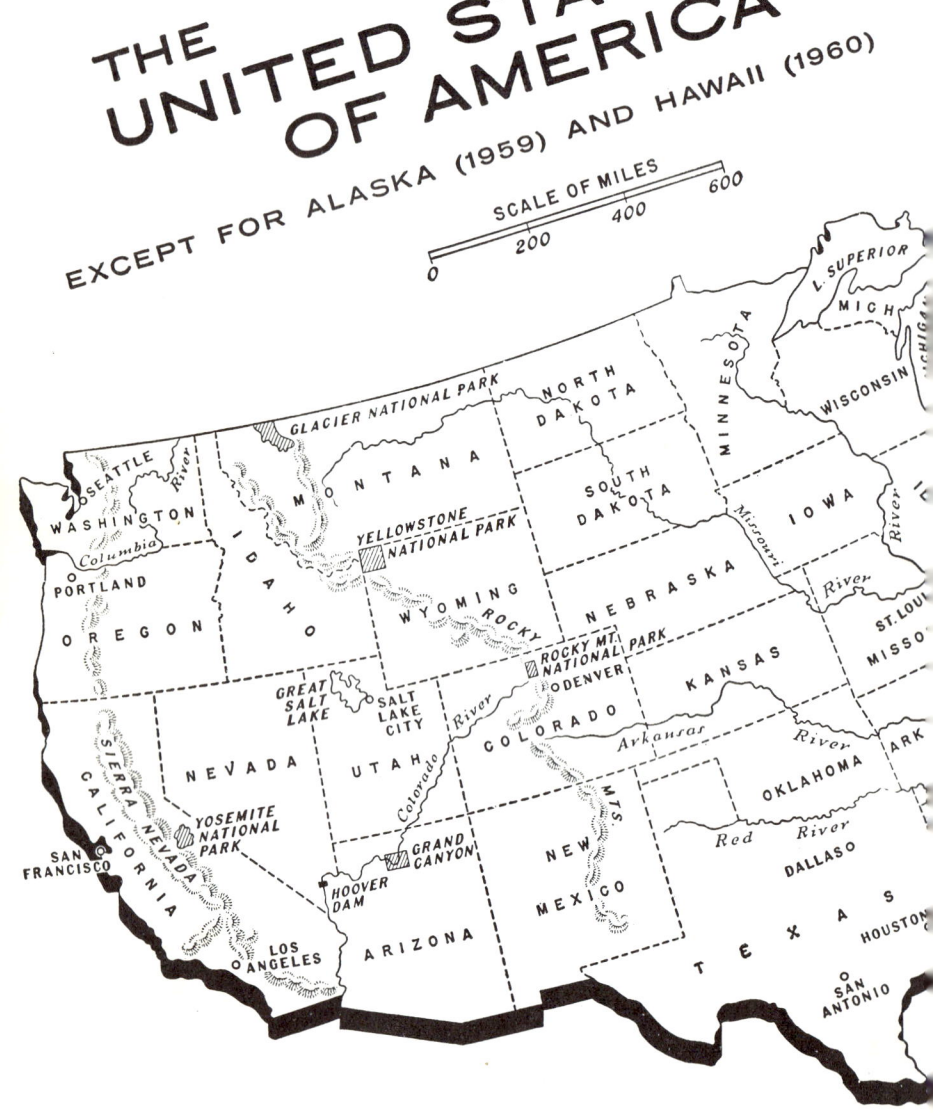

THE UNITED STATES OF AMERICA

EXCEPT FOR ALASKA (1959) AND HAWAII (1960)

SCALE OF MILES
0 200 400 600

SECTION OF THE EASTERN SEABOARD

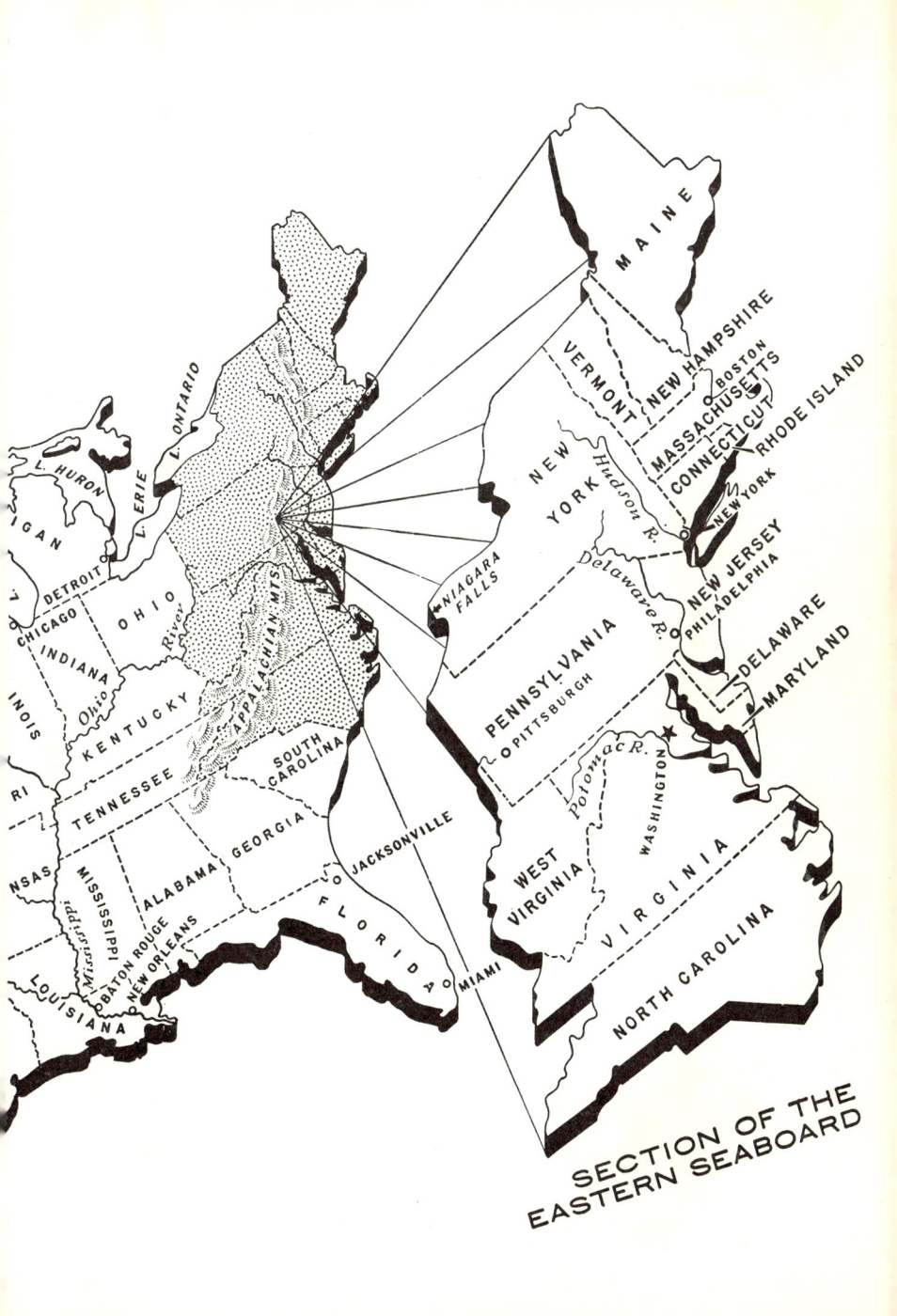

PRACTICE YOUR ENGLISH

AUDREY L. WRIGHT

AMERICAN BOOK COMPANY

PRACTIQUE
SU INGLES

Second Edition

New York

COPYRIGHT © 1960 BY AMERICAN BOOK COMPANY UNDER
UNIVERSAL COPYRIGHT CONVENTION,
INTERNATIONAL COPYRIGHT CONVENTION, and
PAN-AMERICAN COPYRIGHT CONVENTIONS

Maps and diagrams by L. Robert Tschirky

Wright: *Practice Your English*, Practique Su Inglés.

Made in the United States of America. Certain portions of this work copyright 1953, 1952, and 1949; Philippines copyright, 1954 and 1953; Formosan copyright, 1955, by AMERICAN BOOK COMPANY. All rights reserved. No part of this book protected by the copyrights hereon may be reproduced in any form without written permission of the publisher.

A   30

PREFACE

This book is a simple, concise review of the essentials of English grammar, designed to meet the special needs of Spanish-speaking students. The correlated readings offer information about some of the customs, geography, history, and economic life of the United States. For two years prior to revision into its present form, *Practice Your English* had the advantage of actual use in the adult classes at the Centro Colombo-Americano of Bogotá, Colombia.

Since this book attempts to teach informal, conversational English rather than literary English, it has departed somewhat from the traditional approach of many language textbooks. It is more intensive than comprehensive. Although the rules are given, briefly stated in simple English, the emphasis in teaching or in learning should be placed on oral practice with the basic patterns of English sentences. Where both formal and informal constructions are acceptable, preference is often given to correct informal usage. Special attention is paid to those constructions which differ from the Spanish. *Practice Your English* offers practical aid to the student who has already studied English for one or two years, but who needs abundant practice in order to understand it and speak it with ease.

Within the limits of the subjects treated, the vocabulary represents good oral usage in the United States, but it does not include the many slang expressions in current use. It is based on the actual needs of students as shown by the author's experience in Bogotá. In the vocabulary of each lesson and the vocabulary at the end, meanings given are those which apply to the subject matter of the respective lessons.

The pronunciation indicated is that of General American, which is spoken by the majority of North Americans. Phonetic symbols are included in brackets for the benefit of those teachers who wish to use them in order to teach a more accurate differentiation of sounds.

By special arrangement of the American Book Company, certain materials in this text are based on *An Intensive Course in English for Latin-American Students* by Dr. Charles C. Fries of the English Language Institute of the University of Michigan. The author is greatly indebted to Dr. Charles N. Staubach, also of the University of Michigan, for his careful reading and constructive criticism of the original manuscript while he was an exchange professor in Bogotá, as well as for permission to draw upon material from his book *Two-Word Verbs*, published by the Centro Colombo-Americano in Bogotá in 1945. The author wishes to express her appreciation to the staff of the Centro Colombo-Americano of Bogotá for their contributions and suggestions; to Mrs. Wilbur C. Douglas, News Editor of Louisiana State University, for her help in securing the photographs for Lessons I, IV, VII, and XII; to Mr. Arturo Serrano of Bogotá and Mr. Hernán Lineros of Santiago, Chile, for their assistance in the preparation of the vocabulary; and to Dr. Harvey L. Johnson of Northwestern University, Evanston, Illinois, for his reading of the revised manuscript. Her thanks also go to Dr. José M. Gallardo, Latin-American Editor of the American Book Company, with whom it has been a pleasure to work.

A. L. W.

CONTENTS

PRONUNCIATION   xvii

PART I

I. VIRGINIA LOPEZ   3

the order of words in a sentence — gender — subject pronouns — the definite and indefinite articles — the plural of nouns — the form and position of adjectives — the present tense of **be, have** — the simple present tense and the present tense with **ing**

II. THE HOUSE WHERE MR. AND MRS. MILLER LIVE   12

the irregular plural form of some nouns — object pronouns — the prepositions **in, on, at** — questions with **be** — **there is** and **there are** — irregular verb forms in the third person singular

III. AT THE GROCERY STORE   22

the auxiliary verb **do** — the verb **like** — the use of the definite and indefinite articles — the prepositions **beside, besides, next to, near, far from, in front of, behind, opposite**

Review Lesson I   31

IV. INTRODUCTIONS, GREETINGS, LEAVE-TAKINGS   34

the negative form of the present tense — negative statements with **be** — negative questions — the use of **no** and **not** — the position of adverbs of frequency — the prepositions **of** and **from**

xi

V. AMERICAN NAMES — 45
the past tense of **be** — the past tense with **ing** — future time with **going to** — possessive nouns, adjectives, and pronouns — demonstrative adjectives and pronouns

VI. A LETTER FROM VIRGINIA — 55
the simple past tense of regular verbs — the negative and interrogative forms of the simple past tense — nouns used as adjectives — the order of adjectives before a noun — the prepositions **to, at; before, after; until, as far as**

Review Lesson II — 64

VII. THE MOVIES — 69
the simple past tense of irregular verbs — **used to** — adverbs or adverbial expressions and their position in a sentence — the expressions of quantity **much, many, a lot of, lots of, a great deal of** — the prepositions **above, below; over, under; toward, to; into, out of; through**

VIII. WHAT IS THE OBJECT? — 82
imperative sentences — indirect objects — **say** and **tell** — questions with **how, how far, how much,** and **how many** — the prepositions **between, among; upon, off**

IX. A TELEPHONE CONVERSATION — 91
the future auxiliary **will** — the attached question — the expressions of purpose **in order to, to, for** — other uses of the preposition **for** — **why** or **what . . . for** in questions of purpose

Review Lesson III — 100

X. A RIDE ON A BUS — 106
the use of **it** as subject — the interrogative words **which** and **what** — the use of **one** after adjectives — reflexive pronouns — the preposition **by**

XI. AT THE DOCTOR'S OFFICE 117

some and **any** used after verbs — the infinitive as a substitute for the Spanish subjunctive — comparison of the past tense with **ing** and the simple past tense — review of the prepositions **for, by, to; to** as part of the infinitive

XII. EDUCATION IN THE UNITED STATES 127

comparisons of inequality with **more, less,** and the ending **er** — comparisons of equality with **the same . . . as, as . . . as, so . . . as** — comparisons with **similar, like, alike,** and **different** — the superlative: **most** and the ending **est** — some irregular comparisons

Review Lesson IV 138

PART II

XIII. A TRIP THROUGH THE UNITED STATES; MIAMI, FLORIDA 147

the formation and uses of the present perfect tense — comparison of the present perfect and the simple past tenses — the auxiliary verbs **shall, will; should, would**

XIV. WASHINGTON, D. C. 162

the formation and uses of the past perfect tense — the auxiliary verbs **can, could; may, might**

XV. PHILADELPHIA, PENNSYLVANIA 171

the passive voice — the use of **be** (estar) with the past participle — the auxiliaries of obligation **have to, must, should, ought to**

Review Lesson V 181

XVI. NEW YORK, NEW YORK 188

the auxiliaries **had better, would rather** — **used to, be used to, get used to** — **still, any more, any longer** — **already** and **yet**

xiii

XVII. BOSTON, MASSACHUSETTS — 198
shortened sentences with **be, have,** and auxiliaries — shortened sentences with **hope to, want to, expect to,** etc.

XVIII. FROM BOSTON, MASSACHUSETTS, TO CHICAGO, ILLINOIS — 208
clauses — noun clauses used as direct objects — infinitive and participial constructions used after verbs of the senses and others — the direct object followed by a noun — the direct object followed by an adjective or a past participle

Review Lesson VI — 220

XIX. THE MISSISSIPPI VALLEY AND NEW ORLEANS, LOUISIANA — 225
adjective clauses — prepositions at the end of adjective clauses — prepositions at the end of questions — indefinite pronouns

XX. FROM TEXAS TO DENVER, COLORADO — 238
adverbial clauses of time — adverbial clauses of concession — adverbial clauses of cause or reason — adverbial clauses of purpose — adverbial clauses of result

XXI. SALT LAKE CITY, UTAH — 249
conditional sentences — prepositions used after certain verbs — prepositions used after certain adjectives and past participles

Review Lesson VII — 259

XXII. THE SOUTHWEST — 266
the formation and use of the present subjunctive — the formation and use of the past subjunctive — the formation and use of the past perfect subjunctive — the gerund

XXIII. CALIFORNIA: LOS ANGELES AND SAN FRANCISCO 277

various uses of the five common verbs **do, make, have, get, take**

XXIV. THE NORTHWEST 292

two-word verbs — a few things to remember about verbs, prepositions, and common English constructions

Review Lesson VIII 301

APPENDIX 309

conjugation of the regular verb **ask** — principal parts of irregular verbs — numerals — months, days, and seasons — the United States of America and their abbreviations — some rules for English spelling — capitalization — syllabication

ENGLISH–SPANISH VOCABULARY 323

SPANISH–ENGLISH VOCABULARY 357

INDEX 363

PRONUNCIATION

BRIEF OUTLINE OF THE SOUNDS IN ENGLISH INDICATED BY THEIR PHONETIC SYMBOLS

I. Vowel Sounds.

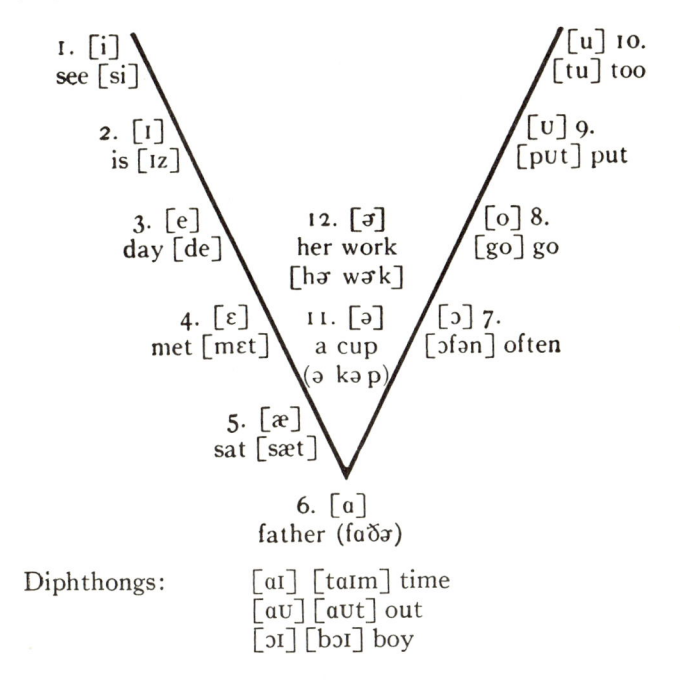

1. [i] see [si]
2. [ɪ] is [ɪz]
3. [e] day [de]
4. [ɛ] met [mɛt]
5. [æ] sat [sæt]
6. [ɑ] father (fɑðɚ)
7. [ɔ] [ɔfən] often
8. [o] [go] go
9. [ʊ] [pʊt] put
10. [u] [tu] too
11. [ə] a cup (ə kəp)
12. [ɚ] her work [hɚ wɚk]

Diphthongs: [aɪ] [taɪm] time
[aʊ] [aʊt] out
[ɔɪ] [bɔɪ] boy

II. Consonant Sounds.

[b]	[bi]	be	[p]	[pɛn]	pen	[θ]	[θɪn]	thin
[d]	[de]	day	[r]	[rɛd]	red	[ð]	[ðe]	they
[f]	[faɪn]	fine	[s]	[si]	see	[ʃ]	[ʃi]	she
[g]	[gɛt]	get	[t]	[tek]	take	[ʒ]	[plɛʒɚ]	pleasure
[h]	[hæt]	hat	[v]	[vɔɪs]	voice	[tʃ]	[mətʃ]	much
[k]	[kɑr]	car	[w]	[wɛl]	well	[dʒ]	[dʒun]	June
[l]	[laɪk]	like	[y]	[yɛs]	yes	[hw]	[hwɛn]	when
[m]	[mi]	me	[z]	[zon]	zone			
[n]	[naɪn]	nine	[ŋ]	[rɪŋ]	ring			

III. Voiced and Voiceless Sounds.

Voiced sounds are produced by the vibration of the vocal cords. The corresponding *voiceless* sounds keep the same lip and tongue positions, but there is no vibration of the vocal cords.

Voiced sounds include all the vowels and most of the consonants. The voiceless consonants with their voiced equivalents are listed below.

Pronounce the following pairs of consonant sounds:

| Voiceless: | [p] | [t] | [k] | [f] | [s] | [θ] | [ʃ] | [tʃ] | [h] |
| Voiced: | [b] | [d] | [g] | [v] | [z] | [ð] | [ʒ] | [dʒ] | |

IV. Unstressed Syllables.

One of the principal characteristics of English pronunciation is the quality of the vowel sounds in unstressed syllables. For instance, the [æ] in **fast** becomes [ə] in **breakfast** because the stress is no longer on **fast**. Thus the vowels in unstressed syllables are usually pronounced [ə] or [ɪ], and sometimes they disappear completely in rapid speech.

| breakfast | [ə] | occasion | [ə] | minute | [ɪ] |
| student | [ə] | lettuce | [ə] | package | [ɪ] |

PART I

McVadon's Studio

LESSON I

Louisiana State University

VIRGINIA LOPEZ

The doorbell rings. I answer the door, and I find the postman there with a letter. It is from my sister Virginia, who is in the United States now. She has one of the scholarships which the Institute of International Education gives to worthy students each year. My sister says that she is learn-

3

ing a great deal at the university which she is attending. We expect to see her again next summer. We know that she is having a good time, but we miss her very much.

VOCABULARY

again	otra vez	postman	cartero
to attend	asistir a	to ring	sonar
doorbell	timbre	scholarship	beca
each	cada	that	que
to expect	esperar	which	que
to learn	aprender	worthy	digno

IDIOMS

a great deal (of)	mucho
to answer the door	ir a ver quién llama a la puerta
every year	todos los años
to have a good time	divertirse, estar contento
How do you say *beca* in English?	¿Cómo dice Vd. *beca* en inglés?
Is it correct to say . . . ?	¿Es correcto decir . . . ?
to miss a person	echar de menos a una persona
next summer	el verano próximo
What does *beca* mean?	¿Qué significa *beca*?
What is the meaning of *beca*?	¿Cuál es el significado de *beca*?

WORD STUDY

The verb **esperar** has four meanings in English.

1. **to hope,** tener esperanza

   I **hope** to see you again soon.
   I **hope** that you can come.

2. **to expect,** estar casi seguro, contar con

   We **expect** to see Virginia next year.
   We **expect** her to be here.
   We **expect** that she will be here.

3. **to wait (a while),** esperar (un rato)

   Wait a minute, please.
   The postman **is waiting** at the door.
   He **is waiting** to see you.

4. **to wait for (someone or something),** esperar (a alguien o algo)

   Please **wait for** me at the corner.
   We **waited** ten minutes **for** the bus.
   We **waited for** it to come.

CONVERSATION

Answer these questions in complete sentences.

1. Who rings the doorbell? 2. From whom is the letter? 3. What is her name? 4. Where is she now? 5. What is she doing there? 6. Where is she studying? 7. Is she learning a great deal? 8. Is she also having a good time? 9. Do we miss her very much? 10. When do we expect to see her again? 11. Who gives scholarships to worthy students? 12. Does Virginia like the United States?

13. Who answers the door at your house? 14. What is your name? 15. Are you living with your family? 16. Where are you studying English? 17. Are you learning a great deal? 18. Are you having a good time in this class? 19. Is your teacher speaking English now? 20. Is there a university in your city? 21. What do people study at a university? 22. Why is it that some people like to go to the United States to study? 23. Is it necessary to know English to get a scholarship? Why? 24. What is the meaning of **who? whom? where? when? how? what?**

PRONUNCIATION

- [I] is, sister, miss, ring, ship, which, university
- [st] study, student, stand, strong, stamp, star
- [ð] the, this, that, there, with, worthy
- [v] very, live, give, have, university, having, living
- [m] man, my, miss, time, room, come, some, sometime
- [ə] but, much, study, summer

GRAMMAR   Section 1

I. The Order of Words in a Sentence.

In an English sentence, the subject usually precedes the verb, except in questions.

On the following page you will see columns of words arranged in no special order. Arrange the words in each column so that they make good sentences. Think of all the things you know about word order before you begin.

1. at a university
   is
   studying
   Virginia

2. is
   difficult
   pronunciation
   English

3. has
   a scholarship
   my sister

4. country
   the
   beautiful
   is

II. The Gender of Words in English.

A. Articles and adjectives are invariable; they do not change to indicate gender. One exception is **blond, blonde,** derived from French.

>   **the little** boy   **the little** girl
>   **the blond** boy   **the blonde** girl

B. The only pronouns which indicate gender are **he** (*masculine*), **she** (*feminine*), and **it** (*neuter*). **He** and **she** refer to persons in the singular, and **it** refers to a thing. For an animal **it** is generally used, but **he** or **she** is often used in speaking of a pet.

>   Where is your father?   **He** is at the office.
>   Where is your sister?   **She** is in the United States.
>   Is that dog friendly?   Yes, **it** is very friendly.
>   Is Fido playing with the   Yes, **he** is playing with them.
>   children?

C. Nouns indicating persons often differ in the masculine and feminine forms. Among the most common ones are the following:

man	woman	male	female
father	mother	bachelor	old maid
husband	wife		single (*adj.*)
son	daughter	king	queen
brother	sister	monk	nun
boy	girl	actor	actress
uncle	aunt	host	hostess
nephew	niece	bridegroom	bride

6

III. The Subject Pronouns I, you, he, she, it, we, you, they.

Subject pronouns are always expressed, except in imperative sentences. I is always written with a *capital letter*. **You** is both singular and plural, polite and familiar. **They** refers to both things and persons in the plural.

Practice changing the words in italics to pronouns.

1. *The university* is very large.

    It is very large.

2. *My sister* is in the United States.
3. *The doorbell* is ringing.
4. *Her scholarship* is a good one.
5. *The scholarships* are for worthy students.
6. *The postman* comes very late.
7. *The students* are taking English lessons.
8. *The letters* are in English.
9. *Her sister* speaks English very well.
10. *The university* has a beautiful campus.

IV. The Definite and Indefinite Articles.

A. The definite article **the** is the same in the singular and the plural. Before a vowel sound it is pronounced [ðɪ]. Before a consonant sound it is pronounced [ðə].

Practice reading aloud:

[ðɪ] 1. the ocean, the oceans, the idea, the ideas, the apple, the apples, the hour, the hours, the uncle, the uncles, the end, the ends, the Andes, the Atlantic, the only girl

[ðə] 2. the sister, the sisters, the doorbell, the doorbells, the scholarship, the scholarships, the student, the students, the letter, the letters, the postman, the house, the country, the **u**niversity [yunɪvɝsɪtɪ], the **U**nited [yunaɪtɪd] States, the **o**ne [wən] girl

Note: The last three examples begin with a consonant sound.

B. The indefinite article has two forms, **a** and **an**. Before a consonant sound **a** [ə] is used. Before a vowel sound **an** [ən] is used.

7

Practice reading aloud:

[ə] 1. a student, a scholarship, a summer, a doorbell, a friend, a house, a university, a great deal, a good time, a good idea, a useful [yusfʊl] thing

[ən] 2. an article, an idea, an American, an Englishman, an (h)our, an (h)onest man, an old hat, an easy lesson, an important point, an excellent class, an interesting letter

Note: For emphasis, **a** is occasionally pronounced [e], and **an** is pronounced [æn].

V. The Plural of Nouns.

A. The plural of nouns is generally formed by adding **s** to the singular. After a voiceless consonant (**f, k, p, t**), the **s** ending is pronounced [s]. After a vowel or a voiced consonant, the **s** is pronounced [z].

Practice reading aloud:

[s] 1. coats, hats, students, books, banks, desks, stamps, maps, scholarships, cuffs, handkerchiefs

[z] 2. letters, summers, sisters, doors, stores, hands, sounds, friends, sons, lessons, doors, doorbells, dogs, customs, boys, girls, hours, ideas, shoes

B. If a singular noun ends in **s, sh, ch,** or **x**, the plural is formed by adding **es**. The ending **es** is pronounced as a separate syllable [ɪz].

Practice reading aloud:

class	class**es**	dress	dress**es**
church	church**es**	watch	watch**es**
dish	dish**es**	wish	wish**es**
box	box**es**	fox	fox**es**

C. If a singular noun ends in **ce, se,** or **ge,** the plural is formed by adding **s,** but the ending **es** is pronounced [ɪz] as in B.

Practice reading aloud:

voice	voic**es**	[sɪz]	sentence	sentenc**es**	[sɪz]
case	cas**es**	[sɪz]	course	cours**es**	[sɪz]
rose	ros**es**	[zɪz]	house	hous**es**	[zɪz]
age	ag**es**	[dʒɪz]	language	languag**es**	[dʒɪz]

VI. The Form and Position of Adjectives.

The form of adjectives does not change in the plural. They usually precede the nouns that they modify.

    the **large** classes   the **interesting** letters
    the **old** houses   the **white** handkerchiefs

Section 2

VII. The Present Tense of the Verb be (ser, estar).

Long Forms		Contracted Forms	
I am	we are	I'm	we're
you are	you are	you're	you're
he is }		he's }	
she is }	they are	she's }	they're
it is }		it's }	

Note: **Be** is the infinitive of this verb and corresponds to the Spanish form ending in **r** (**estar, ser**). The infinitive may be used with or without the word **to**: **be** or **to be**.

The subject pronouns are always expressed except in imperative sentences. The verb contractions are frequently used in conversation. These contractions are not often written, except in friendly personal letters and in writing which reproduces conversation.

Practice reading these sentences using the verb contractions.

1. I am a Colombian.
2. He is a Brazilian.
3. She is an American.
4. They are North Americans.
5. We are South Americans.
6. It is important.
7. You are the teacher.
8. I am a student.
9. It is time to go.
10. They are in the United States.

VIII. The Present Tense of the Verb have (tener, haber).

I have	we have
you have	you have
he has }	
she has }	they have
it has }	

Practice reading these sentences rapidly.
1. I have a sister.
2. She has a scholarship.
3. You have a map in the room.
4. We have a new student.
5. They have a big house.
6. He has a letter.
7. I have a good book to read.
8. You have good pronunciation.

IX. The Present Tense of Other Verbs, Regular or Irregular.

A. In English there are two forms of the present tense, the *simple present* and the *present with ing*. To form the *simple present*, the infinitive without **to**, or *simple form* of the verb, is used in all persons except the third person singular, where the ending is **s**. To form the *present with ing*, the present tense of the verb **be** is used with the present participle or **ing** form of the principal verb.

Simple Present		Present with **ing**	
I learn	we learn	I am learning	we are learning
you learn	you learn	you are learning	you are learning
he learns }	they learn	he is learning }	they are learning
she learns }		she is learning }	
it learns		it is learning	

Note 1: In the simple present tense, the **s** ending of the third person singular is pronounced [s] after a voiceless sound and [z] after a voiced sound.

    Voiceless: likes [ks], speaks [ks], wants [ts], expects [ts], stops [ps]
    Voiced: gives [vz], learns [nz], finds [dz], comes [mz], knows [oz]

Note 2: In the present with **ing**, the present participle is formed by adding **ing** to the simple form of the verb. If the simple form ends in **e**, the **e** is omitted before adding **ing**. If the simple form ends in a single consonant preceded by a single vowel and if the stress is on the last syllable, the consonant is doubled before adding **ing**.

give	giving	stop	sto**pp**ing
live	living	run	ru**nn**ing
come	coming	begin	begi**nn**ing
hope	hoping	omit	omi**tt**ing

B. The two forms of the present tense have different uses.

1. The simple present tense describes a *customary* action or a general truth.

> We always **have** a good time.
> I **study** my English every day.
> I **want** to know English.
> You **learn** best by practice.

*Practice reading each sentence, using **he and she** instead of **I**.*

1. I like the university.
2. I have a scholarship.
3. I want to see you.
4. I speak a little English.
5. I always learn the new words.
6. I expect to see you soon.
7. I have a letter for you.
8. I give English lessons.
9. I answer the door.
10. I find the postman at the door.

2. The present tense with **ing** is the true present. It describes an action which *is happening* at the present moment.

> I **am studying** English now.
> The doorbell **is ringing**.
> We **are having** a good time.

*Practice reading these sentences, using the simple present tense or the present tense with **ing**, as required, of the verbs in parentheses.*

1. Virginia ——— (speak) English very well.
2. She always ——— (want) to practice it.
3. She ——— (learn) a great deal this year.
4. Mr. and Mrs. Miller ——— (build) a new house.
5. The doorbell ——— (ring) very often.
6. The doorbell ——— (ring) now.
7. Virginia always ——— (have) a good time.
8. She ——— (have) a good time now.
9. We ——— (miss) her very much.
10. I ——— (write) many letters to her.
11. I ——— (write) a long letter now.
12. This class ——— (begin) at eight o'clock.
13. Now we ——— (begin) to understand some English.
14. We ——— (study) the present tense now.
15. We ——— (like) this class.
16. The bus ——— (stop) at the corner now.
17. The bus always ——— (stop) there.
18. It ——— (rain) a great deal in the tropics.
19. It ——— (rain) a little now.
20. The Institute of International Education ——— (give) scholarships to worthy students.

Bahnsen from Monkmeyer

LESSON II

THE HOUSE WHERE MR. AND MRS. MILLER LIVE

Virginia López lives with Mr. and Mrs. Miller in a college town. Their address is 431 Clark Street. Mr. Miller is renting the house from a real-estate company. He pays one hundred dollars a month for it.

The house is made of brick and wood. There is a large

12

front porch and a big yard around the house. There is no wall around the yard. The front yard has a nice green lawn, and the back yard has many pretty flowers.

It is an eight-room house with four rooms downstairs and four rooms upstairs. The rooms downstairs are the living room, the library, the dining room, and the kitchen. There are four bedrooms and a bath upstairs.

The living room is large and light. It has a fireplace, several tables and chairs, a sofa, a floor lamp, and three table lamps. There are also a bookcase and a radio with a record player. There is a large rug on the floor, and there are some pictures on the walls.

VOCABULARY

address	dirección	living room	sala
around	alrededor de	made of	hecho de
back	de atrás	nice	bonito, atractivo
bath	baño	picture	cuadro
bedroom	alcoba	porch	pórtico (*Véase el dibujo*)
bookcase	estante para libros		
brick	ladrillo	real estate	bienes raíces
college town	ciudad donde hay una universidad	record player	tocadiscos, fonógrafo
dining room	comedor	to rent	arrendar, alquilar
downstairs	abajo	rug	alfombra
fireplace	chimenea	several	varios
floor	piso	there is	hay
floor lamp	lámpara de pie	there are	
front	de enfrente	upstairs	arriba
(one) hundred	ciento (cien)	wall	pared, tapia
kitchen	cocina	wood	madera
lawn	prado	yard	patio; espacio alrededor de una casa
library	biblioteca		
light	claro		

IDIOMS

Expressions of Time and Measure with the Indefinite Article <u>a</u> or <u>an</u>.

Time

seventy dollars **a** month (por mes)
three classes **a** week (por semana)

one hour **a** day (por día)
forty pages **an** hour (por hora)
a mile **a** minute (por minuto)

Measure

five dollars **a** pair (el par)
twenty cents **a** gallon (el galón)
eighty cents **a** pound (la libra)
fifty cents **a** dozen (la docena)
one dollar **a** bottle (la botella)

five dollars **each** (cada uno)
five dollars **apiece** (cada uno)

Practice using these expressions in original sentences.

CONVERSATION

Answer these questions in complete sentences.

1. With whom is Virginia living? 2. Is she living in a college town? 3. What is her address? 4. What is the house made of? 5. Is there a wall around the yard? 6. Is Mr. Miller renting the house? 7. From whom is he renting it? 8. How much is the rent? 9. How many rooms are there downstairs? Name them. 10. How many rooms are there upstairs? Name them. 11. Is the living room small? 12. What is there on the floor? 13. Are there many lamps? 14. Where is the green lawn? 15. Where are the flowers?

16. What is your address? 17. Are you living in a house or an apartment? 18. Is your house made of brick? 19. Is there a yard around your house, or is there a patio in the center? 20. Is it an eight-room house? 21. Are there two floors in your house? 22. What are the names of the rooms? 23. How many bedrooms are there? 24. Is there a fireplace in your house? 25. Are you renting the house from a real-estate company? 26. Are houses to rent difficult to find in your city? 27. Are the rents high or low? 28. Are there many **new** houses in your city?

PRONUNCIATION

[æ] bath, path, back, can, has
[ɔ] lawn, small, call, talk, taught, bought
[aʊ] down, flower, around, house, out
[ə] month, front, rug, up, upstairs
[ɚ] flow**er,** sist**er,** broth**er,** Mist**er** (*abbreviation:* Mr.), Mill**er**

GRAMMAR   Section 1

I. The Irregular Plural Form of Some Nouns.

A. To form the plural of nouns ending in **y** preceded by a consonant, **y** is changed to **i,** and **es** is added.

>   baby   bab**ies**
>   vocabulary   vocabular**ies**

Note: The following nouns are regular, because the **y** follows a vowel.

>   boy   boy**s**   day   day**s**

B. To form the plural of nouns ending in **f,** final **f** is changed to **v,** and **es** is added. To form the plural of nouns ending in **fe,** final **fe** is changed to **ve,** and **s** is added. (The **e** is silent; **s** is pronounced [z].)

>   leaf   lea**ves**   wife   wi**ves**
>   loaf   loa**ves**   life   li**ves**
>   thief thie**ves**   knife kni**ves**

Exceptions: **handkerchiefs, roofs, proofs,** and **cuffs.**

C. To form the plural of many nouns ending in **o, es** [z] is added.

>   potato   potato**es**   hero   hero**es**
>   tomato   tomato**es**   Negro   Negro**es**

D. A few English nouns are very irregular in their plurals.

>   man   men   goose   geese
>   woman   women   mouse   mice
>   child   children   ox   oxen
>   foot   feet   deer   deer
>   tooth   teeth   sheep   sheep

Practice writing and pronouncing the plural forms of these nouns.

town	loaf	lunch
house	woman	half
company	brick	man
key	university	boy
street	yard	city
porch	foot	potato
library	tomato	room
dollar	wall	child
month	**sandwich**	wife
address	flower	glass

E. The noun **people** is used with a *plural* verb. The noun **news** is used with a *singular* verb.

> There **are** many **people** in front of the theater.
> Those **people speak** English.
> The North American **people are** friendly.
> No **news is** good news.
> The **news is** broadcast at seven o'clock.
> When the **news is** good, **people are** happy.

Practice using the correct form of the verb **be.**

1. The news ———— important this morning.
2. The people ———— renting the house.
3. There ———— many people in the store.
4. There ———— some good news for you.
5. The people ———— happy because she has a scholarship.
6. The news about her ———— very interesting.

II. The Object Pronouns.

A. The object pronouns, direct and indirect, are **me, you, him, her, it, us, you, them.** They follow the verb.

B. The same object pronouns are used after a preposition.

> with **me,** for **you,** from **him,** about **her,** on **it,** to **us,** after **them**

Practice using the correct object pronouns instead of the words in italics.

1. Mr. Miller is renting *the house.*
2. I see *Mr. Miller* every day.
3. Virginia attends *the university.*

4. The students like *Virginia*.
5. We like *her letters* very much.
6. They are speaking with *the teacher* (la profesora).
7. The teacher is explaining *the lesson* to *the students*.
8. Virginia usually answers *the questions* correctly.
9. Virginia is going to the party with *John*.
10. We receive many letters from *Virginia*.
11. You have *the letters* in your pocket.
12. The news is about *George*.
13. She likes *the college town* very much.
14. He is giving *the news* on the radio now.
15. I like *those people* very much.

III. The Prepositions in, on, at.

A. The preposition **in** is used in the following ways:

1. *Time:* with the names of *months*, *years*, and **seasons**.
   in March, in 1946, in the winter

2. *Time:* with parts of the *day* or *night* used in a **general** sense.

   in the morning, in the afternoon, in the evening
   But: **tomorrow morning, yesterday morning**

3. *Place:* inside of something (en, dentro de alguna **cosa**)
   Virginia is in the United States.
   She lives in a college town.
   His office is in that building.
   The letters are in the drawer of the desk.
   Please sit in this chair.

B. The preposition **on** is used in the following ways:

1. *Time:* with *days* of the week, and *days* of the month.
   on Tuesday, on the tenth of March, on March 10th
   But: **next Tuesday, next March, last Tuesday, last March**

2. *Place:* to indicate *contact* with a surface.
   The rug is on the floor.
   The pictures are on the wall.
   She lives on Clark Street.
   Please sit on this sofa.

Note: A sofa is large and sometimes armless; therefore one does not sit *in* it.

17

C. The preposition **at** is used to indicate a *definite* time or place.

1. *Time:* for *hours* and *minutes*, and with **noon, night, midnight.**

    at six o'clock, **at** ten minutes to two, **at** half past five
    at noon, **at** night, **at** midnight

2. *Place:* for a *definite* position.

    They are **at** home.
    The postman is **at** the door.
    She lives **at** 431 Clark Street.
    She writes her name **at** the end of the letter.
    We are studying English **at** the university.

D. Different prepositions are used after the verb **arrive** (llegar a).

1. In English **llegar a** is never translated by **arrive to.**

2. The correct expressions are **arrive in** a country, **in** or **at** a city, and **at** other places.

    She arrives **in** the United States next Sunday.
    She arrives **in** (at) New York on Monday.
    She always arrives **at** school a little early.
    It is necessary to arrive **at** the airport early.

Practice using the correct preposition, if one is needed.

——— Sunday
——— First Street
——— 431 Clark Street
——— the evening
——— night
——— next Sunday
——— December 7 (seventh)
——— December
——— the spring
——— 1941

——— the summer
——— Saturday
——— last Saturday
——— 1950
——— the top of the page
——— July 4 (fourth)
——— noon
——— Fifth Avenue
——— 1025 Fifth Avenue
——— the morning

1. She is ——— the university this morning.
2. He is sitting ——— the table.
3. The lamp is ——— the desk.
4. Mrs. Miller is ——— home.
5. They live ——— Clark Street.

6. There are many flowers ——— the yard.
7. The name is ——— the door of the house.
8. His birthday is ——— June.
9. His birthday is ——— June 4 (fourth).
10. He arrives ——— Miami ——— six o'clock ——— the morning.

Section 2

IV. Questions with the Verb be.

In the present tense the principal verb **be** or the auxiliary **be** precedes the subject in questions, except when the subject is **who** or **what**.

Is Virginia in the United States?   **Who is** coming to the door?
Is the doorbell ringing?   **What is** on the table?

Practice changing the following sentences to questions.

1. The house is on Clark Street.
2. The bedrooms are upstairs.
3. They are renting the house.
4. The front porch is large.
5. The address is 431 Clark Street.
6. The doorbell is ringing.
7. Mr. Miller is coming now.
8. He is late for dinner.
9. Virginia is having a good time.
10. We are expecting her next year.
11. John is very busy now.
12. He is writing a letter.
13. They are standing at the door.
14. His name is Smith.
15. They are speaking to Mr. Miller.
16. Virginia is a good student.
17. The lessons are easy.
18. They are living in an apartment.
19. The news is very interesting.
20. The people are ready to go.

V. There is, there are (hay).

There is is used for **hay** before a singular noun, and **there are** is used for **hay** before a plural noun. The interrogative forms are **is there?** and **are there?**

There is a good drugstore on the corner.
Is there a good drugstore on the corner?

There are some new books in the library.
Are there some new books in the library?

19

Replace each blank with the correct translation of **hay;** *then change the sentences to questions.*

1. (Hay) ——— many students in the room.
2. (Hay) ——— a big map on the wall.
3. (Hay) ——— classes on Tuesdays and Thursdays.
4. (Hay) ——— a lecture tomorrow night.
5. (Hay) ——— five children in the family.
6. (Hay) ——— a nice front lawn.
7. (Hay) ——— four bedrooms upstairs.
8. (Hay) ——— a telephone downstairs.
9. (Hay) ——— some letters on the desk for you.
10. (Hay) ——— twelve months in a year.

Practice making sentences about your classroom, using **there is** *and* **there are.**

VI. Irregular Verb Forms in the Third Person Singular of the Simple Present Tense.

The following changes in spelling and pronunciation occur in the *third person singular* of the simple present tense:

1. To verbs of one syllable that end in **o,** the ending **es** is added. The sound of **es** is [z].

   He goes.

2. With verbs that end in **y** preceded by a consonant, the **y** is changed to **i,** and the ending **es** is added. The sound of **es** is [z].

   He flies.

3. To verbs that end in **s, sh, ch, x,** or **z,** the ending **es** is added. The **es** is pronounced as a separate syllable [iz].

   He misses.

4. To verbs that end in **ge, ce,** or **se,** the ending **s** is added. The **es** is pronounced as a separate syllable [iz].

   He uses.

Note: Compare these with the plural forms of nouns in Lesson I.

*Practice reading these forms with **he** or **she** as subject.*

goes	misses	washes
does	passes	wishes
studies	expresses	cashes
flies	notices	catches
cries	pronounces	watches
replies	ceases	teaches
pays	closes	fixes
buys	uses	mixes
says	changes	buzzes

Lass from F. Lewis

LESSON III

AT THE GROCERY STORE

Virginia López goes to the grocery store with Mrs. Miller. She listens to Mrs. Miller talking with the clerk, Mr. Brown.

Mrs. Miller: Good morning, Mr. Brown.
Mr. Brown: Good morning, Mrs. Miller.

22

Mrs. Miller: Can you wait on me?
Mr. Brown: Yes. What can I do for you?
Mrs. Miller: I have a lot of groceries to buy this morning.
Mr. Brown: What would you like?
Mrs. Miller: Are your vegetables fresh? I need some radishes, tomatoes, and lettuce for a salad.
Mr. Brown: How do you like these tomatoes? They are fresh this morning. Some are a little green; but if you put them in the sun, they will be all right for tomorrow.
Mrs. Miller: I think they will do. Now, do you have string beans and cauliflower?
Mr. Brown: Yes, the beans are fifteen cents a pound, or two pounds for a quarter. The cauliflower is thirty cents. Will one cauliflower be enough?
Mrs. Miller: Yes; please give me two pounds of beans and one cauliflower. I also need a quart of milk, a pound of butter, a dozen eggs, a loaf of bread, and a pound of steak.
Mr. Brown: Is that all, Mrs. Miller?
Mrs. Miller: Yes, that's all this morning.
Mr. Brown: All right. If you want to go to the meat counter and pick out your steak, I will get the rest of your order ready in a minute.
Mrs. Miller: Thank you, Mr. Brown.
Mr. Brown: You're welcome.

VOCABULARY

a lot of	muchos	**to listen to**	escuchar
butter	mantequilla	**loaf of bread**	pan
to buy	comprar	**meat**	carne
cauliflower	coliflor	**to need**	necesitar
clerk	dependiente	**order**	pedido
counter	mostrador	**to pick out**	escoger
egg	huevo	**pound**	libra
enough	suficiente	**to put**	poner
fresh	fresco	**quarter**	moneda de 25 centavos
groceries	víveres, abarrotes		
grocery store	almacén de víveres	**radish**	rábano
lettuce	lechuga	**rest**	resto

salad	ensalada	**sun**	sol
steak	biftec	**to think**	pensar, creer
store	almacén	**vegetable**	legumbre, verdura
string beans	habichuelas tiernas		

IDIOMS

All right.	Muy bien, Está bien.
Can you wait on me?	¿Puede Vd. atenderme?
Good morning.	Buenos días.
How do you like these?	¿Qué tal le parecen éstos?
I think they will do.	Creo que servirán.
I will get it ready.	Lo tendré listo.
What can I do for you?	¿Qué se le ofrece?
What would you like?	¿Qué le gustaría?
You're welcome.	No hay de qué.

CONVERSATION

Answer these questions in complete sentences.

1. Where does Mrs. Miller go this morning?   2. Does Virginia go with her?   3. Does Virginia listen to her conversation with Mr. Brown?   4. Does Mrs. Miller have many groceries to buy?   5. Who is Mr. Brown? Is Mrs. Miller a customer?   6. What does the clerk do?   7. What does Mrs. Miller need for her salad?   8. Why is it necessary to put the tomatoes in the sun?   9. Does Mrs. Miller think that they will do?   10. How much are the string beans? How many does she buy?   11. How much is the cauliflower? How much does she buy?   12. What other things does she need?   13. Where does she go to pick out the steak?

14. Who buys the groceries for your family?   15. Do many North American families have maids?   16. Do you buy meat and vegetables in the same store?   17. Do you like green tomatoes or ripe tomatoes?   18. Which vegetables do you like best?   19. Do you like your steak rare, medium, or well done?   20. How much are eggs now? potatoes? carrots? peas?   21. How much is milk now? butter?   22. Is meat cheap or expensive now?   23. Where do you buy your groceries, at a grocery store or a market?   24. Do you like to go to market?

PRONUNCIATION

[ə] lettuce, cactus, circus, minus, let us, send us
[ɛ] ready, rest, get, egg, letter, fresh
[ˈvɛdʒtəbl] vegetable

[i] bean, meat, need, green, fourteen, fifteen, sixteen
[ɚ] order, quarter, counter, father, mother, brother, flower, cauliflower

GRAMMAR   Section 1

I. The Auxiliary Verb do.

The verb **do** is a principal verb (hacer) and also an auxiliary verb which has no meaning in itself. As an auxiliary, it is used in *questions* with all verbs except **be** (Lesson II) and other auxiliaries. It is equivalent to the inverted question mark in Spanish. In the present tense, the form **do** is used in all persons except the third person singular, where it changes to **does**. The word order in a question is as follows:

Do (Does) → Subject → Principal Verb
(*simple form*)

Do	you	prefer	bananas or oranges?
Do	they	rent	the house?
Do	we	have	a big class?
Does	Virginia	live	on Clark Street?
Does	the house	have	a nice green lawn?
Does	Mrs. Miller	go	to the store every day?

Note 1: The simple form of the principal verb is always used after **do** or **does**.

Note 2: When the affirmative question begins with the subject **who** or **what**, the auxiliary **do** is not necessary.

Who lives in that house?
What costs fifteen cents a pound?

Note 3: In the present tense only, questions with the verb **have** may be expressed in two ways, with or without the auxiliary **do**. In idioms the auxiliary is necessary.

Do you have a book?
Have you a book?
But: **Do you have** to go? (¿ Tiene que ir?)

Practice changing these sentences to questions.
1. Mr. and Mrs. Miller rent the house.
2. It has a nice living room.
3. They have four bedrooms in the house.
4. They speak English and Spanish.
5. He speaks Spanish very well.
6. The students understand their teacher.
7. She wants to study English.
8. We learn the vocabulary and the idioms of each lesson.
9. Mr. Miller has a new car.
10. They go to New York on business.
11. Virginia goes to the grocery store with Mrs. Miller.
12. I have many things to buy today.
13. The clerk waits on Mrs. Miller.
14. She puts the tomatoes in the sun.
15. Mrs. Miller thinks that they will do.
16. I need to buy meat and vegetables.
17. The cauliflower costs thirty cents.
18. You have my order ready.
19. Mrs. Miller picks out a good steak.
20. We listen to the radio after dinner.

II. The Verb like.

A. The verb **like** is conjugated in the same way as other verbs, with the personal pronoun subjects. It is the reverse of the Spanish verb **gustar** because:

1. The indirect object of **gustar** becomes the subject of **like**.

2. The subject of **gustar** becomes the direct object of **like**.

I like it.	Me gusta.	**We like them.**	Nos gustan.
You like it.	Te gusta.	**You like them.**	Os gustan.
He likes it.	Le gusta.	**They like them.**	Les gustan.

Interrogative: **Do you like it?** ¿ Le gusta a Vd. ?
Does he like it? ¿ Le gusta a él ?

Notice the idiom: **How do you like it?** ¿ Qué tal le parece ?
I like it very much. Me gusta mucho.

B. An infinitive with **to** is often used after the verb **like**.

We **like to listen** to the radio.
He **likes to study** English.

26

Practice answering these questions in the affirmative, using complete sentences.

1. Do you like the movies?
2. When do you like to go to the movies?
3. Which do you like best, peas, carrots, or cauliflower?
4. Do you like to drink coffee or tea?
5. Does Virginia like the United States?
6. Do you like music?
7. When do you like to listen to the radio?
8. Do you like to speak English?
9. Do they like the English class?
10. Do they like the teacher?
11. Does Virginia like to dance?
12. How do you like her hat?
13. How do you like the house?
14. How do you like the lectures?
15. What do you like to do on Saturday?
16. What do you like to do during your vacation?

Section 2

III. The Use of the Definite and Indefinite Articles.

A. Definite articles are *not* used in the following cases:

1. With nouns used in a general sense.

   Coffee is exported from several Latin-American countries.
   But: **The coffee** which is exported from Colombia is excellent.

   Vegetables contain many vitamins.
   But: **The vegetables** which I like best are peas and string beans.

   Patience is necessary in a good teacher.
   But: He has **the patience** of Job.

2. With the names of persons preceded by a title.

   Virginia López is living with **Mr.** and **Mrs. Miller.**
   President Jones is taking a short vacation now.
   General Green is in Washington now.
   But: **The general** likes to read.

3. With the names of continents, countries, states, lakes, cities, and streets.

Brazil is the largest country in **South America.**
Many people go to **Florida** for the winter.
Lake Michigan is one of the five Great Lakes.
They are going to **Havana** next week.
She lives on the corner of **Fifth Avenue** and **Tenth Street.**

Exceptions: the United States, the British Isles, the Netherlands, the Soviet Union, the Dominican Republic.

4. With the names of languages used without the word **language.**

He understands **English,** but he speaks it badly.
But: He thinks that **the English language** is difficult to learn.

5. Before the words **next** and **last** in expressions that are related to the present moment.

next Sunday	el domingo entrante
next week	la semana que viene
next year	el año que viene
last Sunday	el domingo pasado
last week	la semana pasada
last year	el año pasado

But: **the last Sunday of the month**   el último domingo del mes

6. With the words **breakfast, lunch,** and **dinner,** when used without modifiers.

What do you eat for **breakfast?**
I am going to have **lunch** now.

7. With the noun **home** when it is used without a modifier.

Virginia is at **home.**
Are you going **home** now?
But: No, we are going to **the home of some friends.**

Practice reading these sentences, inserting the definite article if necessary.

1. North Americans usually like ——— sports of all kinds.
2. ——— sports which Americans like best are football and baseball.

3. ―――― exercise is good for one's health.
4. the exercise which he receives from tennis is good for his health.
5. ―― the oil is found in the eastern part of ―――― Texas.
6. ―――― bananas are exported from ―――― Central America.
7. Do you prefer ―――― coffee or ―――― tea?
8. He is from ―――― Argentina, but he lives in ―――― Havana now.
9. Lake Ontario is situated between the United States and ―――― Canada.
10. ―――― Captain Smith is not at ―――― home now.
11. Where does ―――― Professor White live?
12. Does he live on ―――― Seventh Avenue near ―――― Morton Street?
13. I live on ―――― ―――― (Street or Avenue).
14. New York City is in the state of ―――― New York and at the mouth of ―――― Hudson River.
15. Is ―――― English more difficult than ―――― French?
16. People say that the English language is difficult to learn.

B. Indefinite articles *are* used in the following cases:

1. In referring to someone's profession or nationality after the verb **be**.

   Mr. Miller is **a lawyer.** He is **an American.**

Practice answering these questions.

1. Is Mr. Miller a North American?
2. Are you an American?
3. Are you a Latin American?
4. What is your nationality?
5. Is Mr. Brown a clerk?
6. Is he a bank clerk?
7. Are you a salesman?
8. Is Mr. Miller a doctor?
9. Is his friend an engineer?
10. Is she a teacher or a secretary?
11. What is your profession or occupation?

2. In expressing a unit of time or measure. (See Lesson II.)

fifty dollars **a week**   fifteen cents **a pound**
fifty miles **an hour**   twenty cents **a dozen**

3. **A** or **an** is much more common in English than the numeral **one**. **One** is used for emphasis or comparison.

He is **a** doctor, and his wife is **a** nurse.
The Millers have **a** nice house.

29

Virginia is attending **a** large university.
She has **one** class in the morning and three in the afternoon.
One girl is tall, but the other girl is short.

IV. Prepositions.

The following prepositions indicate *place*.

1. **beside** (al lado de)   **next to** (junto a)

    Mrs. Miller is sitting **beside** Mr. Miller.
    She is sitting **next to** Mr. Miller.

Note: **Besides** (además de) is similar in form to **beside** (al lado de) but different in meaning.

    Besides vegetables, Mrs. Miller needs to buy milk, butter, and steak.

2. **near** (cerca de)   **far from** (lejos de)

    They live **near** the corner.
    My house is **far from** the stores.

3. **in front of** (delante de)   **behind** (detrás de)

    There is a nice lawn **in front of** the house.
    The garden is **behind** the house.

4. **opposite** (frente a, al otro lado de la calle)

    They live **opposite** the park.
    The house **opposite** our house is for rent.

Fill each blank with the correct English translation of the Spanish preposition, and practice reading the sentences aloud.

1. She is sitting ——— the door. (cerca de)
2. He always sits ——— the window. (al lado de)
3. The teacher is standing ——— the class. (delante de)
4. He is standing ——— the blackboard. (junto a)
5. The car is ——— the house. (delante de)
6. My sister lives ——— the church. (frente a)
7. Her house is ——— downtown. (lejos de)
8. Washington is ——— New York. (cerca de)
9. ——— a coat, I need a new hat. (además de)
10. His store is ——— the bank. (frente a)

REVIEW LESSON I

I. Give the plural of the following nouns.

address   loaf   glory   rose
American   city   day   dish
boy   chair   son   lesson
fly   foot   house   lunch
banana   month   orange   potato
life   match   week   church
hero   meal   wife   year
room   key   tooth   glass
bridge   fox   man   street
woman   child   handkerchief   sandwich

II. Change the words in italics to personal pronouns.

1. *The money* is on the desk.
2. *The new words* are on the blackboard.
3. *Mr. Miller* is late today.
4. *Mrs. Miller* is always early.
5. Are you going with *George*?
6. Where is *my English book*?
7. I have a surprise for *my friends*.
8. I am waiting for *my sister*.
9. He is taking *his son* with him.
10. *Mr. and Mrs. Miller* rent *the house*.
11. *Virginia* is a student.
12. *The students* are working hard.
13. *The President* is speaking now.
14. *The university* is very old.
15. I have *my books* with me.
16. *The news* is very good.
17. We see *those people* every day.
18. *The maid* opens the door.
19. I see *Virginia* at lunch.
20. Does she have *dinner* early?

31

III. Use the correct form of the simple present tense of the verb.

1. He _comes_ (come) from Brazil.
2. _Are_ (be) you from New York?
3. He _goes_ (go) to class early.
4. You _explain_ (explain) the lesson.
5. He _understands_ (understand) the words.
6. The teachers _are_ (be) North Americans.
7. Virginia _likes_ (like) the university.
8. She _has_ (have) many books.
9. The lesson _is_ (be) important.
10. Mr. Miller _rents_ (rent) the house.
11. The house _has_ (have) a nice green lawn.
12. There _are_ (be) four rooms downstairs.
13. There _is_ (be) a garden in the back yard.
14. Virginia _lives_ (live) on Clark Street.
15. Mrs. Miller _has_ (have) many things to buy.
16. The tomatoes _are_ (be) a little green.
17. She _needs_ (need) to buy vegetables.
18. I ——— (listen) to the radio every night.
19. We ——— (want) to speak English well.
20. There _are_ (be) many Latin Americans in the United States.
21. Those people _are_ (be) North Americans.
22. The news _is_ (be) bad tonight.
23. There _is_ (be) some good news for you in this letter.
24. There _are_ (be) not many people in the bank now.
25. The people in this class _want_ (want) to learn English.

IV. Change these sentences to questions.

1. Virginia is in the United States.
2. She is studying at a university.
3. It is difficult.
4. She is learning a great deal.
5. She is having a good time.
6. The house is made of brick.
7. There are four bedrooms upstairs.
8. The front yard is small.
9. Her friends are expecting her soon.
10. She is a South American.
11. They know Spanish.
12. He likes to speak English.
13. You come to class early.
14. We need butter.
15. She wants to eat now.
16. You understand his English.
17. They listen to the radio in the evening.
18. Mrs. Miller has many things to buy.
19. Mr. Brown waits on Mrs. Miller.
20. Virginia goes to the store with her.

V. Answer these questions in complete sentences.

1. How much is butter? 2. How much is coffee? 3. How much are eggs? 4. How much is sugar? 5. How much is gasoline? 6. How much do tomatoes cost? 7. How much do apples cost? 8. How much does bread cost? 9. How much does milk cost? 10. How much do nylon stockings cost? 11. In what country do you live? 12. In what city do you live? 13. On what street do you live? 14. What is your address? 15. Do you speak Spanish? English? 16. Are you studying English? 17. Where are you studying English? 18. Do you like to study English? 19. Do you like to listen to English? 20. Is English pronunciation difficult? 21. Do you arrive at class on time? 22. Are you going home after class? 23. On what days do you have your English class? 24. How much coffee do you drink a day? 25. Do you like to sit in a chair or on a sofa? 26. Is Virginia a South American? 27. Are you a Mexican? 28. Is your teacher a North American? 29. Are you a student? 30. Are you an engineer? 31. Does it often rain in the tropics? 32. Is it raining now?

Morgan Brassell

LESSON IV

INTRODUCTIONS, GREETINGS, LEAVE–TAKINGS

The customs of one country are often different from those of another. For example, North Americans do not shake hands as much as Latin Americans do. In introductions, a woman sometimes extends her hand to a man or to another woman, but this is not necessary; two men, however, always

34

shake hands. Men also stand up, but women rise only to show special respect to another person because of age or position.

North Americans are friendly, but their greetings and leave-takings are short and informal. When two friends meet or when they say good-bye, they sometimes shake hands, and sometimes not. They do not embrace. This is different from the Latin-American custom, but it does not indicate that North Americans are unfriendly.

Introductions

    A. Mrs. Miller, this is my friend, Mr. Jones.
    B. How do you do, Mrs. Miller?
    C. How do you do? I'm glad to meet you.

    . . .

    B. Good-bye, Mrs. Miller. It was a pleasure to meet you.
    C. Thank you. The pleasure was mine.

Greetings

Formal: A. How do you do, Mrs. Miller?
          B. How do you do, Mrs. Jones? How are you?
          A. Very well, thank you. And you?
          B. Fine, thank you.

Formal: A. Good morning (Good afternoon, Good evening), Mr. Miller.
          B. Good morning, Mr. Jones. I'm glad to see you.

Familiar: A. Hello, Jim (James).
          B. Hello, Virginia. How are you?
          A. Just fine, thanks. And you?
          B. Oh, so-so (fair).

Very Familiar:
    A. Hi, Ginny.
    B. Hi, Jim. What's new?
    A. Oh, nothing in particular. How's everything (with you)?
    B. All right, thank you.

Note· **How do you do?** is only a preliminary greeting. The second person usually repeats the same phrase and then says **How are you?** The answer **Very well** or **Fine** generally follows.

Leave-takings

Formal: A. Good-bye, Mrs. Miller.
         B. Good-bye, James. I am so glad to have seen you.

Formal: A. Good night, Mrs. Miller.
         B. Good night, James. It was nice to see you.

Familiar: A. So long, Jim. I'll see you later.
          B. So long, Ginny. See you tomorrow. (I'll be seeing you.)

Note: At night, **Good night** is used only to say good-bye. The greeting is always **Good evening.**

VOCABULARY

another	otro	**leave-taking**	despedida
as much as	tanto como	**to meet**	conocer (*por primera vez*); encontrarse
because of	por, a causa de		
common	usado		
custom	costumbre	**mine**	mío
to embrace	abrazar	**often**	muchas veces, a menudo
ever	alguna vez; nunca		
to extend (the hand)	tender (la mano)	**pleasure**	placer
		to rise	levantarse
fair	regular	**seldom**	rara vez
familiar	de confianza	**to shake hands**	darse la mano
fine	muy bien	**short**	corto
to follow	seguir	**so long**	hasta luego, hasta la vista
formal	respetuoso; con ceremonia		
friendly	simpático	**sometimes**	algunas veces
generally	generalmente	**so-so**	regular, así así
good-bye	adiós	**to stand up**	ponerse de pie
greeting	saludo	**unfriendly**	poco amistoso
however	sin embargo	**usually**	usualmente, generalmente
introduction	presentación		

IDIOMS

different from	diferente de
for example	por ejemplo
Good afternoon.	Buenas tardes.
Good evening.	Buenas noches.
Good night.	Buenas noches.
How are you?	¿Cómo está Vd.? ¿Qué tal?
How's everything (with you)?	¿Cómo le va?
I am glad to meet you.	Mucho gusto en conocerlo.
I am glad to see you.	Mucho gusto en verlo.
I am so glad to have seen you.	Tanto gusto en haberlo visto.
I'll be seeing you (*familiar*).	Lo veré más tarde.
(I'll) See you later.	Lo veré más tarde.
It was nice to see you.	Mucho gusto en haberlo visto.
Just fine.	Muy bien.
Nothing in particular.	Nada de particular.
What's new?	¿Qué hay de nuevo?

CONVERSATION

Answer the following questions in complete sentences.

1. In introductions, do North Americans shake hands? 2. Do the men shake hands? 3. Do the women shake hands? 4. Does a woman shake hands with a man? 5. In the United States, is it necessary to rise when one is introduced? Is it necessary in your country? 6. Are North American greetings long and formal? 7. Do two North American friends shake hands when they greet each other? 8. Do North American friends sometimes embrace? 9. What greeting do they use at night? 10. When do they use the expression **How do you do?** How do they answer it? 11. What is the usual nickname for James? for Virginia? 12. What is the meaning of **Hi,** and when is it used? 13. Are the customs of one country different from those of another?

14. In your country, do you shake hands with a man when you greet him? 15. Do you shake hands with a woman when you greet her? 16. Do two women shake hands? Do they embrace? 17. Do two men shake hands? Do they embrace? 18. Are greetings the same in all Latin-American countries?

PRONUNCIATION

- [θ] thin, thing, think, thank, north, south
- [ɜ] sir, bird, learn, heard, word
- [e] embrace, shake, later, say, explain, they, steak
- [ʊ] good, book, look, took, shook, put, full
- [ʃ] shake, short, show, shower, shape, ship, shook

GRAMMAR   Section 1

I. The Negative Form of the Simple Present Tense.

In negative sentences in the present tense, the auxiliary verb **do** is used with all verbs except **be** and other auxiliaries. The negative adverb is **not**. The word order is:

Subject → {**do not (don't)** / **does not (doesn't)**} → Principal Verb

I	do not (don't)	have	a good radio.
You	do not (don't)	say	"Hi" to your teacher.
He	does not (doesn't)	notice	the difference.
We	do not (don't)	live	on that street now.
They	do not (don't)	shake	hands.

Note 1: The principal verb is always in the simple form after **do not** and **does not**. The contraction for **do not** is **don't**; for **does not**, it is **doesn't**.

Note 2: The verb **have** (tener) has two negative forms in the present, but the form with **do not** is used in idioms.

        I do not (don't) have a book.
        I haven't a book. (*less frequent*)
Idiom: I do not (don't) have to go. (No tengo que ir.)

Practice reading the following sentences in the negative. Read them (1) without the contractions, (2) with the contractions.

1. He needs to learn French.
2. They like to study English.
3. John has a good pronunciation.
4. They want to live in the United States.
5. My friend has enough time.
6. We need vegetables today.
7. He eats lunch at one o'clock.
8. They come to class early.
9. George studies very hard.
10. We practice our English every day.
11. Virginia speaks Spanish well.
12. It rains a great deal there.
13. They use formal greetings.
14. She notices the difference.
15. I understand Mr. Miller because he speaks slowly and clearly.

II. Negative Statements with the Verb be.

A. The adverb **not** follows the principal verb **be** or the auxiliary **be**. The auxiliary verb **do** is not used. The negative word order with **be** is the following:

Subject → Verb **be** → **not**

I	am	not		a doctor.
I	am	not	studying	medicine.
You	are	not		a lawyer.
You	are	not	studying	law.
He	is	not		busy now.
He	is	not	working	now.
We	are	not		ready to go.
We	are	not	going	with you.
They	are	not		at home now.
They	are	not	living	there now.

B. Contractions of the verb **be** are generally used in conversation and in friendly letters. With a *pronoun* subject, there are two *negative contractions*, except in the first person singular, where there is only one. With a *noun* subject, only the forms **isn't** and **aren't** are used.

(1) I'm not   we're not   (2) ———   we aren't
     you're not   you're not   you aren't   you aren't

     he's not ⎫   he isn't ⎫
     she's not ⎬ they're not   she isn't ⎬ they aren't
     it's not ⎭   it isn't ⎭

Practice reading these sentences in the negative. Read them (1) without the contractions, (2) with the contractions.

1. The lesson is difficult.
2. The classes are small.
3. The students are late.
4. Virginia is speaking English.
5. I am waiting for her.
6. We are writing letters.
7. That is a familiar greeting.
8. They are Colombians.
9. He is a South American.
10. They are shaking hands now.
11. We are leaving tomorrow.
12. She is living on Clark Street.
13. I am studying the lesson now.
14. The teacher is explaining it.
15. They are comin᷄ to class today.
16. He is very glad to see them.
17. We are ready to go now.

III. Negative Questions.

A. Generally, in negative questions the contraction is more common than the long form. For example, **don't you notice** is much more natural than **do you not notice**. However, in the first person singular, present tense, of the verb **be**, no contraction exists. It is necessary to say **am I not**.

B. The order in negative questions with the contractions is as follows:

Don't
Doesn't
Aren't
Isn't   → Subject → Principal Verb

Don't	I	need	a new hat?
Don't	you	want	to go with us?
Doesn't	he	rent	the house?
Doesn't	she	like	to study?
Don't	we	have	a class today?
Don't	they	notice	the difference?
Aren't	you	coming	with us?
Isn't	Virginia		ready to go?

Exception: **Am I not** pronouncing the word correctly?

Practice changing the sentences in I and in II B of this lesson to negative questions.

IV. The Use of the Negatives no and not.

A. **No** is used both as an adverb and an adjective.

1. As an adverb, **no** is used to answer questions in the negative.

   Do you come to class on Saturday? **No.**
   Are you a lawyer? **No,** I am not a lawyer.

2. As an adjective, **no** is used before a noun without an article or before a noun preceded by any adjective except **any, much, many,** or **enough.**

   I have **no** money in my pocket.
   There is **no** paper in the desk.
   There is **no** white paper in the desk.

B. The adverb **not** is used in all other cases.

1. Before a noun with an article.

    Not a person in the class is absent today.

2. Before **any, much, many,** and **enough.**

    There is **not** any paper on the desk.
    Not much time is left.
    Not many students come to class late.
    Not enough students are here to have a class today.

3. To make verbs negative, or in phrases when a verb is understood.

    The classes are **not** large.
    They do **not** want to go with us.
    He is a Bolivian, **not** a Peruvian.
    Sometimes they shake hands, sometimes **not**.
    Do they embrace? **Not** often.
    Are they going? **Not** now. (Ahora no.)
    Are they ready? **Not** yet. (Todavía no.)

Note: The adjective **no** is not used in a sentence containing the word **not**. English, unlike Spanish, does not use a double negative.

> I have **no** class today.
> (**No** tengo **ninguna** clase hoy.)

> I do **not** have a (**any**) class today.

*Practice reading these sentences with **no** or **not**, as required.*

1. He notices ——— difference in their pronunciation.
2. The room has ——— windows in it.
3. That store does ——— sell paper.
4. They have ——— fireplace in their house.
5. They do ——— have a class today.
6. We have ——— time for that now.
7. ——— news is good news.
8. ——— a man in the room speaks English.
9. ——— sentence is complete without a subject.
10. There is ——— heat in the building.
11. ——— many people like to wait.
12. ——— much light enters this room.
13. ——— other class wants to do that.
14. There is ——— time like the present.
15. ——— many students are in the library now.

16. Mr. Miller is ——— at home now.
17. There is ——— a store near our house.
18. There is ——— bread in the house.
19. The teacher is ——— difficult to understand.
20. Is the pronunciation easy? ———.
21. There are ——— students absent today.
22. We have ——— hot water today.
23. She does ——— like to speak English.
24. There are ——— new houses on that street.
25. Do you often go to the movies? ———, ——— often.

Section 2

V. The Position of Adverbs of Frequency.

The adverbs **always, usually, often, sometimes, never, rarely, seldom,** and **ever** precede all principal verbs except **be**. This is the natural word order, and it is always correct; but for emphasis these words are sometimes used in other positions in the sentence.

	Questions			Answers	
Do you	ever	see her?	Yes, I		see her.
Do you	often	see her?	Yes, I	often	see her.
Do you	always	see her?	Yes, I	always	see her.
Do you	usually	see her?	Yes, I	usually	see her.
Do you	sometimes	see her?	Yes, I	sometimes	see her.
Don't you	ever	see her?	No, I	{ never / don't ever	see her.
Don't you	often	see her?	No, I	don't often	see her.
Don't you	always	see her?	No, I	don't always	see her.
Don't you	usually	see her?	No, I	don't usually	see her.
Don't you	sometimes	see her?	No, I	{ rarely / seldom	see her.

Note 1: Several answers, affirmative or negative, can be used after each question.
Note 2: **Ever** is used only in questions and in negative statements. **Never** is the equivalent of **not ever**.

Is he	ever	here on Saturday?	Yes, he is		here then.
Is he	often	here on Saturday?	Yes, he is	often	here then.
Is he	always	here on Saturday?	Yes, he is	always	here then.
Is he	usually	here on Saturday?	Yes, he is	usually	here then.
Is he	sometimes	here on Saturday?	Yes, he is	sometimes	here then.

Isn't he **ever**	here on Saturday?	No, he { is **never** / isn't **ever** }	here then.
Isn't he **often**	here on Saturday?	No, he isn't **often**	here then.
Isn't he **always**	here on Saturday?	No, he isn't **always**	here then.
Isn't he **usually**	here on Saturday?	No, he isn't **usually**	here then.
Isn't he **sometimes**	here on Saturday?	No, he is { **rarely** / **seldom** }	here then.

Note: These adverbs follow the verb **be** except when it is used with an auxiliary.

> I **can never be** there at ten o'clock.
> He **has usually been** here on time.

Practice answering these questions, using different adverbs of frequency (1) in the affirmative, (2) in the negative.

1. Do you ever look at *Life* magazine?
2. Does he ever study his lesson?
3. Does she ever play the piano for you?
4. Do they ever wait for you?
5. Don't you ever see Mr. Miller?
6. Doesn't it ever rain in December?
7. Do you usually write letters on Sunday?
8. Do they sometimes shake hands?
9. Does he often come to class late?
10. Does she always have coffee for breakfast?
11. Are you ever at home in the afternoon?
12. Is there ever a lecture in English?
13. Is she ever ready on time?
14. Are they ever late?
15. Aren't you usually busy in the morning?
16. Isn't he sometimes in that room?
17. Isn't she often there on Saturday?
18. Are you always serious?
19. Are they often out of town?
20. Is it always hot in Panama?

VI. The Prepositions of, from (de).

A. The preposition **of** is used:

1. To indicate a quantity or a part of something.

   a pound **of** sugar   some **of** the students
   a gallon **of** gasoline   all **of** the books
   a glass **of** milk   none **of** the houses

2. To indicate possession when speaking of things.

>   the name **of** the school   the color **of** the walls
>   the capital **of** the country   the present tense **of** the verb

Note: For the treatment of possession referring to persons, see Lesson V.

Practice giving the English equivalent of these phrases.

1. los parques de la ciudad
2. la vista de las montañas
3. el precio del vestido
4. la madre de la familia
5. el nombre de la calle
6. la dirección de la carta
7. las puertas de la casa
8. los dependientes del almacén
9. las costumbres del país
10. el color del sofá

B. The preposition **from** is used:

1. To indicate the *origin* of people and things.

> Where is she **from**? She is **from** California.
> Where does she come **from**? She comes **from** California.
> She has a letter **from** her family.
> Is your bracelet **from** Peru or México?

Practice answering these questions.

1. What country do you come **from**?
2. What part of the country do you come **from**?
3. What city do you come **from**?

2. To indicate the place where, or the time when, an action begins.

> He goes directly **from** his office to class.
> The plane flies **from** Barranquilla to Miami.
>
> They are always happy **from** morning to night.
> The lecture is **from** seven o'clock to eight o'clock.

H. Armstrong Roberts

LESSON V

NORTH AMERICAN NAMES

There are five members in the Miller family. The father's full name is Charles Edward Miller. Charles is his first name or given name, Edward his middle name, and Miller his last name or surname. A North American has only one surname because he never uses his mother's maiden name after his father's name.

45

Mr. Miller's wife is Mrs. Charles Edward Miller, or Mrs. Charles E. Miller. Before her marriage, her name was Alice Grant, but now it is Alice Miller. In business letters, she uses the signature **Alice Miller,** with **Mrs. Charles E. Miller** in parentheses below. On her calling card, however, her name is always written **Mrs. Charles Edward Miller.**

Mr. and Mrs. Miller have two sons and one daughter. The name of one son is Charles Edward Miller, Jr. The word **Junior** (**Jr.**) follows the name of this son in order to distinguish it from the name of his father. The name of the other son is Paul Andrew Miller. The daughter's name is Mary Grant Miller. On her calling card, it is always written **Miss Mary Grant Miller.** The parents select the first two names of their children, either given names or family surnames; but the last name is always the father's surname.

VOCABULARY

Alice	Alicia	**Junior (Jr.)**	hijo
Andrew	Andrés	**last name**	apellido
below	abajo	**maiden name**	apellido de una mujer antes de su matrimonio
business letter	carta comercial		
calling card	tarjeta de visita		
Charles	Carlos	**marriage**	matrimonio
country	país	**member**	miembro
to distinguish	distinguir	**middle name**	segundo nombre
Edward	Eduardo	**only**	solamente
either . . . or	o . . . o	**parents**	padres
first name	nombre	**Paul**	Pablo
full name	nombre completo	**to select**	escoger
		to sign	firmar
given name	nombre de pila	**signature**	firma
in order to	para	**surname**	apellido
is written	se escribe		

WORD STUDY

Other Members of a Family

uncle	tío	**nephew**	sobrino
aunt	tía	**niece**	sobrina

cousin	primo, prima	brother-in-law	cuñado
grandfather	abuelo	sister-in-law	cuñada
grandmother	abuela	son-in-law	yerno
grandparents	abuelos	daughter-in-law	nuera
grandson	nieto	stepfather	padrastro
granddaughter	nieta	stepmother	madrastra
grandchildren	nietos	stepchild	hijastro
great-grandfather	bisabuelo	godfather	padrino
father-in-law	suegro	godmother	madrina
mother-in-law	suegra	godchild	ahijado

Complete the following sentences with the appropriate word.

1. My father's mother is my ———.
2. My mother's brother is my ———.
3. My sister's husband is my ———.
4. My uncle's son is my ———.
5. My nephew is my brother's ———.
6. My sister's daughter is my ———.
7. My father's sister is my ———.
8. My husband's mother is my ———.
9. My father's second wife is my ———.
10. My daughter's husband is my ———.

CONVERSATION

Answer these questions in complete sentences.

1. What does this lesson explain? 2. How many members are there in the Miller family? 3. What is Mr. Miller's full name? 4. What is his first name? his middle name? his surname? 5. Who selects the first two names? 6. Does a North American use his mother's maiden name after his father's name? 7. When does a woman change her name? 8. What is Mrs. Miller's full name? 9. What is the name on her calling card? 10. How is it different from the calling card of a Latin-American woman? 11. How does Mrs. Miller sign a business letter? 12. What are the names of the children? 13. Do they use their mother's maiden name after their father's surname? 14. Why is Jr. sometimes used after the name of a son?

15. Does the teacher explain North American names? 16. Does the teacher understand the Latin-American custom? 17. What is your complete name? 18. What is your

first name? your middle name? 19. How many surnames do you have? What are they? 20. How would the name on your calling card be written (se escribiría) in English? 21. What are the principal differences between the customs of North America and Latin America? 22. How would you sign (firmaría Vd.) your name in the United States? Why?

GRAMMAR   Section 1

I. The Past Tense of the Verb be.

Affirmative	Negative	Interrogative	Negative Interrogative
I was	I was not (wasn't)	was I?	wasn't I?
you were	you were not (weren't)	were you?	weren't you?
he was	he was not (wasn't)	was he?	wasn't he?
she was	she was not (wasn't)	was she?	wasn't she?
it was	it was not (wasn't)	was it?	wasn't it?
we were	we were not (weren't)	were we?	weren't we?
you were	you were not (weren't)	were you?	weren't you?
they were	they were not (weren't)	were they?	weren't they?

*Fill the blanks with the correct form of the past tense of **be**.*

1. There ——— five members in the Miller family.
2. Her name ——— Alice Grant before her marriage.
3. ——— you in class yesterday?
4. He ——— not in the office yesterday.
5. His calling card ——— on the desk this morning.
6. We ——— very busy last week.
7. ——— her signature at the end of the letter?
8. The children ——— not in school last week.
9. He ——— never in the United States.
10. His grandparents ——— from Spain.

II. The Past Tense with ing.

To form the past tense with **ing**, the past tense of the verb **be** is used as an auxiliary with the present participle (**ing** form) of the principal verb.

>   I **was reading** the paper.
>   We **weren't talking**.
>   **Were** you **writing** a letter?
>   **Weren't** they **waiting** for you?

Practice using the correct form of each verb in the past tense with ing. *Then repeat the sentences in the negative.*

1. My niece ——— (visit) us.
2. I ——— (study) my English lesson.
3. They ——— (have) a good time.
4. We ——— (listen) to the radio.
5. She ——— (write) a letter.
6. I ——— (go) to the library.
7. ——— you ——— (sleep)?
8. ——— he ——— (wait) for her?
9. ——— the children ——— (play) in the yard?
10. ——— you ——— (expect) to see her?

III. Future Time with going to.

A. To express future time, the words **going to** are often used with a form of the verb **be**. Here the word **going** does not have the meaning of the verb **go**; it is only an indication of future time. **Going to** is equivalent to the Spanish **ir a.**

I **am going to** write a letter.
You **are going to** be late.
He **is going to** visit his cousin.
We **are going to** study our English.
They **are not going to** go home now.

Answer the following questions in complete sentences.

1. What are you going to do tonight?
2. What are you going to do tomorrow morning?
3. What are you going to do tomorrow afternoon?
4. What are you going to do tomorrow evening?
5. What are you going to do on Saturday? on Sunday?

B. Future time is also expressed by the simple present **tense** or by the present with **ing**. In such sentences there is often an adverbial expression, like **tomorrow,** that indicates the future time.

When **does** he **leave**?	He **leaves** tomorrow morning.
When **is** he **leaving**?	He **is leaving** tomorrow morning.
When **does** he **arrive**?	He **arrives** next Saturday.
When **is** he **arriving**?	He **is arriving** next Saturday.

Answer these questions using the present tense.
1. When are you going downtown?
2. When is he leaving for his vacation?
3. When does the lecture begin?
4. When do you leave for your vacation?
5. When do classes end this year?

Section 2

IV. Possessives.

A. The possessive form of a noun referring to a person or an animal is usually formed by adding an apostrophe and an s. In the case of a plural noun that ends in s, only an apostrophe is added after the s. This possessive form always precedes the noun that is possessed.

> **Paul's** book is on the desk.
> The **doctor's** office is on the second floor.
> **Charles's** middle name is Edward.
> The **men's** hats and coats are in the other room.
> The **girls'** friends are from New York.
> The **Millers'** house is made of brick and wood.

The possessive form of a noun may be used alone as a pronoun.

> This book is **Paul's**.
> That office is the **doctor's**.
> That house is the **Millers'**.

Practice giving the English equivalents of these phrases.
1. los amigos de Virginia
2. la casa de mi padre
3. los libros del estudiante
4. los libros de los estudiantes
5. la casa del presidente
6. la opinión del profesor
7. el automóvil de mi amigo
8. el automóvil de mis amigos
9. la casa de la señora Miller
10. la conferencia del director
11. la pronunciación del señor
12. el perro de Jaime

B. Possessive *adjectives* agree with the possessor and not with the nouns they modify. They agree in person and number; in the third person singular, they also agree in gender. The same form is used before singular or plural nouns.

my habit	**my** habits
your habit	**your** habits
his habit (*m.*)	**his** habits
her habit (*f.*)	**her** habits
its habit (*n.*)	**its** habits
our habit	**our** habits
your habit	**your** habits
their habit	**their** habits

Note: The possessive adjective is used with parts of the body or things associated with the body.

> **My** eyes are blue.
> She sometimes extends **her** hand.
> He is wearing **his** new hat.

C. Possessive *pronouns* also agree with the possessor and not with the thing possessed. They agree in person and number; in the third person singular, they also agree in gender. The same form is used to refer to singular or plural nouns. No definite article is used with the possessive pronouns as in Spanish.

> The book is (The books are) **mine.**
> The book is (The books are) **yours.**
> The book is (The books are) **his.**
> The book is (The books are) **hers.**
> The book is (The books are) **ours.**
> The book is (The books are) **yours.**
> The book is (The books are) **theirs.**

D. A double possessive is possible in English by using the preposition **of**, which shows possession, before a possessive noun or pronoun.

She is a cousin **of John's.**	(Es una prima de Juan.)
He is a friend **of mine.**	(Es un amigo mío.)
They are friends **of ours.**	(Son amigos nuestros.)

E. The possessive form of **who** is **whose**. It is the translation of Spanish **cuyo** and **¿de quién?**

> The boy **whose** father is a doctor is James Brown. (*adjective*)
> **Whose** pencil is this? (*adjective*)
> **Whose** is it? (*pronoun*)

Practice 1. Use the possessive adjective that refers to the person or persons mentioned in the sentence.

1. The boy usually helps ——— sister.
2. The boys usually help ——— sisters.
3. Virginia has a present for ——— sister.
4. We like to visit ——— friends.
5. We are waiting for ——— class to begin.
6. On what days do you have ——— English class?
7. Charles and ——— brother are studying Spanish.
8. Mrs. Miller loves ——— children.
9. Virginia says that ——— North American friends use short greetings.
10. Mr. and Mrs. Miller have three children. ——— last name is Miller, and ——— first names are Charles, Paul, and Mary.
11. The North American man does not use ——— mother's surname.
12. ——— middle name is Edward.
13. On ——— calling card ——— name is written **Miss Mary Grant Miller.**
14. The children do not use ——— mother's surname.
15. ——— name was Alice Grant before ——— marriage.
16. I am learning ——— lesson.

Practice 2. Use a possessive pronoun in place of the words in italics.

1. The signature is *her signature.*
2. Is the book *your book?*
3. The letter is *my letter.*
4. The shoes are *his shoes.*
5. The house is *their house.*
6. Is the hat *your hat* or *Paul's hat?*
7. The room is *his room.*
8. The radio is *my sister's radio.*
9. The car is *Mr. Miller's car.*
10. The calling card is *Charles's calling card.*
11. Here is *my calling card* on the desk.
12. The desk is *my brother's desk.*
13. The coat is *Virginia's coat.*
14. Is the magazine *your magazine?*
15. Is her name the same as *my name?*
16. The dog on the porch is *our dog.*

V. The Demonstratives this, that, these, those.

A. The demonstrative adjectives in English are as follows:

	Singular		Plural
this boy	este muchacho	**these boys**	estos muchachos
this girl	esta muchacha	**these girls**	estas muchachas
that boy	ese (aquel) muchacho	**those boys**	esos (aquellos) muchachos
that girl	esa (aquella) muchacha	**those girls**	esas (aquellas) muchachas

B. The demonstrative pronouns in English are as follows:

	Singular		Plural
this	esto		
this one	éste, ésta	**these**	éstos, éstas
that	eso; aquello		
that one	ése, ésa; aquél, aquélla	**those**	ésos, ésas; aquéllos, aquéllas

Note: When the singular demonstrative pronoun refers to a noun already mentioned, the form **this one** or **that one** is used. In the plural, **these** or **those** is used.

> Do you prefer this book or **that one**?
> I think **this one** is better than **that one**.
> These customs are different from **those** of your country.

C. The order of the words in these questions should be studied carefully. **Whose** is used as an adjective and **this** as a pronoun in questions, contrary to the usage in Spanish.

Whose book is this?	¿De quién es este libro?
This book is mine.	Este libro es mío.
Whose book is that?	¿De quién es ese libro?
That book is yours.	Ese libro es de Vd.
Whose books are these?	¿De quién son estos libros?
These books are hers.	Estos libros son de ella.
Whose books are those?	¿De quién son esos libros?
Those books are ours.	Esos libros son nuestros.

D. Learn the following expressions:

this morning	esta mañana	**this evening**	esta noche (*temprano*)
this afternoon	esta tarde	**tonight**	esta noche

Translate into English.
1. Estos niños están felices hoy.
2. Este perro es muy simpático.
3. Esta casa no es muy grande.
4. Esas casas son pequeñas.
5. Aquel señor es médico.
6. Esta casa es nuestra. Esa es la de él.
7. Esta casa es bonita pero aquéllas no me gustan.
8. Estos anteojos son de Vd. ¿ Dónde están los míos?
9. ¿ De quién es este perro? Es de ellos.
10. ¿ De quién son estos libros? Son de mi hermano.
11. ¿ De quién es esta firma? Es de Virginia.
12. ¿ De quién es aquel automóvil? Es del señor Miller.
13. ¿ Qué es esto? Esto es un borrador.
14. Esta firma es difícil de leer. Esa es fácil.
15. Ese nombre es muy usado en inglés.
16. Esta prima está casada y ésa no está casada.
17. Mi nombre es muy usado; el suyo no es muy usado.
18. Esas tarjetas de visita son diferentes de éstas.
19. Esta estampilla es nueva; ésa es vieja.
20. Estos cuadernos son míos; ésos son de ella.

Charles Phelps Cushing

LESSON VI

A LETTER FROM VIRGINIA

431 Clark Street
Baton Rouge, La.
November 1, 19—

Dear Isabel,

As you know, I am attending Louisiana State University. There are so many things to do and to see that it is hard to

55

find time to write letters. Besides, I have to study very hard, because my courses are difficult, and my English isn't very good yet.

I think that you will be very interested in the American custom of "dating" because it is not like the custom at home. "To have a date" means to have an engagement for a social affair with a friend, usually a friend of the opposite sex. For instance, one has a date to go for a walk, to go to the movies, to go to a party or a dance, to go to a lecture or a concert, to have dinner at a restaurant or at the home of some friends. The young people go without a chaperon. The basis for this American custom is that most parents teach their children to be independent and responsible for their actions whether there are adults present or not.

One of my friends is Robert Anderson. I met him in one of my classes, and of course an introduction is not necessary when you see each other in class every day. One day after class he asked me to go to the drugstore to have a Coke, and then he walked home with me. A week later he invited me to go to the movies, and last night I had a date to go to a college dance with him. He is a very good dancer, so I had a wonderful time.

Now I have to stop, because I have an appointment with my history professor. In my next letter I'm going to write more about my classes and my social life. Please give my regards to your family, and let me hear from you soon.

                                    Affectionately,
                                    Virginia

VOCABULARY

appointment	cita	**engagement**	compromiso
as	como	**to find** (*things*)	encontrar
basis	razón, base	**hard** (*adj.*)	difícil
chaperon	acompañante de los jóvenes	**hard** (*adv.*)	mucho
		interested	interesado
Coke	Coca Cola	**lecture**	conferencia
dance	baile	**like**	como
dancer	bailador, bailarín	**to meet** (**met**)	conocer (conocí)
date	cita	**movies**	cine

of course	por supuesto	to stop (doing something)	dejar de (hacer algo)
opposite sex	el otro sexo	to teach	enseñar
party	fiesta	time	tiempo
regards	recuerdos	whether or not	si o no
to see each other	verse	wonderful	maravilloso
so	así es que	yet	todavía
social affair	función social	young people	jóvenes

IDIOMS

to ask someone to go	pedir a alguien que vaya
for instance	por ejemplo
to go for a walk	ir a pasear(se) (a pie)
to have a wonderful time	divertirse de lo lindo
to have dinner	comer
to have to	tener que
to invite someone to go	invitar a alguien que vaya
to let me hear from you	permitir que yo reciba noticias suyas
so many things to do	tantas cosas que hacer
to walk home with someone	acompañar a casa a alguien a pie

CONVERSATION

Answer these questions in complete sentences.

1. What is the name of the university that Virginia is attending? 2. In what state is the university located? 3. In what city is it located? 4. In what part of the country is Louisiana? 5. Why is it hard to find time to write letters? 6. Does Virginia speak English well? 7. What is the difference between an appointment and an engagement? 8. What is the difference between an engagement and a date? 9. What different kinds of dates are there? 10. Does Virginia often go to the movies? 11. Did Robert invite her to go to the movies? 12. Did a chaperon go with them? Why not? 13. Where did Virginia and Robert go to get a Coke? 14. What other things are sold in an American drugstore? 15. What is Virginia going to tell us in her next letter? 16. How does one usually end a friendly letter? 17. Did Virginia have a good time at the college dance? Why? 18. With whom did she have an appointment? Why?

19. Do you like to write letters? 20. Do you have time to write many? 21. Do you notice any difference between the style of an American letter and one of your letters? 22. Do you live in a college town? 23. Do you buy Cokes at a drugstore? Where do you usually get a Coke? 24. How are your drugstores different from North American drugstores? 25. Do many young people here go to the movies without a chaperon? 26. If several couples go together, is a chaperon necessary? 27. Did you have a date last Saturday or Sunday? Did a chaperon go, too? 28. Do you like to dance? Are you a good dancer? Do you often dance? 29. Did you have an appointment with the doctor or dentist last week? 30. Do you have an engagement for next Saturday?

PRONUNCIATION

[ɪ] it, is, his, him, think, thing, different, difficult, invite, introduction, interested, history, middle, signature, English
[aɪ] find, time, life, wife, five, sign, night, write, besides
[ɑ] not, stop, follow, opposite, economics, Robert
[æ] as, ask, have, had, happy, action, class, last, dance, dancer
[ʃ] she, short, social, action, affectionately, chaperon, Michigan, Chicago

GRAMMAR   Section 1

I. The Simple Past Tense of Regular Verbs.

A. The regular ending of the simple past tense is **ed**; it is added to the simple form of the verb. If the verb ends in **e**, only **d** is added.

B. The ending **ed** or **d** is pronounced [t] after a voiceless sound: [p], [k], [f], [s] [ʃ], [tʃ]. After a voiced sound, it is pronounced [d]. If the verb ends in **t** or **d**, it is pronounced as a separate syllable: [ɪd].

58

Practice reading these forms aloud.

[t]	[d]	[ɪd]
danced	learned	wanted
noticed	listened	waited
pronounced	signed	rented
missed	lived	invited
watched	arrived	selected
walked	used	expected
asked	followed	ended
liked	changed	attended
finished	ordered	needed
distinguished	answered	extended

C. The variations in spelling of the simple past tense are as follows:

1. When the simple form of the verb ends in a single consonant preceded by a single vowel and the stress is on the last syllable, the consonant is doubled before a suffix beginning with a vowel.

    stop   sto**pp**ed   omit   omi**tt**ed

2. When the simple form of the verb ends in **y** preceded by a consonant, the **y** changes to **i** before **ed**.

    study   stud**ied**   marry   marr**ied**

D. The simple past tense is generally used to express an action completed at a definite time in the past.

> Virginia **studied** very hard yesterday.
> Robert **walked** home with her last night.

II. The Simple Past Tense: Negative and Interrogative.

The past tense of the auxiliary verb **do** is **did**. All principal verbs except **be** use **did** in the interrogative and **did not** in the negative. The negative contraction is **didn't**. The principal verb is always in the simple form.

Negative	Interrogative	Negative Interrogative
I **did not** (**didn't**) **walk**	**did** I **walk**?	**didn't** I **walk**?
you **did not** (**didn't**) **walk**	**did** you **walk**?	**didn't** you **walk**?
he **did not** (**didn't**) **walk**	**did** he **walk**?	**didn't** he **walk**?

we **did not (didn't) walk**	**did** we **walk?**	**didn't** we **walk?**
you **did not (didn't) walk**	**did** you **walk?**	**didn't** you **walk?**
they **did not (didn't) walk**	**did** they **walk?**	**didn't** they **walk?**

Practice 1. Read these sentences in (1) the interrogative, (2) the negative.

1. We changed the sentences to questions.
2. We pronounced the words many times.
3. The teacher asked many questions.
4. I answered all her questions.
5. Virginia embraced her mother.
6. Our friends rented the house on the corner.
7. They liked the lecture very much.
8. She received several letters yesterday.
9. Mr. Miller wanted to have his lunch early.
10. Mrs. Miller prepared lunch for him.
11. The streetcar stopped in front of my house.
12. They walked home from class.
13. She selected new calling cards.
14. He lived on College Avenue last year.
15. They needed to buy the tickets early.

Practice 2. Answer these questions in complete sentences in (1) the affirmative, (2) the negative.

1. Did Virginia meet Robert in a class?

    Yes, she met him in a class.
    No, she didn't meet him in a class.

2. Did he ask her to go to the drugstore for a Coke?
3. Did he walk home with her?
4. Did Virginia have a date with him last Saturday?
5. Did she dance with him all the time?
6. Did she have an appointment with her history professor?
7. Did she study hard for her examination?
8. Did you learn your English here?
9. Did the maid answer the door?
10. Did you like the movie last night?
11. Did he pronounce the words well?
12. Did you notice Virginia's new dress?
13. Did you miss me last week?
14. Did they arrive this morning?
15. Did you sign your name?
16. Did he use the correct word?
17. Did they wait for you after class?

18. Did she invite you to her party?
19. Did you expect to see her yesterday?
20. Did you receive a letter this morning?

Section 2

III. Nouns Used as Adjectives Before Other Nouns.

A. In English, a noun is often used as an adjective before another noun. The noun that precedes is always *singular*.

an **evening** dress	(un vestido de noche)
a **grocery** list	(una lista de víveres)
some **silver** bracelets	(unas pulseras de plata)
the **coffee** cups	(las tazas para café)
an **address** book	(una libreta para direcciones)
a **ten-dollar** bill	(un billete de diez dólares)

B. Sometimes, two nouns are used as adjectives before another noun.

the **corner shoe** store (la zapatería de la esquina)

Practice translating these expressions into English.

1. la lección de inglés
2. la clase de historia
3. un vestido de seda
4. un sombrero de verano
5. un abrigo de invierno
6. un vestido de lana
7. un plato de vidrio
8. un vaso para agua
9. el jugo de naranja
10. un plato para ensalada
11. una lámpara de mesa
12. una estación de radio
13. un billete de cinco dólares
14. una estampilla de diez centavos
15. una lista de teléfonos
16. un cheque por cincuenta dólares
17. una taza de plata
18. el orden de las palabras en inglés
19. los programas de radio
20. las clases de la tarde

IV. The Order of Adjectives Before a Noun.

The order of the words that modify these nouns should be noted.

Our first six reading lessons are not difficult.
The teacher's two interesting afternoon classes are large.
That old blue evening dress is beautiful on her.
Several very good American radio programs are beginning this month.

Note: Articles, possessives, demonstratives, indefinite adjectives (**some, any, several, much, many**) come first. An ordinal number precedes a cardinal number. **Very** precedes its adjective. A general descriptive adjective precedes an adjective of *color*. An adjective of *nationality* is next to the noun unless there is another noun used as an adjective. A noun used as an adjective is next to the noun it modifies.

Practice reading these sentences in the correct word order.

1. Do you have { a / book / new / telephone }
2. The library has { English / easy / books / very / several }
3. Mrs. Miller has { suit / pretty / a / green / very }
4. The church has { pictures / very / old / some / Spanish }
5. I like { two / silk / those / dresses / blue }
6. { black / dress / pretty / her / wool } is at the cleaner's.
7. The parents select { names / first / their / two / children's }
8. { these / bills / one-dollar / new / five } are for you.
9. He is { young / a / student / North American }
10. { first / names / daughter's / her / two } are Mary Grant.

V. The Prepositions <u>to</u>, <u>at</u>; <u>before</u>, <u>after</u>; <u>until</u>, <u>as far as</u>.

A. **To** and **at** are prepositions of place. **To** indicates motion. **At** indicates position.

They are going **to** the movies.
He walked **to** the office.

Now they are **at** the movies.
He is **at** the office now.

B. **Before** (antes de) and **after** (después de) are prepositions of time.

>I am going to leave **before** noon today.
>I am going to leave **before** seeing them.
>
>I don't need to work **after** five o'clock.
>I didn't work **after** seeing them.

Note: If a verb follows a preposition, the present participle (**ing** form of the verb) is used.

C. **Until** (hasta — *tiempo*) refers to future time; **as far as** (hasta — *distancia*) refers to distance.

>We waited for them **until** six o'clock.
>We walked **as far as** Fourteenth Street.

Translate the prepositions and read the sentences aloud.

1. He isn't ——— home now. He is ——— the office. (en)
2. They are going ——— the lecture tonight. (a)
3. The train arrived ——— five o'clock. (antes de)
4. I always read the newspaper ——— breakfast. (después de)
5. Our friends were here ——— midnight. (hasta)
6. I like to study ——— class. (antes de)
7. She is going to be busy ——— four o'clock. (después de)
8. We walked ——— the corner together. (hasta)
9. I want to see him ——— writing the letter. (antes de)
10. Robert invited Virginia to go ——— the party. (a)
11. We played bridge ——— dinner. (después de)
12. She listened to the radio ——— going to bed. (antes de)
13. They are going ——— Miami by plane. (hasta)
14. I was tired ——— dancing so much. (después de)
15. Good-bye ——— tomorrow. (hasta)

REVIEW LESSON II

I. Change these affirmative statements to (1) interrogative, (2) negative.

1. Virginia is a South American.
2. She lives with Mr. and Mrs. Miller.
3. She is studying at Lousiania State University.
4. She likes her classes very much.
5. She wants to learn English well.
6. She notices the differences between North American and Latin-American customs.
7. She needs to study very hard.
8. She is going to New York for her vacation.
9. She has history three days a week.
10. She receives many letters from her friends.

II. Give the past tense of the verb in parentheses.

1. I ——— (work) hard yesterday.
2. We ——— (listen) to the radio for an hour.
3. He ——— (learn) a great deal of English last year.
4. They ——— (be) here until eight o'clock.
5. I ——— (walk) as far as the church with them.
6. They ——— (decide) to go to the lecture.
7. They ——— (arrive) ten minutes early.
8. The lecture ——— (be) very good and easy to understand.
9. Mr. and Mrs. Miller ——— (invite) us to their house for dinner.
10. We ——— (play) bridge after dinner.

III. Answer these questions in the negative.

1. Did you attend class yesterday?
2. Did you study your lesson before class?
3. Did you arrive early?
4. Did you walk to class?
5. Did you go to the movies last night?
6. Did you like the movie?
7. Did you ask Virginia to go with you?
8. Did you have a date?
9. Did you go without a chaperon?
10. Did you buy your ticket early?
11. Did it rain yesterday?
12. Did you wear your raincoat?
13. Did you have your umbrella?
14. Did you see Virginia and Robert?

IV. Use the definite article *the* where it is necessary.

Remember: The definite article is omitted (1) before nouns used in a general sense; (2) before continents, most countries, states, cities, streets, and titles.

1. They are from ——— United States.
   We are from ——— Latin America.
   He is from ——— Brazil.
2. She lives in ——— Havana.
   They live in ——— United States.
   He lives in ——— Argentina.
3. They speak ——— English.
   We speak ——— Spanish.
   Do you speak ——— French, too?
4. ——— English language has many consonant sounds.
   ——— English is difficult to pronounce.
   ——— Spanish is easy to pronounce.
   ——— Spanish language has many vowel sounds.
   ——— Spanish is a musical language.
5. ——— Professor Wilson is not here.
   ——— professor is not here now.
   ——— Mrs. Miller speaks ——— English.
   ——— Mr. Miller understands ——— Spanish.
   ——— President Roosevelt died in 1945.
   ——— President never travels alone.
   ——— General MacArthur was in ——— Philippines.
   ——— general likes his work, but it is difficult.

65

6. She lives on ——— Clark Street.
   She lives between ——— Fourth and ——— Fifth Avenues.
   ——— Clark Street has some nice houses.
   ——— streets in this part of the city are very wide.

7. ——— coffee is an important product of Colombia.
   ——— coffee from Colombia is very good.
   I prefer ——— tea now, but I like ——— coffee for breakfast.
   ——— vegetables are good for your health.
   ——— vegetables in that store are fresh every day.
   ——— patience is necessary in a teacher.
   She has ——— patience of Job.

8. We are going ——— home soon.
   ——— Miller home is beautiful inside.

9. Were you in class ——— last Friday?
   I am going to the country ——— next week.
   He didn't study ——— English ——— last year.
   Did you see her ——— last week?
   We are always busy ——— last week of the month.

10. I am going to have ——— lunch at one o'clock.
    ——— lunch at the hotel was wonderful.
    What do you usually have for ——— breakfast?
    Do you have ——— dinner at seven o'clock?

V. Answer these questions in the affirmative or the negative.

Remember: The indefinite article is necessary before nouns indicating a nationality, a profession, or a unit of measure.

1. Is he a North American?
   Is he a South American?
   Is he a Cuban?
   Is he a Venezuelan?
   Is he a Peruvian?
   Is he a Colombian?
   Is he a Canadian?
   Is he a Spaniard?
   Is he an Englishman?
   Is he a Russian?
   Is he a Mexican?
   Is he an Argentinian?

2. Is he a doctor?
   Is he a lawyer?
   Is he a businessman?
   Is he a teacher?
   Is he an engineer?

3. How much is milk?
   How much is butter?
   How much are oranges?
   How much are cigarettes?
   How many classes do you have a week?

VI. Place the adverb of frequency in its proper position, and read each sentence aloud.

1. Mr. Miller goes to the theater. (often)
2. We get up late on Sunday. (usually)
3. Do you drink milk? (ever)
4. I am here on Saturday. (usually)
5. We invite friends for dinner. (sometimes)
6. Does he study his lesson? (always)
7. I don't see him on Mondays. (ever)
8. I take a vacation. (seldom)
9. Do you speak English with your friends? (ever)
10. I speak English outside the class. (never)
11. I don't have a Coke. (often)
12. We go without a chaperon. (rarely)
13. They have lunch at home. (always)
14. We go to English lectures. (sometimes)
15. I am late for class. (seldom)

VII. Fill each blank with the possessive adjective which refers to the subject.

1. Paul broke ——— arm.
2. I signed ——— name twice.
3. She says that ——— history class is interesting.
4. Mr. Miller missed ——— train last night.
5. Do you like ——— new car?
6. Virginia is having ——— English class now.
7. Mr. and Mrs. Smith are living in ——— new apartment.
8. She had a date with ——— friend Robert.
9. He had an appointment with ——— lawyer.
10. They rented ——— house for a year.
11. I have to wash ——— gloves today.
12. She combs ——— hair many times a day.
13. I always brush ——— teeth before going to bed.
14. Do you like ——— blue suit better than ——— gray suit?

VIII. Fill each blank with the possessive form of the noun or pronoun indicated.

1. Is this book ———? (de ella) No, it's ———. (de él)
2. This pen isn't ———. (mía) Is it ———? (de Vd.)

3. Is that car ———— ? (de los señores Miller)   Yes, it's ————.   (de ellos)
4. Is this coat ———— (de su hermano) or ————? (de Vd.) It's ————. (de él)
5. Are those children ————? (de ella) No, they are ————. (de su hermana)

IX. Fill each blank with the correct preposition, and read these sentences aloud.

1. Do you take sugar ———— your coffee?
2. There are many nice stores ———— Fifth Avenue.
3. The train leaves ———— six o'clock.
4. He is going ———— the station early.
5. Mr. Miller's office is ———— the second floor.
6. We have our class ———— the evening.
7. We have our class ———— Mondays, Wednesdays, and Fridays.
8. The book is ———— the drawer of the desk.
9. Virginia is studying ———— Louisiana State University.
10. She arrived ———— Baton Rouge ———— September.
11. She does not like to study ———— the summer.
12. Her birthday is ———— the fifteenth of January.
13. Mr. Miller comes ———— New York, but he lives ———— Baton Rouge now.
14. He and his family live ———— Clark Street.
15. They live ———— 431 Clark Street.
16. Their car was ———— front ———— our house.
17. Why don't you sit ———— a comfortable chair?
18. I take a bus ———— Forty-second Street. (hasta)
19. Are you going ———— the concert tomorrow?
20. Were you ———— the English lecture last night?
21. Those cars are made ———— the United States.
22. We are going ———— Miami by plane. (hasta)
23. He is not going home ———— six o'clock. (hasta)
24. The church is ———— my house. (*Use five prepositions.*)
25. The theater is ———— the hotel. (frente a)
26. I want to review this lesson ———— continuing. (antes de)
27. He has no time to see us ———— tomorrow afternoon. (hasta)
28. What are you going to do ———— class? (después de)
29. My house is ———— the corner. (cerca de)
30. Why don't you walk ———— the corner with me? (hasta)

McVadon's Studio

LESSON VII

THE MOVIES

There was a good picture at the Columbia Theater last week, so Virginia and Robert decided to see it. They arrived at the theater at seven o'clock, in time for the newsreel. (In cities in the United States, shows usually begin at one o'clock in the afternoon and are continuous until midnight.)

Robert wanted to sit in the balcony; but because Virginia preferred to sit downstairs, they sat on the main floor.

After the newsreel they saw a short and a preview of the coming attraction. They heard perfectly because the sound equipment was excellent.

The main feature was about college life, as Hollywood interprets it, and was very entertaining. In the picture, the students played football, went to dances, and sang songs to pretty girls. In fact, they did everything but study. The acting and the music were good, but the film did not show how North American students really live. It is true that students dance and play on week ends, but during the week they study hard.

Virginia sees many movies, and she says that they do not present a true picture of American life. The movies often exaggerate or emphasize the sensational and the exceptional instead of showing how most people in the United States really live. The fact is that North Americans usually go to the movies for amusement; they want to escape from the monotonous routine of everyday life. They do not take the movies seriously, because they know that the films are made especially to entertain the public.

VOCABULARY

acting	actuación	**picture**	película; representación
amusement	diversión		
attraction	atracción, película	**to play**	jugar; divertirse
		preview	escenas de un estreno exhibidas anticipadamente
to be about	tratarse de		
coming	venidero		
to emphasize	dar énfasis a	**really**	verdaderamente
to entertain	divertir	**routine**	rutina
entertaining	divertido	**to show**	mostrar
everyday (*adj.*)	cotidiano, ordinario	**show**	espectáculo
		to sing	cantar
fact	hecho	**song**	canción
film	película	**sound equipment**	aparato de sonido
main feature	película principal		
main floor	luneta	**true**	verdadero, cierto
most	la mayor parte de	**week end**	fin de semana
newsreel	noticiero		

IDIOMS

everything but study	todo menos estudiar
in fact	en efecto
in the balcony	en el balcón
in time for something	a tiempo para algo
on the main floor	en luneta
on time	a tiempo
to take seriously	tomar en serio
the fact is that ...	(el hecho) es que ...

CONVERSATION

Answer the following questions in complete sentences.

1. What time do shows usually begin in the United States? 2. What time do they end? 3. To what theater did Virginia and Robert go? 4. What did they see first? 5. Did they arrive in time for the newsreel? 6. Where did Robert want to sit? 7. Why did they sit downstairs? 8. What did they see after the newsreel? 9. Why did they hear well? 10. What was the main feature about? 11. How were the music and the acting? 12. Do university students play, dance, and sing all the time? 13. Does Hollywood show how North American students really live? 14. What does Virginia say about the movies? 15. Do North Americans take the movies seriously? 16. Why do they go to the movies?

17. Do you like to go to the movies? 18. What time do you usually go? 19. Are the shows continuous? 20. Which theater here do you prefer? Why? 21. Do you like to sit in the balcony or on the main floor? 22. Do you like to sit in the front or in the back of the theater? 23. How much do the movies cost here? 24. Who are your favorite actor and actress? 25. How many times a week do you go to the movies? 26. Did you go to a show last night? last Saturday or Sunday? 27. What was the name of the picture? 28. At what theater was the picture? 29. Who were the principal actor and actress? 30. Did you like the picture? Why? 31. Do you like North American movies? Why? 32. Can you understand what the actors say?

PRONUNCIATION

[tʃ] teacher, picture, lecture, feature
[ɔ] floor, door, more, store
[u] afternoon, cartoon
[ʊ] good, football, Hollywood

[dʒ] John, James, Junior, just, joke, college, marriage
[z] was, news, girls, songs, shows, films, music, present, represent, amusement, emphasize

GRAMMAR   Section 1

I. The Simple Past Tense of the Most Common Irregular Verbs.

Some common verbs have an irregular past tense and are therefore called irregular verbs. It is necessary to learn the spelling and the pronunciation of these forms.

Present	Past	Translation
be	was (were)	ser, estar
become	became	llegar a ser
begin	began	empezar
break	broke	romper
bring	brought	traer
buy	bought	comprar
catch	caught	coger
choose	chose	escoger
come	came	venir
cost	cost	costar
cut	cut	cortar
do	did	hacer
drink	drank	beber
drive	drove	manejar (*un automóvil*)
eat	ate	comer
fall	fell	caer(se)
feel	felt	sentir(se)
find	found	encontrar (*cosas*)
fly	flew	volar
forget	forgot	olvidar(se)
freeze	froze	congelar
get	got	conseguir
give	gave	dar
go	went	ir
grow	grew	crecer

hang	hung (hanged)	colgar
have	had	tener, haber
hear	heard	oír
hold	held	tener, sostener
keep	kept	guardar
know	knew	saber, conocer
lay	laid	colocar
leave	left	salir, dejar
lend	lent	prestar
let	let	permitir, dejar
lie	lay	estar situado, yacer
lose	lost	perder
make	made	hacer
mean	meant	significar
meet	met	encontrar(se), conocer
pay	paid	pagar
put	put	poner
read [rid]	read [rɛd]	leer
ride	rode	montar, pasear en vehículo
ring	rang	sonar, timbrar
rise	rose	levantarse
run	ran	correr
say	said	decir
see	saw	ver
sell	sold	vender
shake	shook	sacudir
shine	shone (shined)	brillar (lustrar)
sing	sang	cantar
sit	sat	sentarse, estar sentado
sleep	slept	dormir
speak	spoke	hablar
spend	spent	gastar, pasar
stand	stood	ponerse de pie, estar de pie
steal	stole	robar
swim	swam	nadar
swing	swung	balancear(se)
take	took	tomar, llevar
teach	taught	enseñar
tear	tore	romper, rasgar
tell	told	decir, contar
think	thought	pensar
throw	threw	echar, lanzar
understand	understood	comprender
wake	woke	despertar(se)

wear	wore	usar, llevar, traer (ropa)
win	won	ganar
write	wrote	escribir

Note 1: The form **hanged** is used only of death by hanging.

Note 2: **Shined** is the past tense of the transitive verb **shine**, and **shone** is the past tense of the intransitive verb **shine**.

Practice answering these sentences in the affirmative.

1. What did he buy?
2. When did he come?
3. Where did they eat?
4. Did you understand well?
5. Why did they run?
6. What time did you get up?
7. Where did you find it?
8. When did you see him?
9. When did you sell your radio?
10. How much did the movie cost?
11. When did you read it?
12. What did they say?
13. Where did they sit?
14. When did he call me?
15. Did you write a letter?
16. Did you have a vacation?
17. Did she forget her book?
18. Where did they go last night?
19. Who put it there?
20. Who sang songs to the girls?
21. Did the class begin on time?
22. Did you bring your notebook?
23. Did he break the glass?
24. Why did you choose that hat?
25. When did she cut her finger?
26. When did he become a doctor?
27. Did you drink all your coffee?
28. Did they drive to the office?
29. Did he feel all right?
30. Did you fly or take a train?
31. Did the lake freeze in the winter?
32. Did he give you his seat?
33. Did Virginia have a wonderful time?
34. Did you hear the serenade?
35. Did he know her before?
36. Where did I leave my gloves?
37. How much money did you lend him?
38. Did she make her sweater?
39. Where did Virginia meet Robert?
40. Did he pay for the tickets?
41. Did you ride on the streetcar?
42. When did you send the package?
43. Did they shake hands?
44. Did you sleep well last night?
45. Did she speak to you?
46. Did he swim across the river?
47. Did she teach English here?
48. Did he tell you the truth?
49. Did you think of me?
50. Did she wear her new hat?
51. Did they take Virginia with them?
52. Did you win the prize?
53. Did she spend a week there?

54. Where did he fall?
55. When did you get the tickets?
56. Where did he hang his coat and hat?
57. Where did they keep their car?
58. Where did I lay my keys?
59. Did the teacher stand?
60. Did you mean that?

II. The Expression used to [yustə].

A. In present time, habit is expressed by the simple present tense. In past time, habit is generally expressed by **used to** and the simple form of the principal verb. An adverb of frequency is sometimes used before **used to**.

> Present: **He** (often) **plays** football.
> Past: **He** (often) **used to play** football.

*Practice changing these sentences from the present to the past tense with **used to**.*

1. We see him every day.
   We used to see him every day.
2. He speaks English well.
3. The two friends often have dinner together.
4. She comes to class early.
5. They go to the movies every Saturday.
6. I write many letters.
7. Robert forgets his books.
8. He takes a bus every morning.
9. Our class begins at six o'clock.
10. I often walk home.
11. She reads a book every week.
12. He sings very well.
13. They go for a walk every Sunday.
14. Virginia studies almost every night until eleven o'clock.
15. She has a date during the week.

B. The interrogative form of **used to** is **did I** (**you, he,** etc.) **use to . . .?** The negative form of **used to** is **I** (**you, he,** etc.) **didn't use to . . .**

> **Did he** (often) **use to play** football?
> No, **he didn't** (often) **use to play** football.

*Practice changing the sentences in A to (1) the interrogative, (2) the negative, using a form of **used to**.*

Section 2

III. Adverbs or Adverbial Expressions and Their Position in a Sentence.

A. Some adverbs, especially adverbs of manner, are formed by adding **ly** to an adjective. This ending corresponds to **mente** in Spanish. If the adjective ends in **y,** the **y** is changed to **i** before **ly** is added. If the adjective ends in **ble** or **ple,** the **e** is omitted, and only **y** is added.

usual	usual**ly**	slow	slow**ly**
general	general**ly**	quick	quick**ly**
frequent	frequent**ly**	sure	sure**ly**
rare	rare**ly**	easy	eas**ily**
actual	actual**ly**	busy	bus**ily**
careful	careful**ly**	simple	simp**ly**
correct	correct**ly**	possible	possi**bly**

B. Adverbs or adverbial expressions usually follow the verb and the direct object, with the exception of the adverbs of frequency, which precede the verb (see Lesson IV). Adverbs and adverbial expressions never come between the verb and the direct object.

The usual word order in a sentence is the following:

Subject→Verb→Object→{Adverb of Place}→{Adverb of Manner}→{Adverb of Time}

> I found the letter on my desk yesterday.
> Virginia met Robert in one of her classes this year.
> They usually go to the movies after dinner.
> We drove the car very fast last night.
> She understands English very well now.

This order is the most natural and is always correct, although other positions of adverbs or adverbial expressions are sometimes possible. For example, the expression of *time* is often placed first in the sentence instead of last, for more emphasis.

> **Yesterday** I found the letter on my desk.
> **Now** she understands English very well.

Practice reading the following sentences in the correct word order.

1. That movie was { last week / at the Columbia
2. Mrs. Gómez was not { on Monday / in class
3. Does he live { now / on Nineteenth Street
4. I saw { a good movie / last week / at the Columbia Theater
5. Please close { when you leave / the door / quietly
6. Please use { in a sentence / this word
7. He explained { yesterday / the lesson / in class
8. He gave { this morning / very slowly / his lecture
9. They live { now / in New York
10. She is { at the university / a student / this year
11. I liked { very much / last night / the program
12. Please read { slowly / that sentence / now
13. She brought { yesterday / a friend / to class
14. I went { once / there
15. She sang { last night / very well / that song

IV. The Expressions of Quantity <u>much</u>, <u>many</u>, <u>a lot of</u>, <u>lots of</u>, <u>a great deal of</u>.

A. **Much** is singular. It is used both in negative and affirmative questions and in negative statements, but rarely in affirmative statements.

B. **Many** is plural. It is used in all types of sentences.

C. **A great deal of** is singular. It is used in all types of sentences.

D. **A lot of** and **lots of** are informal equivalents of **much, many,** and **a great deal of.** They are used before singular or plural nouns in all types of sentences.

Singular: Does he have **much** time? (*interrogative*)
Doesn't he have **much** time? (*negative interrogative*)
No, he doesn't have **much** time. (*negative*)

Yes, he has { **a great deal of** time. / **a lot of** time. / **lots of** time. } (*affirmative*)

Plural: Does Virginia see **many** movies? (*interrogative*)
Doesn't she see **many** movies? (*negative interrogative*)
No, she doesn't see **many** movies. (*negative*)

Yes, she sees { **many** movies. / **a lot of** movies. / **lots of** movies. } (*affirmative*)

Practice 1. Use one of these expressions of quantity to complete each sentence.

1. ——— South Americans speak English.
2. The teacher has ——— patience with the students.
3. They drink ——— water with their meals.
4. There are ——— pretty girls in the class.
5. Do you use ——— sugar in your coffee?
6. They have ——— rain in the tropics.
7. Does he have ——— time to study?
8. Not ——— students wear hats.
9. I don't have ——— money with me.
10. Are there ——— good pictures at the Columbia?

Practice 2. Complete each question with an expression of quantity, and answer the question.

1. Do you have ——— time to study English?
2. Do you have ——— opportunities to speak English?
3. Don't you have ——— work to do now?
4. Does Virginia have ——— social life?
5. Do you see ——— movies?
6. Do you hear ——— English?
7. Do North Americans drink ——— coffee?
8. Doesn't she know ——— people there?
9. Do you write ——— letters?
10. Does she speak ——— English?

V. The Prepositions of Place above, below; over, under.

Above means anywhere *higher than* a certain point. **Over** means *above* a certain point in a perpendicular line. **Below** means anywhere *lower than* a certain point. **Under** means *below* a certain point in a perpendicular line.

A is **above** X but not **over** X.   C is **above** X and also **over** X.
B is **below** X but not **under** X.   D is **below** X and also **under** X.

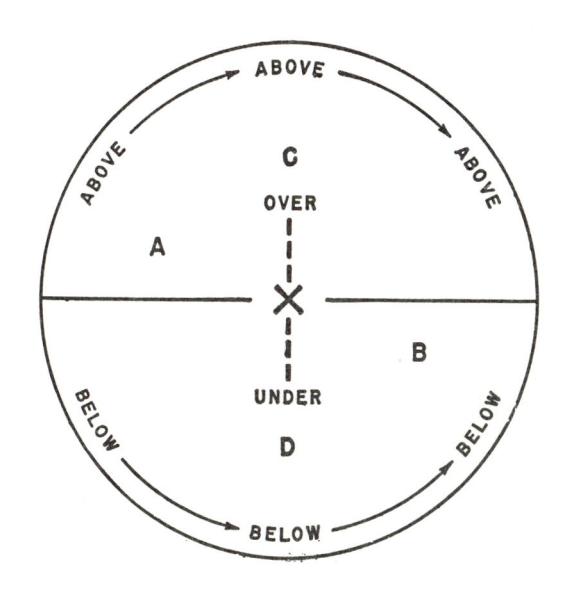

Fill each blank with the correct preposition. (In some cases, two are possible.)

1. Mrs. Miller hung a beautiful mirror ——— the fireplace.
2. In the winter the temperature is sometimes ——— zero (Fahrenheit).
3. Usually it is not so cold, about ten or twenty degrees ——— zero.
4. The money rolled ——— the chair.
5. I live on the fourth floor. He lives ——— me on the fifth floor.
6. During our plane trip, we saw many mountains ——— us.
7. We flew ——— the clouds.
8. He jumped ——— the hole.

79

9. He put his hat ——— the seat in the theater.
10. The wastebasket is ——— the desk.
11. The plane flew ——— the city.
12. She hung her coat ——— mine.

VI. The Prepositions of Motion <u>toward</u>, <u>to</u>; <u>into</u>, <u>out of</u>; <u>through</u>; <u>from</u>.

Toward indicates the direction of the motion. **To** indicates motion continued to a definite place. **Into** indicates a motion that ends inside a place. **Out of** indicates a motion that ends outside a place. **Through** combines the meanings of **into** and **out of**. **From** indicates motion away from a place.

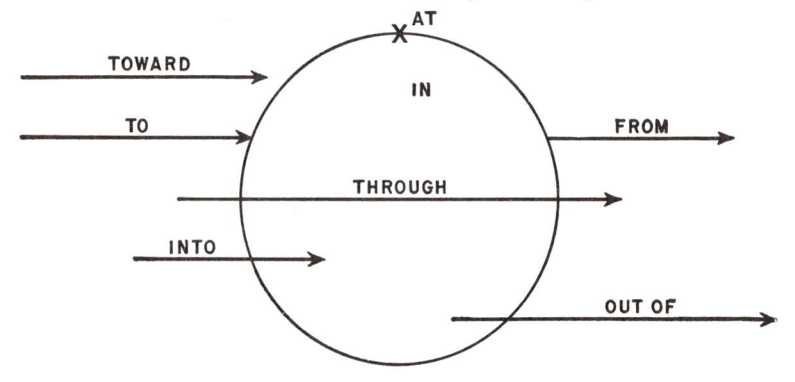

```
                    AT
                    ×
    TOWARD
                    IN
    TO                              FROM

                  THROUGH

    INTO

                                OUT OF
```

Note: The prepositions **in** and **at** indicate place without any idea of motion.

Practice translating the prepositions in parentheses.

1. Robert went ——— the movie. (fué a)
   He went ——— the theater. (entró en)
   Now he is ——— the theater. (está en)
2. He went ——— the house. (salió de)
   He went ——— his office. (fué a)
   He is ——— his office now. (está en)
3. Mr. Miller went ——— the bank. (entró en)
   He was ——— the bank for a few minutes. (estuvo en)
   Then he went ——— the bank. (salió de)
4. They are walking ——— the corner. (hacia)

5. They are going ——— the park. (van a)
6. He took the money ——— his pocket. (sacó de)
7. I didn't see him come ——— the store. (salir de)
8. The thief went ——— the house and jumped ——— the window. (atravesó, saltó por)
9. She was waiting ——— the front door. (esperaba en)
10. We walked ——— the garden. (por)

Keystone

LESSON VIII

WHAT IS THE OBJECT?

One evening when Virginia and some of her friends were together, Robert said, "Let's play a game called *What Is The Object?*" The others agreed, and the game began.

One person went out of the room; and while he was outside, the other people picked out an object. Then the person outside returned and tried to guess the name of the object. When it was Virginia's turn to leave the room, the object that they chose was the sofa. She asked different people many questions about it.

Virginia: Is the object inside the room or outside?
Answer: It's inside the room.
Virginia: Is it in front of me or behind me?
Answer: It isn't in front of you, and it isn't behind you.
Virginia: Is it beside me then?
Answer: Yes, it's beside you.
Virginia: What size is it? Is it large or small?
Answer: It's rather large.
Virginia: What shape is it? Is it round, square, or rectangular?
Answer: It's rectangular, more or less.
Virginia: Is it long or short?
Answer: It's quite long.
Virginia: I know. It's the piano.
Answer: No, not the piano.
Virginia: Is the object hard or soft?
Answer: It's soft.
Virginia: Is it heavy or light?
Answer: It's rather heavy.
Virginia: How much does it weigh?
Answer: Oh, about a hundred pounds, perhaps.
Virginia: What color is it?
Answer: It's brown.
Virginia: Is it light brown or dark brown?
Answer: I think it's light brown.
Virginia: Oh, dear, this is so difficult. I can't guess it. I give up.
Answer: Don't give up. Please ask another question.
Virginia: Well, is it high or low?
Answer: It's low.
Virginia: Is the object yours or mine?
Answer: It belongs to Mr. and Mrs. Miller, but many of us use it.
Virginia: When do we use it?
Answer: When we want to read or to talk.

Virginia: Do I often use it?
Answer: Yes, you use it every day.
Virginia: Is it the sofa?
Answer: Yes, that's it.

Choose different objects in your classroom, and play this game.

VOCABULARY

about	acerca de; aproximadamente	**outside**	fuera de; afuera
to agree	convenir (en)	**perhaps**	tal vez
to belong to	pertenecer a	**quite**	bastante
brown	pardo, carmelita	**rather**	bastante
to choose	escoger	**to return**	volver
dark	obscuro	**round**	redondo
game	juego	**shape**	forma
to guess	adivinar	**size**	tamaño
hard	duro	**so**	tan
heavy	pesado	**soft**	blando
high	alto	**square**	cuadrado
inside	dentro de	**then**	entonces, pues
light	ligero; claro	**to try to**	tratar de
long	largo	**to weigh**	pesar
low	bajo	**well**	pues
object	objeto	**while**	mientras

IDIOMS

to ask someone a question	hacer una pregunta a alguien
to be one's turn	tocarle a uno
to give up	darse por vencido
Oh, dear!	¡Dios mío!
That's it.	Eso es.
the Millers	los señores Miller

CONVERSATION

A. Repeat the following questions, and answer them as rapidly as possible.

1. Is it large or small?   It's **large**.
2. Is it big or little?   It's ———.
3. Is it long or short?   It's ———.
4. Is it high or low?   It's ———.

5. Is it hard or soft? It's ———.
6. Is it wide or narrow? It's ———.
7. Is it round or square? It's ———.
8. Is it heavy or light? It's ———.
9. Is it light brown or dark brown? It's ———.
10. Is it yours or mine? It's ———.
11. Is it ugly or beautiful? It's ———.
12. Is it inside or outside? It's ———.
13. Is it behind me or in front of me? It's ———.
14. Is it near me or far from me? It's ———.
15. Is it above me or below me? It's ———.

B. Answer these questions in complete sentences.

1. Are you tall or short? 2. How tall are you? 3. How much do you weigh? 4. Are you rather heavy, or are you thin? 5. What color is your hair? 6. What color are your eyes? 7. What color is your English book? 8. How many colors can you name? 9. What shape is this room? the chalk? the light switch?

PRONUNCIATION

[ɔ] soft, long, belong, often, bought, small, call, all, wall, talk, walk

[o] go, home, sofa, low, know, below

[ɪ] it, it's, give, fifty, which, Miller, picked, inside, English

[y] you, yes, yard, young, yellow

[e] play, shape, name, game, weigh

[aʊ] out, outside, round, pound, about, brown, town

[aɪ] size, while, light, high, behind, quite, mine, beside, tried

GRAMMAR   Section 1

I. Imperative Sentences.

A. The simple form of the verb is used in imperative sentences. The subject **you** is understood but not expressed.

Wait for me at the corner.
Listen to my pronunciation.

B. **Do not** (**don't**) is used before the simple form of the verb to make the negative imperative.

Don't give up.
Don't wait for me.

C. Several polite expressions are used before the simple form of the verb. They all have approximately the same meaning.

Please	play the piano.
Will you	play the piano?
Will you please	play the piano?
Won't you	play the piano?
Won't you please	play the piano?
Would you	play the piano?
Would you please	play the piano?

Note: The only polite negative form is **Please don't ...**

Practice making polite imperative sentences that contain the following verbs (1) in the affirmative, (2) in the negative.

ask	give	repeat
be	help	sit (down)
choose	open	try
explain	put	write

D. Imperatives in the first person plural are expressed with the auxiliary **let us** (**let's**). This expression is used when the speaker is included. The simple form of the verb is used after **let's**.

Let's go to the movies.
Let's not go to the movies.

Practice making sentences with let's and the verbs in C.

Section 2

II. Indirect Objects.

A. Some verbs often have two objects, direct and indirect. If both are expressed, the indirect object comes before the direct object and is used without a preposition. The indirect object is usually a person.

Subject	→ Verb →	Indirect Object →	Direct Object
This book	cost	**me**	one dollar.
The teacher	asked	**us**	many questions.
Robert	sent	**his brother**	a check.
Did you	write	**Virginia**	a letter?

B. The indirect object can usually be replaced by a **phrase with to** or **for**. The phrase then follows the direct object. Notice the change in word order in the two forms of each sentence.

Please bring **me** the newspaper.   Please bring the newspaper **to me.**
Did you buy **me** the ticket?   Did you buy the ticket **for me?**

Note: If the direct object is a personal pronoun, the indirect object *must* be replaced by a phrase with **to** or **for**.

Did you give **me** the books?
Did you give them **to me?**

Change the words in italics to indirect objects, and read the sentences in the correct word order.

1. Yes, I bought the ticket *for you*.
2. She gave the book *to him*.
3. He read the letter *to us*.
4. We sent the photograph *to her*.
5. She is getting a glass of water *for you*.
6. I am going to leave my book *for him*.
7. He sold his car *to his brother*.
8. Please show your photographs *to Mrs. Miller*.
9. They sang some North American songs *for Virginia*.
10. I took the flowers *to my friend*.
11. She taught Spanish *to North Americans*.
12. She told a story *to the class*.
13. When are you going to write a letter *to Virginia?*
14. I sent a book *to Virginia* for her birthday.
15. He lent a dollar *to his sister*.

C. The following verbs are always used with the preposition **to** or **for** instead of the indirect object.

Please **explain** that sentence **to me** (**for me**).
Please **describe** your experience **to me** (**for me**).

III. Say and <u>tell</u> (decir).

A. If the exact words of the speaker are given, the verb **say** must always be used. **Say** cannot be used with an indirect object but must be followed instead by a phrase with **to**.

She **said to** the clerk, "Do you have a good steak?"
Then she **said,** "How much is it?"

B. The verb **tell** is often followed immediately by an indirect object without **to**. When the exact words of the speaker are not given, you *say something*, but you *tell someone something*.

>She **said** (that) the movie was good.
>She **told them** (that) the movie was good.
>Please **tell me** his name.

Note: The conjunction **that** is often omitted in conversation.

C. The verb **tell** is used in the following special expressions:

tell the truth	decir la verdad	**tell about some-**	
tell a lie	decir una mentira	**thing**	contar algo
tell the time	decir la hora	**tell fortunes**	decir la buena
tell a story	contar una historia		ventura

Practice using the past tense of **say** *or* **tell,** *as required, in the sentences.*

1. The man ——— me (that) my suit was ready.
2. He ——— (that) the suit was ready.
3. She ——— (that) those people were not at home.
4. She ——— us (that) they were not at home.
5. She ——— (that) she went to the lecture last night.
6. She ——— me (that) she went to the lecture last night.
7. She ———, "The lecture was wonderful."
8. She ——— to me, "I understood almost all the lecture."
9. She ——— me (that) she understood almost all the lecture.
10. Mr. Miller ——— his wife (that) he was going to New York.
11. My friends ——— (that) English was difficult.
12. I ——— (that) I didn't understand English.
13. He ——— me (that) he was sick yesterday.
14. What did you ———?
15. What did you ——— her?
16. Did he ——— you about his vacation?
17. He always ——— the truth.
18. Did you ever ——— a lie?
19. Did she ——— your fortune with tea leaves?
20. He ——— "the people is" instead of "the people are."
21. Virginia ——— (that) she liked Baton Rouge very much.
22. They ——— some good stories last night.
23. What did she ——— when you saw her?
24. She ——— to me, "I don't believe everything he ——— us."

IV. Questions Which Begin with how.

A. The interrogative word **how** is used in questions before adjectives or adverbs.

    How old is your brother?   He is twenty years old.
    How soon is he going?   He is going in an hour.

Practice completing these questions and answering them.

1. How tall ——— ?
2. How big ——— ?
3. How long ——— ?
4. How wide ——— ?
5. How cold ——— ?
6. How expensive ——— ?
7. How early ——— ?
8. How late ——— ?
9. How fast ——— ?
10. How well ——— ?

B. The interrogative expression **how far** is used in questions that refer to distance.

How far is your house from here?   It's three blocks from here.
How far is it from here to your house?   It's half an hour by bus.
How far is it to your house?   It's not very far.

Practice answering the following questions.

1. How far is New York from here?
2. How far is New York from Washington?
3. How far is it from New York to San Francisco?
4. How far is it from Cuba to Miami?
5. How far is it to Buenos Aires? to Panama?
6. How far is the ocean from here? the river?
7. How far is the hotel from here? the church?

C. The interrogative expressions **how much** and **how many** are used in questions that refer to quantity.

How much bread did you buy?   I bought one loaf.
How much time did you spend there?   I spent a week there.
How many children do the Millers have?   They have three.
How many people are there in the class?   There are twenty.

Note: **How much** is singular; **how many** is plural.

Complete these questions, using **much** *or* **many**, *as required, in the first blank of each, and answer them.*

1. How ——— fingers ——— ?
2. How ——— students ——— ?
3. How ——— milk ——— ?

4. How ——— people ———?
5. How ——— money ———?
6. How ——— toes ———?
7. How ——— languages ———?
8. How ——— mistakes ———?
9. How ——— paper ———?
10. How ——— noise ———?

V. The Prepositions between, among; upon, off.

A. **Between** is used in speaking of two things, **among** in speaking of more than two.

> She is sitting **between** Mr. and Mrs. Miller.
> **Among** other things, there were lots of sandwiches.

*Complete these sentences with **between** or **among**, as required, and practice reading them aloud.*

1. The bookstore is ——— the bank and the theater.
2. Virginia found a program ——— her souvenirs.
3. Her calling card was ——— those on the desk.
4. Thursday comes ——— Wednesday and Friday.
5. I am going to look for it ——— my papers.
6. They will arrive ——— five and six o'clock.
7. You will find your book ——— the magazines on the table.
8. There is no comparison ——— this book and that one.
9. The teacher distributed the papers ——— the students.

B. **Upon** means the same as **on** in expressions of place but is not so common in conversation as **on**.

> I laid the keys **on** the table near the door.
> **Upon** the table is a large dictionary.

C. **Off** is the opposite of **on** in expressions of place.

> The pencil was **on** the table.
> The pencil rolled **off** the table.
>
> Mrs. Miller put the flowers **on** the table.
> Mrs. Miller took the flowers **off** the table.

Lambert from F. Lewis

LESSON IX

A TELEPHONE CONVERSATION

Is there anything more difficult than to speak in a foreign language over the telephone? Even if you make yourself understood, the chances are that you will not understand the the person at the other end of the line. When you know what he is saying, the difficulty is to answer him immediately before he becomes impatient and hangs up.

Robert wanted to call Virginia; so when he didn't find her number in the telephone book, he dialed Information.

Voice: Information.
Robert: Will you please give me the telephone number of Mr. C. E. Miller at 431 Clark Street?
Voice: Just a moment, please . . . The number is 8974.
Robert: 8-9-7-4? Thank you very much.

Robert then dialed 8974, but a constant buzz indicated that the line was busy. He waited a few minutes and dialed again.

Voice: Hello.
Robert: Hello. Is this Mr. Miller's residence?
Voice: No, it isn't.
Robert: Isn't this 8974?
Voice: No, you have the wrong number. This is 8975.
Robert: I'm sorry. I made a mistake.

Robert hung up the receiver. After a minute, he picked it up and tried again, being very careful to dial the right number this time.

Voice: Mr. Miller's residence.
Robert: I'd like to speak with Virginia López if she's there.
Voice: I'm sorry, but she isn't here right now. Who's calling, please?
Robert: This is Robert Anderson speaking. Will Virginia be back soon?
Voice: Yes, probably about five o'clock. Do you want to leave a message?
Robert: Well, just tell her that I called, please.
Voice: Wait a moment. I think she's coming in now.
Robert: All right, I'll wait.

Virginia: Hello.
Robert: Virginia, this is Bob.
Virginia: Oh, hello, Bob. How are you?
Robert: Just fine, thanks. And you?
Virginia: Very well. It's nice to hear your voice.

Robert: Virginia, are you going to be busy tomorrow evening?
Virginia: Well, I planned to study my English.
Robert: How about a date for a movie? There's a good picture at the Columbia this week. We'll go early, and then you can study afterwards.
Virginia: All right, Bob, I'd like to go. Thanks a lot.
Robert: Then I'll call for you a little before seven.
Virginia: O.K. I'll be ready.
Robert: Good-bye, Virginia. I'll be seeing you.
Virginia: So long, Bob, and thanks for calling.

VOCABULARY

afterwards	después	just a moment	un momento (nada más)
anything	cualquier cosa	line	línea de comunicación
to be back	estar de regreso		
to become impatient	impacientarse	message	recado, razón
busy	ocupado	to pick up (*a receiver*)	descolgar
buzz	zumbido, sonido prolongado	receiver	audífono, auricular
to call for	ir a buscar		
to call (up)	telefonear, llamar por teléfono	right now	en este momento
		right number	número correcto
chance	probabilidad	telephone book	guía telefónica, lista de teléfonos
to dial	marcar el número en el cuadrante		
		time	vez
even if	aun si	what	lo que
foreign	extranjero	wrong number	número equivocado
to hang up	colgar		

IDIOMS

to be careful	tener cuidado
How about ...?	¿Qué le parece ...?
I'd like to ...	Me gustaría ...
I'm sorry.	Lo siento.
It's nice to hear your voice.	Mucho gusto en oírlo.
Just tell her that ...	Dígale nada más que ...
to make a mistake	equivocarse
to make oneself understood	hacerse entender
to talk over the telephone	hablar por teléfono
The line is busy.	La línea está ocupada.

WORD STUDY

Other Useful Telephone Expressions

long distance	larga distancia
Here's your party.	Está comunicado con «la persona».
Your party is on the line.	Está comunicado con «la persona».
The phone is out of order.	Está dañado el teléfono.
He isn't in now.	No está aquí ahora.

CONVERSATION

Answer the following questions in complete sentences.

1. Whom did Robert want to call up? 2. Why did he have to call Information? 3. What did he say to the operator? 4. Why did he get the wrong number the first time? 5. Was Virginia at home when he called? 6. Did Robert leave a message for her? 7. Where did Robert ask her to go? 8. Did she accept his invitation? 9. What did she say? 10. What time was he going to call for her? 11. What is the usual nickname for Robert?

12. Do you have a telephone at home? 13. Is it a dial phone? 14. What is your telephone number? 15. Is it difficult for you to speak English over the telephone? 16. Can you make yourself understood? 17. Can you understand what the other person says? 18. When you use the telephone, what do you pick up first? 19. How do you know that the line is busy? 20. What do you say in English when you answer the phone? 21. What do you say when someone dials incorrectly and your phone rings? 22. Is it difficult to get the right number? 23. How do you answer the question "Who's calling?" 24. Do you often call up your friends? 25. What do you do when you finish your call?

GRAMMAR   Section 1

I. The Future Auxiliary will.   (See also Lesson XIII.)

Will is an auxiliary which indicates future time. It is followed by the simple form of the principal verb. The contraction of **will** in the affirmative is **'ll**. The contraction in the negative is **won't**.

AFFIRMATIVE		NEGATIVE	
Long Forms	Contracted Forms	Long Forms	Contracted Forms
I will go	I'll go	I will not go	I won't go
you will go	you'll go	you will not go	you won't go
he will go	he'll go	he will not go	he won't go
we will go	we'll go	we will not go	we won't go
you will go	you'll go	you will not go	you won't go
they will go	they'll go	they will not go	they won't go

Practice answering the following questions (1) in the affirmative, (2) in the negative. Use the contractions.

1. Will you call her up later?
   Yes, I'll call her up later.
   No, I won't call her up later.
2. Will he call for her before seven o'clock?
3. Will she be ready on time?
4. Will you see her today?
5. Will they be back at six o'clock?
6. Will you dial that number again?
7. Will he answer the phone?
8. Will she accept his invitation?
9. Will you talk English with her?
10. Will they wait for us if we go now?

II. The Equivalent of <u>¿no es verdad?</u>

A. In English the translation of **¿no es verdad?** depends on the verb in the first part of the sentence. If a form of **be** is the principal verb or the auxiliary verb, that form of **be** is repeated in the short question at the end. If the principal verb (not **be**) is in the simple present tense, **do** or **does** is used in the question; if the principal verb (not **be**) is in the simple past tense, **did** is used in the question. If an auxiliary, such as **will,** is used in the statement, that auxiliary is repeated in the question.

B. The subject of the principal verb is repeated in the short question in its pronoun form.

C. If the first verb is affirmative, the verb in the short question at the end is negative. If the first verb is negative, the verb in the short question is affirmative.

Affirmative Statement	Negative Question
It **is** difficult to learn English,	isn't it?
They **are** talking over the phone,	aren't they?
She **writes** good letters,	doesn't she?
You **like** to go to the movies,	don't you?
Robert **called** Virginia yesterday,	didn't he?
They **will** wait for us,	won't they?

Negative Statement	Affirmative Question
It **isn't** difficult to learn English,	is it?
They **aren't** talking over the phone,	are they?
She **doesn't** write good letters,	does she?
You **don't** like to go to the movies,	do you?
Robert **didn't call** Virginia yesterday,	did he?
They **won't** wait for us,	will they?

Complete these sentences with the correct translation of ¿no es verdad?

1. It is difficult to speak English over the telephone, ———?
2. You make yourself understood, ———?
3. The other person sometimes becomes impatient, ———?
4. Robert didn't find her number in the book, ———?
5. He dialed Information, ———?
6. Mr. Miller lives on Clark Street, ———?
7. The line was busy, ———?
8. He had the wrong number, ———?
9. Virginia wasn't at home, ———?
10. Robert didn't leave a message, ———?
11. Virginia is coming in now, ———?
12. Virginia wants to see the picture, ———?
13. Virginia isn't going to study very much, ———?
14. Bob hung up the receiver, ———?
15. Bob called for her before seven, ———?
16. You have a telephone, ———?
17. It is a dial phone, ———?
18. The phone isn't out of order, ———?

19. You didn't call me up yesterday, ———?
20. You weren't at home yesterday, ———?
21. The telephone didn't ring, ———?
22. Your number is in the telephone book, ———?
23. You usually answer the phone, ———?

III. The Expressions of Purpose in order to, to, and for.

A. **To** and **in order to** are used with the simple form of the verb in expressions of purpose. The short form **to** is more common.

>I came here **to** learn English.
>I came here **in order to** learn English.

*Practice reading these sentences with **to** and **in order to**.*

1. Robert called for Virginia ——— take her to the movies.
2. They went early ——— get a good seat.
3. Let's take a taxi ——— arrive on time.
4. I called Mrs. White ——— ask her about the lesson.
5. Mrs. Miller went to the store ——— buy some vegetables.

B. **For** is used with a noun in expressions of purpose.

>She went to the store **for** some vegetables (to buy some vegetables).
>I am going to the hotel **for** lunch (to have lunch).

*Practice reading these sentences with **to** or **for**, as required.*

1. She went to the post office ——— mail a letter.
2. Then she went to the florist's ——— buy some flowers.
3. We invited Virginia to our house ——— have dinner.
4. We invited Virginia to our house ——— dinner.
5. They stayed after class ——— the lecture.
6. They stayed after class ——— sing.
7. Robert is studying tonight ——— an examination.
8. Robert is doing his homework ——— his Spanish class.
9. Robert called Virginia ——— ask her for a date.
10. Robert called up Virginia ——— a date.

C. It is sometimes possible to use **for** with a gerund (**ing** form of the verb), but this is not common.

>I wear glasses **for reading.**
>He uses a pen **for writing** letters.

IV. Other Uses of the Preposition for.

A. In the sentence below, **for** indicates duration of time. In this sense, **for** is often omitted, but it is always understood.

> I read (**for**) an hour before going to bed.

Answer these questions using for to show duration of time.

1. How long did you wait for her?
2. How long did you play tennis yesterday?
3. How long were you downtown this morning?
4. How long was he sick?
5. How long did you stay in the country?

Note: The preposition **during** indicates a period of time in which something occurs. Compare **for** and **during** in these sentences.

> It rained **for** an hour **during** the afternoon.
> I went to the lake **for** a week **during** my vacation.
> I saw him twice **during** the week.
> I seldom go to the movies **during** the week, but I like to go on week ends.

B. **For** also means **in exchange for;** in this sense it is often used before sums of money.

> He rented the house **for** one hundred dollars a month.

C. **For** sometimes has the meaning of **for the pleasure of.**

> Virginia sang some Spanish songs **for** us.

D. **For** sometimes means **instead of** or **in (the) place of.**

> I am busy now. Will you please go to the post office **for** me?

E. **For** often follows the verb **be** and an adjective when the sentence is completed by an infinitive.

> It is difficult **for** Virginia to understand English over the telephone.

Practice completing the following sentences with for and a personal noun or pronoun.

1. It is too hot **for me** to live there.
2. North American movies are difficult ——— to understand.
3. That radio is expensive ——— to buy.
4. This book is easy ——— to understand.

5. It is necessary ——— to call her up.
6. It is important ——— to dial the right number.
7. It is possible ——— to make herself understood.
8. It is difficult ——— to speak English over the telephone.
9. I think that it is too late ——— to go to class.

V. <u>Why</u> or <u>what . . . for</u> in Questions of Purpose.

What for is used in conversation as an equivalent of **why**.

> **Why** are you studying English?
> **What** are you studying English **for**?
>
> I am studying English **because** I want to go to the United States.
> I am studying English **in order to** get a better job.
> I am studying English **to** be able to speak and understand it when I go to Chicago.
> I am studying English **for** pleasure.

*Practice repeating these questions using **what . . . for** instead of **why**. Then answer the questions, using **because, in order to, to,** or **for**.*

1. Why did Virginia go to the United States?

   What did Virginia go to the United States for?
   Virginia went to the United States because . . .

2. Why did Robert call her up?
3. Why did he hang up the receiver at first?
4. Why did they go to the Columbia Theater?
5. Why did they sit downstairs?
6. Why did you go to the drugstore?
7. Why did you go to the library?
8. Why did you take a taxi?
9. Why did you go to the bank this morning?
10. Why were you absent yesterday?

REVIEW LESSON III

I. Place the expression in parentheses in its correct position, and practice reading the complete sentences.

1. She brought a magazine. (me)
2. She brought a magazine. (to me)
3. Did you lend a dollar? (to him)
4. Yes, I lent a dollar. (him)
5. Did he write a letter? (her)
6. Yes, he wrote several letters. (to her)
7. Did she show her new hat? (you)
8. Yes, she showed her new hat. (to me)
9. Robert sent some flowers. (to Virginia)
10. Robert sent some flowers. (Virginia)
11. Mr. Miller gave ten dollars. (his wife)
12. He took the tickets. (to his brother)
13. She gave a book for Christmas. (Robert)
14. He told a story. (the guests)
15. Virginia asked a question. (Mrs. Miller)

II. Practice reading these sentences in the correct word order.

1. Is he living { now / on Fifth Avenue
2. She went { on Monday / at the university / to her first class
3. She saw { her friends / yesterday / at the party

4. Where is the book I saw { yesterday / on your desk

5. I was { yesterday / there

6. Please write { correctly / on your paper / the sentences

7. She seldom plays { now / the piano

8. We had { our coffee / after dinner / in the living room

9. I was { all afternoon / downtown

10. There is { a new movie / this week / at the Columbia

11. Robert spoke { yesterday / over the telephone / to Virginia

12. He found { the number / in the telephone book / easily

13. He dialed { very carefully / the number / the second time

14. He hung up { after a minute / the receiver

15. She answered { immediately / the phone

III. Use the correct form of <u>say</u> or <u>tell</u>, as required, in the following sentences.

Present Tense

1. What do you ——— when you answer the phone?
2. You ——— Information the number you want.
3. The voice ———, "You have the wrong number."
4. What does Virginia ——— Robert over the phone?
5. Virginia ——— Robert (that) she plans to study English.

6. Robert ——— (that) there is a new picture at the Columbia.
7. He ——— Virginia (that) he will call for her at seven.
8. She ——— him (that) she will be ready on time.
9. She ——— to him, "I'll be ready on time."
10. He ——— (that) he is studying for examinations.
11. Will you please ——— me the meaning of that word?
12. How do you ——— that in English?
13. Mr. Miller ——— (that) he is going out of town tomorrow.
14. Mrs. Miller ——— to him, "How long are you going to stay?"
15. He ——— Mrs. Miller (that) he will be back next Monday.

Simple Past Tense

16. They ——— (that) the movie was very entertaining.
17. They ——— us (that) they understood the English in the movie.
18. Virginia ——— (that) she preferred to sit downstairs.
19. She ——— me about the movie afterwards.
20. She ——— (that) the acting was very good.
21. I think (that) she ——— the truth.
22. She ——— (that) she had a wonderful time at the party.
23. She ——— me (that) she had a wonderful time.
24. She ——— him (that) she had to be home early.
25. She ——— (that) she had to write many letters.
26. Robert ——— me (that) she wasn't at home when he called.
27. He ———, "I'll call her up later."
28. She ——— Robert (that) it was nice to hear his voice.
29. She ———, "It's nice to hear your voice."
30. She ——— to Robert, "It's nice to hear your voice."

IV. Practice reading these sentences in the past tense.

1. Did you send the letters? Yes, I (send) them this morning.
2. How did you sleep last night? I (sleep) well, thank you.
3. I (wake) up very late, and I (get) up immediately.
4. Did you go to bed early? Yes, I (go) to bed about ten o'clock.
5. Where did you leave your book? I (leave) it at the office.
6. She (forget) to bring her book, so I (lend) her mine.
7. Robert (hang) up the receiver because the line (be) busy.

8. The two men (shake) hands when I (introduce) them.
9. We (take) the bus and (ride) as far as Thirty-fourth Street.
10. Virginia (think) that she (lose) her pen, but she (find) it later.
11. Did he drink all his milk? Yes, he (drink) it all.
12. They (sit) downstairs and (hear) very well.
13. We (stand) on the corner waiting for a streetcar.
14. I (know) that she (buy) the picture, but I didn't know how much she (pay) for it.
15. They (come) early and (read) the lesson before class.
16. When he (give) his lecture, he (speak) slowly, and I (understand) quite well.
17. I didn't know what he (mean) in one part of the lecture.
18. I (write) several letters yesterday and (mail) them this morning.
19. Did she make the dress that she (wear) yesterday?
20. He (sell) his old car, but his new car (cost) him a thousand dollars more.
21. When he (become) a doctor, his family (feel) very proud of him.
22. They (choose) the best seats in the theater.
23. Robert (fall) in love with Virginia the first time he (see) her.
24. When did you begin to study English? I (begin) last year.
25. Did they fly all the way to New York? No, they (fly) only to Miami.
26. The child (cut) his finger and (run) to his mother.
27. How long did you swim? I (swim) for an hour.
28. The plant (grow) very well in the house.
29. It (be) very cold there, and he almost (freeze) his ears one day.
30. She (keep) the dinner hot for us, and we (eat) it about eight o'clock.

V. Change the following statements to (1) the interrogative, (2) the negative.

1. Virginia lives with Mr. and Mrs. Miller.
2. Mr. Miller says he is going to fly to New York.
3. He often eats his lunch downtown.
4. Robert likes to speak Spanish with Virginia.
5. She came to class late this morning.
6. She went to bed early last night.
7. She feels better today.

8. You had time to study your lesson.
9. You understand your teacher very well.
10. He speaks very clearly in class.
11. You understood the lecture.
12. They will have lunch at one o'clock.
13. Robert called Virginia last night.
14. She answered the phone.
15. They went to a movie.
16. The movie was very entertaining.
17. You often go to a movie on Saturday.
18. Virginia wants to stay there two years.
19. You will remember their names.
20. They are going to study English next year.

VI. Use the verb be or the necessary auxiliary in the translation of ¿no es verdad?

1. Virginia went out of the room, ———?
2. She didn't guess the name of the object, ———?
3. The people chose a difficult object, ———?
4. The object is inside the room, ———?
5. It weighs about fifty pounds, ———?
6. Virginia doesn't give up easily, ———?
7. It belongs to Mr. and Mrs. Miller, ———?
8. Many of us use it, ———?
9. Robert dialed the wrong number, ———?
10. It was the wrong number, ———?
11. He will call her (up) again, ———?
12. She will be ready on time, ———?
13. You won't tell her a lie, ———?
14. He will tell the truth, ———?
15. It was a good picture, ———?
16. The shows are continuous, ———?
17. They sat on the main floor, ———?
18. They were there for the newsreel, ———?
19. The students study hard during the week, ———?
20. They don't usually study on Saturday night, ———?
21. Virginia sees many movies, ———?
22. The movies don't really represent American life, ———?
23. People usually go to the movies to be entertained, ———?
24. You always like to dance, ———?
25. You are married, ———?
26. You aren't married, ———?

27. She is a pretty girl, ———?
28. She speaks English well, ———?
29. You mailed that letter for me, ———?
30. The bus doesn't stop here, ———?

VII. Answer these questions, using <u>to</u>, <u>for</u>, or <u>because</u>.

1. What are you studying English for?
2. What are you listening to the radio for?
3. What are you waiting for?
4. What did you go to the bank for?
5. What did you go to the shoe store for?
6. What did you go to the drugstore for?
7. What did you go to the library for?
8. What did you buy that notebook for?
9. What did you call (up) Information for?
10. What did you hang up the receiver for?

Charles Phelps Cushing

LESSON X

A RIDE ON A BUS

One Saturday afternoon while Virginia was in New York on her vacation, she went to the Paramount Theater for a matinee. Mrs. Miller was already downtown; so Virginia had to take a bus alone. First she went to the bus stop near her hotel. After a few minutes, a crowded bus came along; she got on, but she had to stand up.

Virginia: Does this bus go down Broadway?
Driver: No, down Fifth Avenue. Where do you want to go?
Virginia: To the Paramount Theater.
Driver: Well, then you will have to transfer at Fifth Avenue and Forty-second Street. There you catch a crosstown bus marked Forty-second Street and go to Times Square.
Virginia: What's the fare, please?
Driver: Fifteen cents.
Virginia: Can you change a dollar bill for me?
Driver: Yes, I think so.
Virginia: Please give me a transfer, too.
Driver: I'm sorry, I can't. The Forty-second Street bus is on a different line. You'll have to pay another fare on that bus.
Virginia: Will you please let me know when we get to Forty-second Street?
Driver: Yes, of course.
Virginia: Thank you.

Virginia got off and had to wait only a few minutes for her second bus. As she got on the crosstown bus, she gave the driver fifteen cents.

Virginia: Does this bus stop in front of the Paramount Theater?
Driver: No, but it will take you near there. You get off at Forty-second Street and Broadway; then you walk one short block straight ahead, turn right, and you'll see the theater sign ahead on Broadway. You can't miss it.
Virginia: Thank you very much.

VOCABULARY

ahead	adelante	**to catch**	coger
already	ya	**to come along**	venir
bill	billete	**crowded**	concurrido
block	manzana, cuadra	**downtown**	centro comercial
bus stop	paradero, parada		de una ciudad

driver	chófer	**right**	derecha
fare	tarifa, valor del pasaje	**sign**	letrero
		square	plaza
to go down the street	bajar la calle	**to stand up**	estar de pie
		to stop	parar(se)
left	izquierda	**to take**	llevar
line	compañía (*de autobuses*)	**to transfer**	transbordar
		to turn	doblar, dar vuelta
ride	paseo en vehículo o a caballo	**vacation**	vacaciones

IDIOMS

to be downtown	estar en el centro
to get on a bus	subir a un bus
to get off a bus	bajarse de un bus
to get to a place	llegar a un lugar
to go downtown	ir al centro
to let someone know	avisar a uno
to think so	pensar que sí
to walk straight ahead	seguir todo derecho
You can't miss it.	No puede Vd. equivocarse.

WORD STUDY

Other Useful Expressions

crosstown bus	autobús que corre en Nueva York de este a oeste, o viceversa
to get into a taxi(cab)	subir a un taxi
to get out of a taxi(cab)	bajarse de un taxi
heavy traffic	mucho tráfico
Is this taxi free?	¿Está libre este taxi?
Is this taxi taken?	¿Está ocupado este taxi?
to tip the driver	dar una propina al chófer

CONVERSATION

Answer the following questions in complete sentences.

1. Is there a bus stop near your house? 2. How far is it from your house? 3. Do you usually take a bus or a streetcar to go downtown? 4. Which do you prefer, a bus or a

streetcar? Which is faster? Which is more comfortable?
5. Do the buses stop at every corner in your city? 6. How
much is the bus fare in your city? 7. Is the streetcar fare
the same? 8. Do you use a system of transfers in your city?
9. Do you get on at the front door of the bus? 10. Where
do you get off the bus? 11. Do you pay your fare as you
get on? 12. To whom do you pay your fare? 13. Can you
always get a seat? 14. Do you sometimes have to stand
up? 15. Does a man sometimes give a woman his seat?
16. How do you indicate that you want to get off? 17. If
the bus is crowded, what do you say in order to pass through
the crowd? 18. Did you take a bus this morning? Which
bus? 19. Did you have to wait a long time for the bus?
20. Where did you get on? Where did you get off? 21. Did
you have to stand up, or did you find a seat? 22. Are the
taxis in your city cheap or expensive? 23. Are they more
comfortable than the buses? 24. Do you usually tip the taxi
driver? How much? 25. How often do you take a taxi?

PRONUNCIATION

[ɔ] off, along, cost, cross, Broadway

[ɑ] stop, got, block, dollar

[aʊ] how, down, downtown, crowded, crosstown, Paramount

[b] bus, but, bill, block, Broadway

[v] very, vacation, five, avenue, driver

[f] first, fare, few, front, after, afternoon, left, transfer

GRAMMAR

I. The Use of *it* as the Subject of a Sentence.

A. The pronoun **it** is used as subject to refer to a **neuter** antecedent.

>Does this **bus** go down Broadway?
>No, **it** goes down Fifth Avenue.

B. The pronoun **it** is also used in subject position, without an obvious antecedent. (In all English sentences, except imperative sentences, it is necessary to express a subject.) This **occurs**:

1. In expressions of identification.
    What is it? It is a transfer.
    Who is it? It is Mr. and Mrs. Miller.
    Who is it? It is I. (*Colloquial:* It's me.)
2. In expressions of weather.
    Was it a nice day yesterday?
    Yes, it was pleasant, but it wasn't very warm.
    Is it cold there in the winter?
    Yes, it's very cold in New York.
3. In expressions of time.
    What time is it? (*interrogative*)
    It is five o'clock. (*affirmative*)
    It isn't very late. (*negative*)
    Isn't it time for lunch? (*negative interrogative*)
4. In expressions of distance.
    How far is it to the Paramount Theater?
    It is two blocks from the bus stop.
5. In impersonal sentences like the following:
    Is it correct to use "chauffeur" for "driver?"
    Is it possible to say "have you" instead of "do you have"?

Practice answering the following questions with it as subject.

1. What time is it now?
    Is it early or late?
    Is it time to go now?
    Is it time for the class to end?
2. Is it hot today? warm? cool? cold?
    Does it ever snow here?
    Did it rain yesterday?
    Was it a nice day yesterday?
3. How far is it from here to your bank?
    How far is it to the business district?
    How far is it to the nearest bus stop?
    How far is it to the park? to the nearest church?
    How far is it from here to other cities in your country?
4. Which is it, a Broadway bus or a Fifth Avenue bus?
    Who is it, Charles or his brother Paul?
    Virginia answered the phone. Who was it?

5. Is it easy to learn English?
    Is it correct to say "go down from the bus?"
    Is it customary here to pay immediately when you get on a bus?
    Is it necessary to buy theater tickets in advance?
    Is it necessary to stand in line?
    Is it important to be on time?
    Is it time to go now?

II. The Interrogative Words which and what.

A. **Which** is used in questions to indicate a choice from a limited group. It is either a pronoun or an adjective.

> Here come two buses. **Which** bus goes to the Paramount?
> **Which** (one) of these buses goes to the Paramount?
> **Which** students in the class do not have books?
> **Which** ones do not have books?
> **Which** (one) of you plays the piano?

B. **What** is used in questions to ask for general information and definitions. It is either a pronoun or an adjective.

> **What** time is it now?
> **What** do you want to eat?
> **What** bus goes to the Paramount Theater?
> **What** is the meaning of that word?
> **What** is a crosstown bus?

*Fill the blanks with **which** or **what**, as required; then practice reading and answering the questions.*

1. ——— is the name of this book?
2. ——— is your first name? middle name?
3. ——— is the building opposite the library?
4. ——— is the bus fare?
5. ——— is that man's surname?
6. ——— is the price of the theater tickets?
7. ——— is our homework for tomorrow?
8. ——— is the best way to go to the theater?
9. ——— was the result of the election?
10. ——— was the reason for your absence?
11. ——— did the bus driver say?
12. ——— are you eating now?
13. ——— building across the street is the library?
14. ——— language does he speak, English or Spanish?
15. ——— kind of music do you like, classical or popular?

16. ——— is more comfortable, a bus or a streetcar?
17. ——— man in the class is Mr. Rodríguez?
18. ——— students in the class understood the lecture?
19. ——— book are you reading?
20. ——— book (of the three from the library) are you reading?

III. The Use of the Word one after Adjectives.

The word **one** (plural: **ones**) usually follows an adjective when the noun to which the adjective refers is not repeated.

> Two buses came along. Virginia took the **first one**.
> The yellow buses go faster than the **green ones**.
> This theater is larger than **that one**.
> One girl is a blonde, and the **other one** is a brunette.

Note: The plural form **ones** is not used after **these** and **those**.

Practice reading these sentences with **one** *or* **ones***, as required.*

1. The first bus was full, so I took the second ———.
2. This bus goes down Fifth Avenue, and the other ——— goes down Forty-second Street.
3. Is this taxi taken? Yes, but that ——— isn't.
4. I don't like to ride in the old taxis. I like the new ———.
5. The green buses are new. The red ——— are old.
6. This seat is more comfortable than that ———.
7. This street and the next ——— have some good stores.
8. This lesson is easy. The last ——— was more difficult.
9. We have a blue book and a light brown ———.
10. In the library there are books of all sizes, big ——— and little ———.
11. We are going to sing old songs and new ———.
12. In the living room we have one large lamp and two small ———.
13. That camera is small, but it is a good ———.
14. She has a new red dress and also a new black ———.
15. He sent his brown suit and his dark blue ——— to the cleaner's.

IV. The Reflexive Pronouns.

A. The forms of the reflexive pronoun are **myself, yourself, himself, herself, itself, ourselves, yourselves, themselves.**

B. These pronouns are sometimes used as the object of a verb or preposition and always refer to the subject of the sentence.

>The children amused **themselves** all afternoon.
>She was talking to **herself**.
>The little boy played by **himself** (alone).

Note: The reflexive pronoun objects are more frequently used in Spanish than in English. The following verbs are reflexive in Spanish, but not in English.

acordarse de	**to remember**	levantarse	**to get up**
acostarse	**to go to bed**	marcharse	**to leave**
afeitarse	**to shave**	olvidarse	**to forget**
apresurarse	**to hurry**	pararse	**to stop**
atreverse	**to dare**	parecerse	**to resemble**
casarse con	**to marry**	peinarse	**to comb one's hair**
despertarse	**to wake up**	quejarse	**to complain**
fijarse en	**to notice**	reír(se)	**to laugh**
imaginarse	**to imagine**	sentarse	**to sit down**
lavarse (las manos)	**to wash (one's hands)**	sonreír(se)	**to smile**

C. The reflexive pronouns are also used for emphasis in English just as in Spanish. In this sense they correspond to **yo mismo, él mismo,** etc. In English these emphatic reflexives are often separated from the noun or pronoun which they emphasize and placed at the end of the sentence.

>**Mr. Miller himself** wrote the letter. (*more emphatic*)
>**Mr. Miller** wrote the letter **himself**.

Fill the blanks with the correct form of the reflexive pronouns, and practice reading the sentences aloud.

1. Virginia took the bus by ———.
2. I need to buy ——— a new hat.
3. She lives by ———.
4. Why don't you speak for ———?
5. Did you hurt ——— when you fell?
6. He locked ——— out of the house. Did you ever lock ——— out?
7. We excused ——— because we had to leave.
8. Please read to ———, not aloud. (*imperative*)
9. Sometimes you have to introduce ——— to other people.
10. She doesn't like to eat by ———.

11. The taxi ——— was all right, but the driver wasn't careful.
12. I ——— prefer to take a streetcar.
13. Mrs. Miller answered the phone ———.
14. Mr. Miller ——— came to the door.
15. I gave the telegram to Mr. Miller ———. (*two forms*)
16. The house ——— is not large, but it is comfortable.
17. The theater ——— is not beautiful, but the shows are good.
18. Please do the work ———. (*imperative*)
19. If you do it ———, you know that it is done.
20. The trip ——— is very expensive, even without the cost of hotel rooms.

V. The Preposition by.

A. **By** is used with a noun to indicate a *means* (medio) or an *agent* (agente).

    Virginia went downtown **by bus**. (*means*)
    She sent a message **by the boy**. (*agent*)

B. **By** is used with a reflexive pronoun to mean **without help, alone**.

    I cleaned the room **by myself**.
    She sat at the table **by herself**.

Practice answering these questions, using a construction with **by**.

1. How did you come to class today, **by** bus, **by** streetcar, or **on** foot?
2. How did you send the letter, **by** air mail or **by** ordinary mail?
3. Do you prefer to travel **by** boat, **by** train, **by** plane, or **by** car?
4. Is that handkerchief made **by** hand?
5. Did you pay **for** it **by** check?
6. Did she order her groceries **by** telephone?
7. Did you ever read a book written **by** Mark Twain?
8. Did he send you the money **by** his brother?
9. Did you do your homework **by** yourself?
10. Does that train run **by** steam or **by** electricity?

C. **By** is also used with a gerund to indicate means.

> How does one get to the Paramount Theater?
> One gets there **by taking** a bus to Forty-second Street and Broadway, and then **by walking** one block straight ahead and two to the right.

Practice answering these questions, using by and the ing form of the verb (gerund).

1. How does one get to the bank?
   (*Substitute other places in your city.*)
2. How does he earn his living?
3. How did you remember her name?
4. How did you finish your work on time?
5. How did you find the street?
6. How did you get those good tickets?
7. How did you learn English so well?

D. **By** is used in expressions of motion when a person passes near another person or an object and then continues without stopping.

> He walked **by** me without seeing me.
> He walks **by** your house when he goes to school.

Practice reading these sentences, using the preposition by.

1. He drove ——— me in his car, but he didn't see me.
2. I pass ——— the park every day when I go downtown.
3. Many buses go ——— my house every day.
4. Perhaps I went ——— your house, but I didn't recognize it.
5. On your way to the hotel, you will pass ——— a church.
6. I went ——— the drugstore and forgot to get the medicine.

E. **By** is used in expressions of time to mean **not later than**.

> We want to finish this book **by** the end of the year.

Practice using an expression of time with by to complete these sentences.

1. If you write today, you will have an answer **by next week.**
2. Are you going to finish your work ———?
3. Let's be there ——— in order to get good seats.
4. They are leaving the city ———, perhaps before.
5. You will know more English ———.

115

F. By is used in the following idiomatic expressions.

They sat **side by side,** reading the paper. (uno al lado del **otro)**
Little by little, you will learn to speak English. (poco a poco)
They came into the room **one by one.** (uno a uno)
I know him only **by sight.** (de vista)
I took your book **by mistake.** Please forgive me. (por equivocación**)**
They **took** me **by surprise.** (de sorpresa)
By the way, what are you doing tonight? (a propósito)
I am going **by way of** Miami. (por la vía de)
That is **by far** the best movie in town. (sin duda, en mucho**)**
Please learn these expressions **by heart.** (de memoria)

Welgos from F. Lewis

LESSON XI

AT THE DOCTOR'S OFFICE

One day Virginia wasn't feeling very well, so she decided to see Dr. Stone. She went to his office in the National Bank Building. Since there were many people in his waiting room, Virginia sat down to wait for her turn. While she was reading a magazine, the nurse opened the inner door and said to her, "The doctor will see you now. Come in, please."

Dr. Stone looked very professional in his white coat. He told Virginia to sit down and then asked her many questions.

Doctor: What is the matter with you, Miss López?
Virginia: Well, I have a bad cold and a fever.
Doctor: Hmm. Do you have a sore throat, too?
Virginia: No, not today, but I have a cough, and it's hard for me to breathe through my nose.
Doctor: Do you have a headache?
Virginia: Yes, doctor, and I ache all over.
Doctor: And how is your appetite?
Virginia: Not very good.

Dr. Stone then felt Virginia's pulse and took her temperature. Her pulse was a little fast, and the thermometer showed that she had two degrees of fever. Next the doctor examined her nose carefully with a small light. "All right. Now open your mouth, please, and let me see your throat. Say 'ah.'" Then he took his stethoscope and listened to her chest. "Take a deep breath, please." Last, he checked her blood pressure and found it a little low.

"Now, Miss López, you seem to be a little run-down — too much studying, perhaps, or too many parties. I am going to give you a shot for your cold; and here are two prescriptions, one for some pills and one for a tonic. I advise you to rest, to stay at home for a couple of days, and to go on a light diet. If you don't feel better then, come back and see me again; and I'll give you another injection."

"Thanks, Dr. Stone. I feel better already. How much do I owe you?"

"That will be three dollars. You can pay the girl; or, if you prefer, I'll send you a bill at the end of the month. Good-bye, Miss López."

Virginia left the doctor's office and went directly to a drugstore, where a druggist filled her prescriptions while she waited.

VOCABULARY

| to ache | doler | all over | por todas partes |
| to advise | aconsejar | bill | cuenta |

blood pressure	tensión arterial	**next**	luego
to breathe	respirar	**nose**	nariz
chest	pecho	**nurse**	enfermera
cold	resfriado	**office**	consultorio
cough	tos	**to owe**	deber
degree	grado	**pill**	píldora
druggist	farmacéutico, boticario	**prescription**	receta, fórmula
		to rest	descansar
fee (*medical*)	honorarios	**to seem**	parecer
fever	fiebre	**shot**	inyección
headache	dolor de cabeza	**since**	puesto que
inner	interior	**stethoscope**	estetoscopio
last	finalmente	**throat**	garganta
to let	permitir, dejar	**too**	también
light	luz; ligero	**too many**	demasiados
to look	parecer	**too much**	demasiado
magazine	revista	**waiting room**	sala de espera

IDIOMS

a couple of days	un par de días
to be run-down	estar agotado
come and see me	venga a verme
to fill a prescription	preparar una receta
to go on a light diet	ponerse a una dieta ligera
to have a bad cold	estar con un fuerte resfriado
to have a sore throat	dolerle a uno la garganta
to take a deep breath	respirar profundo
(the) day before yesterday	anteayer
What is the matter (with you)?	¿Qué tiene Vd.?

CONVERSATION

Answer the following questions in complete sentences.

1. Why did Virginia go to see the doctor? 2. Where was the doctor's office? 3. Why did she have to wait to see him? 4. Who finally opened the inner door? 5. What was the doctor's name? 6. What was the matter with Virginia? 7. Did she have a sore throat? a headache? 8. What was the doctor wearing? 9. How was Virginia's appetite? 10. What did the doctor use to listen to her chest? 11. Did he examine her throat? 12. Did he check her blood pressure,

too? 13. What did he advise her to do? 14. Did he give her a shot for her cold? 15. How much was the doctor's fee? 16. How many prescriptions did he give her? 17. Who filled the prescriptions for her?

18. Do you sometimes have a headache? an earache? a toothache? a stomach-ache? 19. Do you ever have a sore throat? 20. Do you often have a cold? bronchitis? 21. What do you do when you have a cold? 22. Do you sometimes have shots for a cold? 23. Do you have high blood pressure or low? 24. Do you sometimes feel run-down? When? 25. Do you like to go on a light diet? 26. Does a doctor usually wear a white coat? Why? 27. Where is your doctor's office? 28. What is his office fee? What is his fee if he goes to your house? 29. Do you pay your doctor at the end of the month? 30. In the United States, is a dentist called "doctor"? Is a lawyer? Is an engineer?

PRONUNCIATION

[ɪ] sit, fill, pill, bill, since, inner, listen, prescription
[aɪ] light, white, while, appetite, decide, finally, diet, sign, ride
[ə] pulse, run, much, studying, drug, druggist, couple, nothing, month
[o] only, open, cold, told, owe, home, show, low, nose, throat
[ɚ] inner, matter, fever, over, doctor, pressure, perhaps
[θ] thanks, throat, thermometer, mouth, breath, nothing, stethoscope

GRAMMAR   Section 1

I. Some and any Used after Verbs.

A. **Some** is used as an adjective or a pronoun in affirmative statements.

> Here is **some** money, if you need it. (*singular*)
> I have **some,** thank you.
> Here are **some** pills for your headache. (*plural*)

B. **Any** is used as an adjective or a pronoun after negative verbs.

There weren't **any** people in the waiting room, were there?
No, I didn't see **any** there. (No, I saw **none** there.)
You don't have **any** fever now, do you?
No, I don't have **any** now. (No, I have **none** now.)

Note: The pronoun **none** is sometimes used in the place of **not any**.

C. Both **some** and **any** are used in questions. **Some** indicates that the speaker expects an affirmative answer. **Any** is more indefinite and indicates that the speaker does not know what answer to expect.

>Do you have **some** ink? Do you have **any** ink?
>Are there **some** people in the waiting room?
>Are there **any** people in the waiting room?

*Practice 1. Replace each blank by **some** or **any**, as required, and read the sentences aloud.*

1. There are ——— magazines on the table.
2. There aren't ——— magazines on the table.
3. There is ——— paper in the desk.
4. There isn't ——— paper in the desk.
5. Would you like ——— dessert now?
6. Did you buy ——— stamps?
7. She didn't have ——— mistakes on her paper.
8. You don't need ——— coat today.
9. His father gave him ——— money.
10. I met ——— North Americans there.

Practice 2. Answer these questions affirmatively and negatively.

1. Is there any good music on the radio?
2. Do you have any money for a tip?
3. Is there any sugar in the house?
4. Do you have any time to write it this afternoon?
5. Are there any classes on Saturday?
6. Do you have some paper for dictation?
7. Do you need some stamps?
8. Did you receive some letters today?
9. Did you buy some vegetables for dinner?
10. Are there some seats in the center of the theater?

*Practice 3. Replace each blank by **any** or **no**, as required, and read the sentences aloud. (See Lesson IV.)*

1. He doesn't notice ——— difference in their pronunciation.
   He notices ——— difference in their pronunciation.

2. The room doesn't have ——— windows in it.
   The room has ——— windows in it.
3. They don't have ——— fireplace in their house.
   They have ——— fireplace in their house.
4. We don't have ——— time for that now.
   We have ——— time for that now.
5. There isn't ——— heat in the building.
   There is ——— heat in the building.
6. There isn't ——— time like the present.
   There is ——— time like the present.
7. There aren't ——— students absent today.
   There are ——— students absent today.
8. We don't have ——— hot water today.
   We have ——— hot water today.
9. I didn't receive ——— letters today.
   I received ——— letters today.
10. She doesn't ask ——— questions in class.
    She asks ——— questions in class.

Section 2

II. The Infinitive as a Substitute for the Spanish Subjunctive.

A. In Spanish the subjunctive is used after many verbs; in English an infinitive is used after most of the same verbs, whether the sentence is in present or past time. (See Lesson XXII.)

    The doctor **asks** Virginia **to sit down.** (que se siente)
    The doctor **asked** her **to sit down.** (que se sentara)

B. The infinitive construction is used whether the two verbs in the sentence refer to different people or to the same person.

    The **doctor** wanted to take a vacation.
    The **doctor** wanted **Virginia** to take a vacation.

C. Here are a few common verbs that require the infinitive in English:

advise	aconsejar	**beg**	rogar
allow	permitir	**invite**	invitar
ask	pedir	**let**	permitir

permit	permitir	**urge**	urgir
tell	decir	**want**	querer

Note: The word **to** is omitted after the verb **let**.

The teacher **let** her **go** early.

Practice 1. Use the infinitive construction to translate the words in parentheses.

1. The nurse asks Virginia (que espere).
   The nurse asked her (que esperara).
2. She allows Virginia (que use) the telephone.
   She allowed her (que usara) the telephone.
3. The doctor asks her (que abra) her mouth.
   The doctor asked her (que abriera) her mouth.
4. He says, "Please let me (que vea) your throat."
5. He tells her (que respire profundo).
   He told her (que respirara profundo).
6. He advises her (que descanse).
   He advised her (que descansara).
7. He wants her (que se quede en casa).
   He wanted her (que se quedara en casa).
8. He urges her (que vuelva) if she isn't better.
   He urged her (que volviera) if she wasn't better.
9. Robert invites Virginia (que vaya) to a party.
   Robert invited her (que fuera) to a party.
10. I beg you (que repita) these sentences many times.
    I begged you (que repitiera) these sentences many times.

Practice 2. Answer these questions, using the infinitive construction.

1. Did Robert ask Virginia to dance?
2. Did she ask him to wait for her?
3. Who advised you to enter this class?
4. Does your teacher advise you to study?
5. Do you want me to help you with your pronunciation?
6. Do you want them to go with you?
7. Do parents here let their daughters go to the movies without a chaperon?
8. Did you let her use your book?
9. Did she tell the druggist to fill her prescriptions?
10. Where did he tell us to buy that book?

III. Comparison of the Past Tense with <u>ing</u> and the Simple Past Tense.

The *past tense with* **ing** is used to describe a continuous or unfinished action in the past. It is often used to indicate a continuous past action which was interrupted by another action of short duration. The *simple past tense* is used to indicate only a completed action of long or short duration.

What **were** you **doing**? I **was writing** letters.
Virginia **was reading** a magazine when the nurse **entered**.
The nurse **entered** while she **was reading** a magazine.

Practice 1. Use the past tense with **ing** *in the following sentences.*

1. Virginia ——— (go) to see the doctor when I met her.
2. She ——— (read) a magazine while she ——— (wait).
3. She ——— (sit) in the waiting room when the doctor arrived.
4. He ——— (take) her temperature when the nurse came in.
5. He ——— (listen) to her chest when he said, "Take a deep breath."
6. He ——— (examine) her throat when the phone rang.
7. While the druggist ——— (fill) her prescriptions, she called up a friend.
8. She ——— (sleep) while I ——— (write) those letters.
9. It began to rain while I ——— (wait) for the bus.
10. People ——— (get on) the bus while others ——— (get off).

Practice 2. Use the past tense with **ing** *or the simple past, as required.*

1. I ——— (write) a letter last night.
   I ——— (write) a letter last night when they came.
2. The doctor ——— (give) her a shot for her cold.
   The doctor ——— (give) her a shot when she fainted.
3. The sun ——— (shine) brightly all morning.
   The sun ——— (shine) brightly when we left.
4. It ——— (rain) hard last night.
   It ——— (rain) hard last night when we arrived.
5. I ——— (walk) down Madison Avenue to the theater.
   I ——— (walk) down Madison Avenue when you drove by me.

6. We ——— (take) a streetcar to go downtown yesterday.
   We ——— (ride) on a streetcar when you passed us in your car.
7. She ——— (have) her dinner early last night.
   She ——— (have) her dinner when he called her.
8. Virginia ——— (wait) for us for half an hour.
   While Virginia ——— (wait) for us, she saw an accident.
9. The doorbell ——— (ring) only once this morning.
   While I ——— (listen) to the radio, the doorbell rang.
10. She ——— (lose) the money yesterday afternoon.
    While she ——— (go) to the doctor's, she lost the money.

Practice 3. Answer these questions in complete sentences.

1. Where were you going when I saw you?
2. Was the sun shining when you got up this morning?
3. What was the teacher saying when you came in?
4. What was Virginia doing while she was waiting for the doctor?
5. What was the druggist doing while Virginia was telephoning?

IV. Review of Prepositions: <u>for</u>, <u>by</u>, <u>to</u>; <u>to</u> as Part of the Infinitive.

Complete the following sentences with the correct one of the above prepositions, and read the sentences aloud.

1. I would like ——— leave class early today.
2. We learned the address ——— asking a friend.
3. We will stay ——— two hours; we have to leave ——— ten.
4. They sold the desk ——— fifty dollars.
5. Those shoes are too wide ——— me ——— wear.
6. Did you go ——— the movies last night?
7. Robert called Virginia ——— ask her ——— a date.
8. Mrs. Miller gave a party ——— Virginia.
9. Are you going ——— way of Miami or Mexico City?
10. We hope ——— leave ——— two o'clock.
11. Do you wear glasses ——— reading?
12. We waited ——— fifteen minutes and then took a taxi.
13. Let's ask Virginia ——— have dinner with us.
14. She got to the theater ——— taking two buses.
15. I sent the letter ——— air mail yesterday.
16. I hope ——— learn ——— speak English some day.

17. I have a little notebook ——— addresses.
18. He earns his living ——— selling shoes.
19. Please call me ——— Friday morning.
20. Robert is going to the drugstore ——— some ice cream.
21. They lived there ——— five years before coming here.
22. He waited after class ——— talk with the teacher.
23. If you write now, you will have an answer ——— Monday.
24. Virginia needs ——— have more rest and ——— stay at home a few days.
25. The bus goes ——— my house every half hour.
26. They stayed after class ——— the singing.
27. They stayed after class ——— learn some new songs.
28. They are learning ——— speak English ——— practicing it with North Americans.
29. Robert called Virginia up ——— ask her ——— go ——— the movies.
30. People usually use a pen ——— writing letters.
31. ——— the way, do you know the idioms ——— heart?
32. Paul went ——— his room ——— get a book.
33. It is important ——— you ——— come ——— class regularly.
34. Virginia is going ——— the grocery store ——— buy some fruit.
35. He drove ——— me in his car, but he didn't see me.
36. I am going early ——— get a good seat.
37. On your way to the hotel, you will pass ——— a large church.
38. I arrived on time ——— taking a taxi.
39. We do not expect ——— see them tomorrow.
40. English is difficult ——— pronounce.

Morgan Brassell

LESSON XII

EDUCATION IN THE UNITED STATES

Virginia: How many years did you go to school before you came to the university?

Robert: Thirteen years.

Virginia: What a long time! And it didn't cost you a cent?

Robert: No, because I went to public schools, as most Americans do.

Virginia: How old were you when you started to school?
Robert: I was five years old when I went to kindergarten.
Virginia: And after kindergarten?
Robert: Then I went into first grade, second grade, and so on, through eighth grade. That made eight years in elementary school.
Virginia: Do all children go to high school then?
Robert: Well, almost all, because education is compulsory until a certain age, and in most states the age is sixteen.
Virginia: Was the high school in the same building as the elementary school?
Robert: No, there are five big high schools in my home town, and I went to the nearest one, Monroe High School. It was five blocks from my home.
Virginia: How many students were there in the school?
Robert: If I remember correctly, there were about fifteen hundred boys and girls. Most of our public schools are coeducational, you know.
Virginia: And how many years did you go to high school?
Robert: Four years. The first year we are freshmen, the second year sophomores, the third year juniors, and the fourth year seniors.
Virginia: And when you finished high school, did you get the degree of bachelor?
Robert: No. When we graduate from high school, we get a diploma. A student does not receive a bachelor's degree until he graduates from college.
Virginia: Then what is a college? I thought that it was the same as a high school or *colegio*.
Robert: No, not at all. A *colegio* is similar to our high school; when we graduate from high school, we are ready to go to college.
Virginia: Then a college is like a university?
Robert: Yes, Virginia, that's it. The principal difference is that a university has several colleges or schools, such as the College of Engineering, the School of Medicine, and the School of Law; but the largest unit of the university is usually the College of Liberal Arts. There are also many separate liberal arts

	colleges which are not connected with any university. They offer a general four-year course and give a bachelor's degree to the graduates just as the corresponding college of a university does. In any case, a college or university student does not begin to major in a special field until his junior year.
Virginia:	Did you have to take an examination to enter the university?
Robert:	No, fortunately, but that depends on the college or university. If we graduate from high school with good grades, many colleges or universities will accept us without requiring an examination. It is necessary, however, to make an application for entrance many months in advance. The school year always begins in September or October and ends in May or June.
Virginia:	Did you ever fail an examination?
Robert:	Oh, yes, but I never "flunked" a course, thank goodness!
Virginia:	What does "flunk" mean?
Robert:	"Flunk" is a colloquial expression used by students instead of "fail."
Virginia:	How large are the colleges and universities?
Robert:	There are schools of every size and description: large and small, public and private, coeducational and for men or women alone, schools with a campus and without, schools in large cities and in small towns. Some universities have twenty thousand students or more, whereas some liberal arts colleges have three hundred students or even fewer.
Virginia:	Do many girls go to college?
Robert:	Oh, yes, the ratio in general is about three men students to two women students.
Virginia:	Is it very expensive to go to college?
Robert:	Yes, it is. But remember that education through high school is free, and most young people finish high school. Many cannot go to college because it costs too much.
Virginia:	How much does it cost?

Robert: Well, about two thousand dollars a year, more or less. That's an average, and it includes tuition, board and room, books, laboratory fees, travel expenses, and some clothes. It really depends on the school and also on the person.

Virginia: Please forgive me for asking you so many questions, Bob, but it is all very interesting. I understand your educational system much better now than before. Thanks a million.

VOCABULARY

age	edad	**field** (*of study*)	campo, ramo
almost	casi	**to flunk**	
and so on	etcétera	(*colloquial*)	fracasar
application	solicitud	**to forgive**	perdonar
average	promedio	**fortunately**	afortunadamente
bachelor	bachiller	**free**	gratuito
campus	terrenos que rodean la universidad y le pertenecen	**grade**	año escolar; calificación
		high school	instituto de educación secundaria
certain	cierto	**to include**	incluír
clothes	ropa	**law**	derecho
coeducational	para ambos sexos	**to major in**	especializarse en
		most (*adj.*)	la mayoría de
colloquial	familiar, de uso corriente	**to offer**	ofrecer
		private	particular
compulsory	obligatorio	**ratio**	proporción
degree	título académico	**similar**	parecido
engineering	ingeniería	**such as**	tal(es) como
to enter	entrar (en)	**system**	sistema
entrance	admisión, ingreso	**travel** (*adj.*)	de viaje
		tuition	valor de la enseñanza
expenses	gastos		
to fail	fracasar	**unit**	unidad
fees (*laboratory*)	derechos	**whereas**	mientras que

IDIOMS

board and room alojamiento y alimentación, cuarto y comida

to depend on depender de

to fail an examination	salir suspenso en un examen
to go to college	seguir estudios universitarios
in advance	con anticipación
in any case	de todas maneras
to start to school	empezar la escuela
to take an examination	presentarse a examen, sufrir examen
Thank goodness!	¡ Gracias a Dios !
Thanks a million!	¡ Un millón de gracias !
What a long time!	¡ Qué tiempo tan largo !

CONVERSATION

Answer the following questions in complete sentences.

1. Are there more public or private schools in the United States? in your country? 2. Do most children go to public schools in the United States? in your country? 3. Do all children go to kindergarten in the United States? in your country? 4. How many years do they go to elementary school in the United States? in your country? 5. How many years do they go to high school in the United States? in your country? 6. Are American high schools larger than yours? 7. Do you have high schools which are coeducational? 8. Why do most American children finish high school? 9. Is a college the same as a *colegio* or a *liceo* in your country? 10. What is the difference between an American college and a university? 11. Do you have a university in your city? What is its name? Is it very old? Where is it situated? How many students attend it? How many women students? Is it very expensive? 12. What degree is given after four years at an American university? What degree is given to the graduates of your universities? 13. When does the school year begin and end in the United States? in your country? 14. Explain in English the meaning of **tuition** and **board and room.** 15. If the teacher gives you an examination on these questions, do you think you will "flunk" it?

PRONUNCIATION

[ɝ] first, third, thirteen, turn, nurse, certain

[tʃ] teacher, fortunately, temperature, lecture, feature

[æ] as, ask, advance, travel, thanks, examination, laboratory, understand

[ə] diploma, American, several, elementary, liberal, general, separate (*adj.*), entrance, campus, difference, student, system, freshmen, women

[dʒ] college, average, large, largest, major, engineering, general, junior, education, coeducation, graduate

[ʃ] tuition, examination, application, description, prescription, vacation

GRAMMAR

I. Comparisons of Inequality with more, less, and the Ending er.

A. Adjectives and adverbs of one syllable and a few of two syllables form their comparatives by adding **er**. The word **than** is used in the second part of the comparison (más ... que).

He is **younger than** I (am).
She is **prettier than** her sister (is).
You write **faster than** I (do).

Note: Adjectives and adverbs ending in **e** add only **r**.

larger   bluer   later

B. Adjectives and adverbs of three or more syllables, and sometimes those of two syllables, form their comparatives by placing **more** before the word compared (más ... que).

Washington is **more beautiful than** New York (is).
Our teacher speaks **more slowly than** you (do).

C. Adjectives and adverbs are also compared by placing **less**, the opposite of **more**, before them. The word **than** is used in the second part of the comparison (menos ... que).

This coat is **less expensive than** that one.
She speaks Spanish **less often than** English.

Practice using the following comparisons in sentences.

Adjectives

{ taller than / shorter than } (*people*)   { higher than / lower than } (*things*)

{ older than / younger than } (*people*)   { older than / newer than } (*things*)

{ longer than } (*things*) more common than
{ shorter than }   more friendly than
{ larger than }   more entertaining than
{ smaller than }   less important than
                            less interesting than
{ colder than }   less expensive than
{ warmer than }

Adverbs

later than   more frequently than
oftener than   less carefully than
faster than   less clearly than
more slowly than

Note: The following changes in spelling occur.

pretty	prettier	funny	funnier
easy	easier	hungry	hungrier
busy	busier	early	earlier
ugly	uglier	big	bigger
heavy	heavier	thin	thinner

II. Comparisons of Equality with the same . . . as, as . . . as, so . . . as.

A. **The same . . . as** is used with nouns or when a noun is understood.

> Virginia has **the same** address **as** Mrs. Miller.
> My address is not **the same as** yours.

B. **As . . . as** is used with adjectives and adverbs in affirmative sentences.

> Virginia is **as** tall **as** Robert.

C. **As . . . as** is used with adjectives and adverbs after a negative verb.

> Virginia is not **as** tall **as** Robert.

Note: So . . . as is sometimes used after a negative verb instead of **as . . . as**.

Practice repeating these sentences in the affirmative, then in the negative.

1. The high school was in **the same** building **as** the elementary school.

2. A high school is **the same as** a *colegio*.
3. Virginia's classes come at **the same** time **as** Robert's.
4. Virginia is **as** old **as** Robert.
5. She studies English **as** much **as** he studies Spanish.
6. This course is **as** difficult **as** that one.
7. The School of Medicine is **as** large **as** the School of Law.
8. This college is **as** good **as** that one.
9. This college campus is **as** large **as** that one.
10. Tuition is **as** expensive **as** board and room.

III. Comparisons with similar, like, alike, and different.

Besides the usual comparisons with **more, less,** and **as,** there are other ways to show the idea of comparison.

Type 1

A is { **like** / **similar to** / **different from** } B.   A *colegio* is { **like** / **similar to** / **different from** } a high school.

Type 2

A and B are { **alike.** / **similar.** / **different.** }   A *colegio* and a high school are { **alike.** / **similar.** / **different.** }

Practice changing these comparisons from Type 1 to Type 2.

1. Virginia is **like** her mother in many ways.
   She and her mother are alike in many ways.
2. His new coat is **similar to** his father's.
3. The new clothes are **different from** the old ones.
4. Your telephone number is **similar to** ours.
5. The customs of one Latin-American country are much **like** those of another.
6. North American customs are often **different from** South American customs.
7. The Colombian flag is **similar to** the Venezuelan flag.
8. A Bachelor of Arts degree is **different from** a *bachillerato*.
9. A high school diploma is **similar to** a *bachillerato*.
10. A separate liberal arts college is **like** the corresponding college of a university.
11. The schools in one state are **similar to** the schools in another state.
12. This application blank is **like** that one.

13. Robert's program of studies is **different from** Virginia's.
14. His tuition is not **like** Charles's.
15. This engineering course is **similar to** that one.

IV. The Superlative: <u>most</u> and the Ending <u>est</u>.

A. Adjectives and adverbs of one or two syllables form their superlatives by adding **est.** This ending is similar to the comparative ending **er.**

>My **oldest** brother is a lawyer.
>That is the **highest** building in the city.
>John runs the **fastest**.

Note: Adjectives and adverbs ending in **e** add only **st**.

>largest   bluest   latest

B. Adjectives or adverbs of three or more syllables, and sometimes those of two syllables, form their superlatives by placing **most** before the word compared. The preposition **in** often follows the superlative instead of **of**.

>That is the **most beautiful** building **in** the city.
>Of all the students he does his work the **most carefully**.

C. Adjectives and adverbs also have a superlative with **least,** the opposite of **most**.

>This is the **least difficult** lesson in the book.
>She writes the **least clearly** of all the students.

D. The definite article **the** or a possessive adjective is used before the superlative.

Practice using these superlatives in sentences.

>the shortest girl   his easiest examination
>the tallest student   the most difficult thing
>my busiest day   our most interesting lesson
>my nearest bus stop   the least important part
>the smallest colleges   the most clearly
>the largest universities   the most frequently

V. Some Irregular Comparisons.

Adjectives

good	better . . . than	best
bad	worse . . . than	worst

much	more ... than	most
many	more ... than	most
little	less ... than	least
few	fewer ... than	fewest

Adverbs

well	better than	best
badly	worse than	worst

Note: **Little** is singular; **few** is plural. The expressions **a little** and **a few** have a positive implication; **little** and **few** have a negative implication, as do their Spanish equivalents.

    Do you speak English? Yes, **a little.** (un poco)
    I speak **a little** English. (un poco de)
    I speak **little** English. (poco)
    There are **a few** private schools. (unas pocas)
    There are **few** private schools. (pocas)

Practice completing these sentences, using the comparative and superlative forms of the adjective or adverb.

1. This is a **good** college.
   This is a **better** college **than** that one.
   This is **the best** college **in** the state.

2. I have a **bad** cold.
   My cold is ——— ——— yours.
   I am having my ——— cold **of** the year.

3. Robert doesn't have **much** money.
   Robert has ——— money ——— some of the university students.
   His friend George has the ——— money **of** all.

4. There are **many** colleges in the state of Ohio.
   There are ——— colleges in the state of Pennsylvania ——— in Ohio.
   New York has the ——— colleges **of** any state.

5. There is **little** difference between the English of the East and that of the West.
   There is ——— difference between the English of Boston and Chicago ——— between the English of the North and the South.
   There is the ——— difference between the English of Chicago and that of San Francisco.

6. **Few** children go to private schools in the United States.
    ———— children go to private schools ———— to **public** schools.
    This class has the ———— students **of** all.
7. He speaks English very **well.**
    He speaks it ———— ———— his brother.
    He speaks it the ———— **of** anyone in his class.
8. He writes **badly,** and it's hard to read his writing.
    He writes ———— ———— his brother.
    He writes the ———— **of** anyone in his family.

REVIEW LESSON IV

I. Change the following sentences to questions.

1. Virginia is studying in the United States.
2. She likes the university.
3. She lives with the Miller family.
4. The house is made of brick and wood.
5. Mr. Miller doesn't own the house.
6. The house has a nice green lawn.
7. Mr. Brown waited on Mrs. Miller at the store.
8. Mr. Brown didn't get the steak for her.
9. The parents select the given name and the middle name.
10. The children don't use the mother's maiden name after the father's surname.
11. Virginia met Robert in one of her classes.
12. He asked her to have a Coke with him.
13. He invited her to go to the movies with him.
14. The telephone is ringing.
15. The buzz indicates that the line is busy.
16. Robert didn't leave a message.
17. People usually go to the movies to be entertained.
18. Virginia wanted to sit on the main floor.
19. The doctor advised Virginia to stay at home for a few days.
20. The druggist filled her prescriptions.

II. Answer the following questions, both in the affirmative and the negative.

1. Is Virginia having a good time?
2. Do you expect her to return soon?

3. Does her family miss her very much?
4. Does the doorbell often ring at your house?
5. Do they pronounce English well?
6. Do you live on Clark Street?
7. Do you rent your house?
8. Does he earn seventy-five dollars a week?
9. Do you know her very well?
10. Does this class meet three times a week?
11. Do you have a five-cent stamp?
12. Did you prepare your homework for today?
13. Did you make many mistakes in your sentences?
14. When the news is good, are people happy?
15. Does he live opposite the park?
16. Did they come to class early today?
17. Did you buy a new hat yesterday?
18. Do they sell notebooks in that store?
19. Does she understand the new lesson?
20. Did he go to New York on business?
21. Did you speak English with your North American friends?
22. Does she take sugar in her tea?
23. Did they arrive in this country last week?
24. Does that custom resemble the Latin-American custom?
25. Did you write any letters on Sunday?
26. Did you visit your friends last evening?
27. Is this notebook yours?
28. Are you going to cash the check today?
29. Is Virginia from Peru?
30. Did you attend class last week?
31. Did you like the movie last night?
32. Did you call her up this morning?
33. Did they drive to the airport?
34. Did you sleep well last night?
35. Did you attend the lecture last week?
36. Did she leave her book at home?
37. Did she leave early this morning?
38. Did you forget your pen today?
39. Did he fly to New York?
40. Did it rain yesterday?
41. Did she think that it was going to rain?
42. Did you take a streetcar?
43. Did you use to play the piano?
44. Did he use to have many colds?
45. Did they use to listen to the radio every night?

46. Was he in the city during his vacation?
47. Were they going to the movies when you saw them?
48. Was the sun shining this morning when you left?
49. Were you waiting for us when we phoned?
50. Were they expecting you when you arrived?

III. Use a form of the verb <u>be</u> and <u>going to</u> to express future time.

1. When ——— she ——— begin her classes?
2. He ——— take an examination tomorrow.
3. They ——— study French next year.
4. They ——— visit the United States soon.
5. They ——— travel by plane.
6. They say that they ——— spend two months there.
7. When ——— you ——— have a vacation?
8. I ——— take my vacation in December.
9. Which train ——— he ——— take?
10. I ——— see those people again tomorrow.
11. Where ——— you ——— meet them?
12. We ——— take a ride this afternoon.
13. They ——— play bridge this evening.
14. When ——— Virginia ——— return from the United States?
15. When ——— you ——— write her another letter?

IV. Complete these sentences, using an infinitive construction.

1. I asked him **to wait a few minutes.**
2. Her mother permitted her ———.
3. His father didn't allow him ———.
4. Will his father let him ———?
5. They begged us ———.
6. We wanted you ———.
7. They urged him ———.
8. Did you tell her ———?
9. She invited us ———.
10. The teacher advised us ———.

V. Use <u>one</u> or <u>ones</u>, as required, in the blanks.

1. There are more public schools than private ——— in the United States.
2. There were five high schools in Robert's home town, and he went to the nearest ———.

3. The first year in high school or college, students are freshmen, the second ——— sophomores, and so on.
4. The first examination was easier than the second ———.
5. The small universities are often as good as the large ———.
6. There are colleges of every size and description: large ——— and small ———, public ——— and private ———.
7. The tuition at this college is higher than at that ———.
8. North American schools begin in September; South American ——— usually begin in February or March.
9. That university is the oldest ——— in the United States.
10. There are fifty states. The largest ——— is Alaska, and the smallest ——— is Rhode Island.
11. Her new clothes are more expensive than her old ———.
12. This taxi is better than that ———.
13. The first train leaves at six-thirty. The next ——— leaves at nine.
14. The yellow buses go in one direction, and the blue ——— go in another direction.
15. This bus goes down Fifth Avenue, but the crosstown ——— goes along Forty-second Street.

VI. Complete the sentences in A with *some* or *any, as required;* complete the sentences in B with *any* or *no, as required.*

A.
1. First the doctor asked Virginia ——— questions.
2. Then he gave her a prescription for ——— pills.
3. I need to buy ——— medicine, but I don't have ——— money with me.
4. Would you please lend me ——— until tomorrow?
5. She received ——— letters, but I didn't get ———.
6. Are there ——— students who don't have books?
7. I didn't have ——— breakfast this morning.
8. Do you have ——— paper for a dictation?
9. I'm sorry, but I don't have ———.
10. There are ——— seats in the balcony, but there aren't ——— downstairs.

B.
1. There were ——— buses for half an hour.
2. There weren't ——— buses for half an hour.
3. I have ——— small change.
4. I don't have ——— small change.
5. There is ——— bus stop near my house.
6. There isn't ——— bus stop near my house.

7. There are ——— classes tomorrow.
8. There aren't ——— classes tomorrow.
9. A high school gives ——— courses in philosophy.
10. A high school doesn't give ——— courses in philosophy.

VII. Use the definite article where it is necessary.

1. ——— coffee is grown in some Latin-American countries.
2. ——— coffee from Guatemala is very good.
3. Do you like ——— coffee or ——— tea for breakfast?
4. ——— high schools are similar to ——— *colegios*.
5. Some of ——— big city high schools have two thousand students.
6. ——— education in the United States is compulsory until a certain age.
7. Most young people finish ——— high school.
8. ——— education which he received was like that of most Americans.
9. He studied ——— Spanish at ——— Monroe High School.
10. ——— Madison Avenue has some beautiful old homes.
11. Some of ——— Madison Avenue homes are very elegant.
12. The hotel is on ——— corner of ——— State Street and ——— Lafayette Avenue.
13. He comes from ——— Argentina, but his home is in ——— Havana now.
14. ——— President Hoover thought of the Good Neighbor policy, and ——— President Roosevelt established it.
15. ——— President is a very busy man.

VIII. Prepositions. Fill each blank with the correct preposition.

Robert was going ——— the bank ——— West Third Street to cash a check. Virginia came ——— her house as he was passing ———, so they walked ——— the street together. They talked ——— many things, half ——— Spanish and half ——— English. They stopped when they arrived ——— the drugstore ——— the corner, because Virginia needed to buy some ink. They went ——— the drugstore, and then Robert said, "Let's sit down ——— this little table and have a Coke or some ice cream." There were some other young students ——— another table, and ——— them they noticed two of their friends. The waiter placed two glasses ——— water ——— the table ——— them and then wrote their orders ——— a piece of paper. They stayed ——— only a quarter of an hour because Virginia remembered that she had appointment ——— the doctor ——— three o'clock. ——— walking fast, they arrived ——— the doctor's ——— time. Before Robert left her, he asked her ——— a date ——— (para) Saturday night. She accepted, but she said that she had to be home ——— (no más tarde que) midnight. Then Robert went ——— (a) the bank ——— (frente a) the doctor's office. There were many people ——— (delante de) the bank waiting ——— a bus, but there were more people ——— (en) the bank standing ——— line to get some money before the bank closed ——— three-thirty.

IX. Complete the following sentences with the English equivalent of ¿no es verdad?

1. It was Saturday afternoon, **wasn't it?**
2. Virginia went to the Paramount Theater, ———?
3. Mrs. Miller was downtown, ———?
4. The bus was crowded, ———?
5. This bus doesn't go down Broadway, ———?
6. It goes down Fifth Avenue, ———?
7. The fare is fifteen cents, ———?
8. Buses are usually faster than streetcars, ———?
9. The bus stops at this corner, ———?
10. You get off at Forty-second Street, ———?
11. The theater isn't hard to find, ———?
12. Virginia wasn't feeling very well, ———?
13. There were many people in the waiting room, ———?
14. Dr. Stone looked very professional, ———?
15. Virginia has a bad cold, ———?
16. She doesn't want anything to eat, ———?
17. Her pulse was a little fast, ———?
18. The doctor gave her a shot, ———?
19. You don't have a headache, ———?
20. She doesn't like to go on a diet, ———?
21. A college is not the same as a high school, ———?
22. Robert didn't take an entrance examination, ———?
23. It is very expensive to go to college, ———?
24. Some universities are very large, ———?

X. Idiom Review. Translate the following sentences, which contain idioms from Lessons I–XII.

1. La sirvienta fué a ver quién llamaba a la puerta.
2. Virginia está estudiando mucho, pero también se divierte.

3. La echamos mucho de menos.
4. Ella vive con los señores Miller.
5. El señor Miller arrienda la casa por $100 al mes.
6. Tenemos tres clases a la semana.
7. ¿Viven ellos frente al teatro Columbia?
8. ¿Qué se le ofrece esta mañana?
9. ¿Qué tal le parecen estos tomates?
10. Están un poco verdes pero creo que servirán.
11. ¿Le gustaría bailar o ir al cine?
12. Mucho gusto en haberlo visto. Hasta luego.
13. ¿De dónde es Vd.? ¿Viene de la costa?
14. ¿De quién es este abrigo? ¿Es de Vd. o de su hermano?
15. Hágame el favor de comprar unas estampillas de cinco centavos.
16. ¿Puede Vd. cambiar este billete de diez pesos?
17. ¡Tengo tantas cosas que hacer mañana!
18. Conocí a varios americanos en una fiesta anoche.
19. Fuimos al cine el sábado y nos sentamos en luneta.
20. ¿Llegaron Vds. a tiempo para el noticiero?
21. ¿Toman Vds. en serio las películas?
22. ¿Asistieron Vds. a la conferencia en inglés la semana pasada?
23. Traté de adivinar, pero al fin me di por vencido.
24. Ella nos hizo muchas preguntas.
25. Su traje nuevo es pardo obscuro; el mío es azul claro.
26. ¿Cuál de los dos colores prefiere Vd.?
27. Dice que puede hacerse entender en inglés.
28. Tenga cuidado. Hay mucho tráfico a esta hora.
29. Me gustaría aceptar su invitación. Siento tener otro compromiso.
30. ¿Está dañado el teléfono? No me contestan.
31. Hágame el favor de avisarme con anticipación.
32. ¿Me bajo del bus en esta esquina para ir al teatro?
33. ¿Qué tiene Vd.? Estoy un poco agotado.
34. Me duele una muela, pero eso es todo.
35. ¿Le dijo el médico que se quedara en casa un par de días?
36. ¡Qué tiempo tan largo para aprender el inglés!
37. Depende mucho de la persona y del tiempo que estudie.
38. Poco a poco vamos a aprender mucho.
39. Gracias a Dios, no necesitamos sufrir examen ahora.
40. ¿Quién puede traducir todas estas frases perfectamente?

PART II

Miami Beach News Bureau

LESSON XIII

Miami Beach

A Trip through the United States

When Latin Americans think of the United States, they usually think of New York City; for them New York *is* the United States because it is the largest city in the country. Nothing is more erroneous. It is especially important for a foreigner to realize that New York is not the most typical

North American city. In a nation as large and as varied as the United States, there are many other cities, large and small, that seem more representative of North American life. Now, in order to know the United States better, we are going to take an imaginary trip through the principal cities of the East, and then across the mountains and plains to the cities of the Middle West, the South, and the Far West.

MIAMI, FLORIDA

The gateway to the United States for most Latin Americans who travel by plane is Miami. This city of about 270,000[1] inhabitants is beautifully situated on the southeastern coast of the state of Florida. Miami itself is not on the ocean, but on a large bay called Biscayne Bay. Its wide streets are lined with palms, and its white cement houses are covered with bougainvillea. Across the bay is its neighbor, Miami Beach, which we reach by road over a long causeway. This is a residential town of about 52,000 inhabitants, built between the ocean and Biscayne Bay. It has many beautiful homes; and among the five hundred hotels in Miami Beach and Miami, the most magnificent ones are on the ocean beach. As a matter of fact, no one who lives in Miami or Miami Beach is far from the ocean, and it is possible for everyone to go swimming or sun himself on the beach every day, if he wishes to.

Because of its warm, subtropical climate the year round, the Miami region has become a popular winter resort. Each year it attracts many thousands of wealthy tourists, who prefer its sunshine and flowers to the cold and snow of the North. It is easy, therefore, to understand why Miami's main occupation and largest business is entertaining tourists.

Other important occupations around Miami are fishing and agriculture. This region produces large quantities of citrus fruits such as oranges, grapefruit, and lemons. The city also sends pineapples, papayas, avocados, guavas, coconuts, and vegetables to northern markets during the winter. Miami is also important as a manufacturing center.

[1] Population figures in this book are usually given in round numbers.

Historically, there is little of interest in Miami. The Spanish explorer Menéndez found a large Indian village there in 1567; but the present city has really developed since 1896, when the Florida East Coast Railway chose Miami as its southern terminal.

We cannot stay long, however, in this modern vacation city, since we have our Pullman reservations for next week. Then we are going to travel along the eastern coast to Jacksonville, Florida, and from there we shall pass through the states of Georgia, South Carolina, North Carolina, and Virginia on our way to Washington, D. C. This is a total distance of eleven hundred miles, which takes about a day and a night on the train.

VOCABULARY

across	al otro lado de	no one	nadie
along	a lo largo de	orange	naranja
to attract	atraer	pineapple	piña
avocado	aguacate	plain	llano, llanura
bay	bahía	plane	avión
beach	playa	Pullman	coche dormitorio de un tren
business	negocio		
causeway	calzada	quantity	cantidad
coast	costa	railway	ferrocarril
coconut	coco	to reach	llegar a
covered with	cubierto de	to realize	darse cuenta de
to develop	desarrollar	resort	lugar para pasar temporadas
east	este		
everyone	todos, cada uno	situated	situado
fishing	pesca	snow	nieve
foreigner	extranjero	to stay	quedarse
gateway	puerta de entrada	to sun oneself	tomar el sol
grapefruit	toronja	sunshine	brillo del sol
guava	guayaba	to swim	nadar
instead of	en vez de	therefore	por eso
lined with	bordeado de	trip	viaje
main	principal	village	pueblo
mountain	montaña	wealthy	rico
neighbor	vecino	west	oeste
		wide	ancho

149

IDIOMS

    as a matter of fact   en efecto
    to go swimming   ir a bañarse
    it takes one day   se necesita un día, se echa un día
    on our way to   (en) camino de, rumbo a
    to stay long   demorar
    to take a trip   hacer un viaje
    the year round   durante todo el año
    to think of   pensar en

CONVERSATION

Answer the following questions in complete sentences.

1. Are you thinking of going to the United States some day? 2. Will you go by plane or by boat? 3. How long is the trip to Miami by plane? by boat? 4. When you think of the United States, do you think of New York first? 5. What is it important for a foreigner to realize? 6. What are the names of the different regions of the country? 7. Where is Miami located? In which state? In which part of the state? On the Atlantic Ocean? 8. Where is Miami Beach? 9. How do people reach it from Miami? 10. What is the population of Miami? Miami Beach? 11. Why is Miami called a vacation city? 12. What would you do if you lived in Miami Beach? 13. What kind of climate does Miami have? 14. What is Miami's largest business? 15. What are the other important occupations? 16. What does this region produce in large quantities? 17. Is Miami an interesting old city? 18. How is it connected with the North? 19. Is it sometimes difficult to get Pullman reservations from Miami? During which season? 20. How far is Washington, D. C., from Miami? 21. What states does one pass through on the way? 22. Why do some people prefer to take a train from Miami instead of a plane? 23. What cities do North Americans think of first when they think of South America? 24. What are the vacation spots in your country?

PRONUNCIATION

[tʃ] **ch**oose, **ch**ose, bea**ch**, rea**ch**, ca**tch**
[dʒ] **G**eor**g**ia, Vir**g**inia, brid**g**e, re**g**ion, oran**g**es, ve**g**etable

[ʃ] fish, fishing, sunshine, Spanish, ocean, especially, occupation, vacation, reservation
[θ] north, south, month, nothing, wealthy, through, thousand
[ð] this, that, they, then, there, therefore, another, northern, southern

GRAMMAR   Section 1

I. The Formation of the Present Perfect Tense.

A. The present perfect is formed from the present tense of the auxiliary verb **have** (haber) and the past participle of the principal verb. The past participle of regular verbs ends in **ed** like the simple past tense and is pronounced in the same way.

Note 1: As in the simple past, if the verb ends in **e**, only **d** is added.
Note 2: As with the auxiliaries **do** and **be**, in the negative, **not** (or its contraction **n't**) separates the auxiliary **have** and the participle; in the interrogative, the subject separates the auxiliary and the participle. In the negative interrogative, both **not** and the subject separate the verb and the participle.

	Long Forms	Contracted Forms
Affirmative:	I have asked you have asked he has asked we have asked you have asked they have asked	I've asked you've asked he's asked we've asked you've asked they've asked
Negative:	I have not asked you have not asked he has not asked we have not asked you have not asked they have not asked	I haven't asked you haven't asked he hasn't asked we haven't asked you haven't asked they haven't asked
Interrogative:	have I asked? have you asked? has he asked? have we asked? have you asked? have they asked?	

Negative
Interrogative: have I not asked?   haven't I asked?
                have you not asked?   haven't you asked?
                has he not asked?   hasn't he asked?
                have we not asked?   haven't we asked?
                have you not asked?   haven't you asked?
                have they not asked?   haven't they asked?

Note: The contracted forms of the negative interrogative are much more common in conversation than the long forms.

B. The three principal parts (present, simple past, and past participle) of the most common irregular verbs are given below. Some of the past participles are like the simple past tense, some are completely different, and a few verbs are the same in all three forms. (For the Spanish equivalents, see the Appendix.)

TYPE 1

Present	Past	Past Participle	Present	Past	Past Participle
bring	brought	**brought**	mean	meant	**meant**
buy	bought	**bought**	pay	paid	**paid**
catch	caught	**caught**	say	said	**said**
die	died	**died**	sell	sold	**sold**
feel	felt	**felt**	send	sent	**sent**
find	found	**found**	shine	shone,	**shone,**
get	got	**got, gotten**	sit	shined sat	**shined** **sat**
hang	hung, hanged	**hung, hanged**	sleep spend	slept spent	**slept** **spent**
hear	heard	**heard**	stand	stood	**stood**
hold	held	**held**	swing	swung	**swung**
keep	kept	**kept**	teach	taught	**taught**
lay	laid	**laid**	tell	told	**told**
leave	left	**left**	think	thought	**thought**
lend	lent	**lent**	understand	understood	**understood**
lose	lost	**lost**	win	won	**won**
make	made	**made**			

TYPE 2

| be | was | **been** | begin | began | **begun** |
| become | became | **become** | break | broke | **broken** |

choose	chose	**chosen**	ring	rang	**rung**
come	came	**come**	rise	rose	**risen**
do	did	**done**	run	ran	**run**
drink	drank	**drunk**	see	saw	**seen**
drive	drove	**driven**	shake	shook	**shaken**
eat	ate	**eaten**	show	showed	**shown, showed**
fall	fell	**fallen**			
fly	flew	**flown**	sing	sang	**sung**
forget	forgot	**forgotten**	speak	spoke	**spoken**
freeze	froze	**frozen**	steal	stole	**stolen**
give	gave	**given**	swim	swam	**swum**
go	went	**gone**	take	took	**taken**
grow	grew	**grown**	tear	tore	**torn**
know	knew	**known**	throw	threw	**thrown**
lie	lay	**lain**	wear	wore	**worn**
ride	rode	**ridden**	write	wrote	**written**

TYPE 3

cost	cost	**cost**	put	put	**put**
cut	cut	**cut**	read [rid]	read [rɛd]	**read [rɛd]**
let	let	**let**			

Note 1: **Died** or **dead**. **Died** is the past participle used with **have** (haber). **Dead** is an adjective used after the verb **be**.

He **has died**.   He **is dead**.

Note 2: **Got** or **gotten**. The verb **get** in American English now has two past participles, **got** and **gotten**. North Americans usually use **I've gotten** for **I've obtained** (he conseguido) and **I've become** (he llegado a ser), in preference to **I've got**. On the other hand, they sometimes use **I've got** with the meaning **I have** (tengo) or **I must** (debo). (See Lesson XXIII.) However, these uses of **got** and **gotten** are avoided in good English.

Possible	Better
He's gotten the tickets.	**He's obtained** (**bought**) the tickets.
He's gotten tired of his work.	**He's become** tired of his work.
I've got only five cents in my pocket.	**I have** only five cents in my pocket.
I've got to go now.	**I must** go now.

Note 3: **Hung** or **hanged**. **Hanged** is used only of death by hanging.

Note 4: **Shone** and **shined.** **Shone** is used intransitively, while **shined** is used transitively.

    The sun **has shone** brightly all afternoon.
    The little boy **has shined** my shoes well.

Note 5: **Shown** and **showed.** There is no difference in meaning or use between **shown** and **showed.**

II. Uses of the Present Perfect Tense.

The present perfect tense refers to events in the past, but it is always connected in some way with present time.

    1. This tense is used to describe an action which took place at an indefinite time in the past, or which was repeated within a period of time extending from the past to the present.

        Have you **been** in Miami?
        No, I **have** never **been** there.
        Yes, I **have been** there twice. (*hasta ahora*)

Note: The present perfect with **just** translates the Spanish **acabar de** with an infinitive.

        They **have just left** the house.
        (Acaban de salir de la casa.)

Change the verbs in parentheses to the present perfect tense, and read these sentences aloud.

1. We ——— (miss) Virginia a great deal this year.
2. We ——— (learn) many new words.
3. I ——— never ——— (meet) her.
4. Mr. Miller ——— (be) in New York many times.
5. Modern Miami ——— (develop) only since 1896.
6. ——— you ever ——— (take) a trip by boat?
7. Yes, I ——— (travel) by boat many times.
8. I ——— (lose) my book.
9. ——— you ——— (see) that movie?
10. Miami ——— (become) a popular winter resort.
11. He ——— just ——— (finish) high school.
12. His brother ——— just ——— (graduate) from college.
13. Our friends ——— just ——— (leave) for New York.
14. They ——— just ——— (reach) Miami today.
15. We ——— just ——— (receive) a telegram from them.

2. This tense is also used to describe an action that began in the past and has continued into the present. The **ing** form (present perfect of **be** and the **ing** form of the principal verb) is often used to emphasize the action of the verb.

>**I have studied** English for two years. (*I am still studying.*)
>(Hace dos años que estudio el inglés.)
>
>**I have been studying** English for two years. (*I am still studying.*)
>(Hace dos años que estoy estudiando el inglés.)
>
>**I have studied** English since last May. (*I am still studying.*)
>(Estudio el inglés desde el mayo pasado.)
>
>**I have been studying** English since last May. (*I am still studying.*)
>(Estoy estudiando el inglés desde el mayo pasado.)

Note: **For** is used to indicate the duration of time. **Since** (desde, desde que) indicates when the action began.

Read each sentence aloud, changing the verb in parentheses to (1) the present perfect, (2) the ing form of the present perfect.

1. He ——— (work) there for one year.
   He ——— (work) there since last June.
2. He ——— (live) in Miami for one year.
   He ——— (live) in Miami since he left here last year.
3. He ——— not ——— (smoke) for a month.
   He ——— not ——— (smoke) since he was sick.
4. I ——— (study) with this class for five months.
   I ——— (study) with this class since February.
5. We ——— (wait) for them for half an hour.
   We ——— (wait) for them since five-thirty.
6. How long ——— you ——— (drive) that car?
   I ——— (drive) this car for five years.
   I ——— (drive) this car since I came here.
7. How long ——— you ——— (feel) that way?
   I ——— (feel) this way for a week.
   I ——— (feel) this way since last Sunday.

8. How long ――― you ――― (practice)?
   I ――― (practice) for two hours.
   I ――― (practice) since dinner.
9. How long ――― Virginia ――― (live) with the Millers?
   She ――― (live) with them for six months.
   She ――― (live) with them since September.
10. How long ――― he ――― (teach) here?
    He ――― (teach) here for a month.
    He ――― (teach) here since last month.

III. Comparison of the Present Perfect and the Simple Past Tenses.

A. If a definite time in the past is mentioned or implied, the simple past tense is used to refer to a completed action. The present perfect is used only to refer to an indefinite time in the past, or to an event in past time that is connected with the present.

> **I was** there twice **last year.**
> **I have been** there twice.
> **I have been** there twice **this morning.** (*It is still morning.*)

B. If the word **ago** occurs in a sentence, the simple past tense is always used, because **ago** indicates a definite past time. It is placed immediately after the expression of time.

> It **rained** an hour **ago.** (*It is not raining now.*)
> But: It **has been raining** for an hour. (*It is still raining.*)

Practice 1. Answer these questions, using the past tense and *ago.*

1. How long **ago** did Virginia leave?
2. How long **ago** did you begin to study English?
3. How long **ago** did you enter this class?
4. How long **ago** did you meet Mr. X?
5. How long **ago** did you see your dentist?
6. How long **ago** did you write to your sister?
7. How long **ago** did you send the letter?
8. How long **ago** did you buy that car?
9. How long **ago** did you read that book?
10. How long **ago** did you have a vacation?

Practice 2. In these sentences use the present perfect or the simple past tense, as required.

1. I ―― often ―― (think) of them since they left.
2. I ―― (think) of going, but then it rained.
3. He ―― (travel) by boat several times.
4. He ―― (take) a boat trip during his vacation.
5. ―― you ―― (read) this book?
6. Yes, I ―― (read) it a month ago.
7. Our friends ―― (leave) on the first of the month.
8. I ―― (study) English for two years when I was in school.
9. I ―― (study) English here for two years.
10. I ―― (come) here to live in 1948.
11. I ―― (live) here since 1948.
12. It ―― (rain) very hard yesterday.
13. It ―― (rain) every day this week.
14. She ―― (be) in this class since February.
15. She ―― (be) in this class when it began.
16. The Millers ―― (be) married for twenty years.
17. The Millers ―― (be) married twenty years ago.
18. We ―― (finish) that lesson last week.
19. We ―― (learn) many new words in this lesson.
20. We ―― just ―― (finish) this exercise.

Section 2

IV. The Auxiliary Verbs shall, will; should, would.

A. Shall and **will** are auxiliary verbs used to indicate future time, promise or determination, or volition.

1. Like the auxiliaries **do** and **did,** these are used with the simple form of the principal verb.

2. The rules for the use of **shall** and **will** in formal English are as follows:

a. To indicate simple future, **shall** is used in the first person and **will** in the second and third persons.

I (We) **shall take** a taxi to the station.
He **will take** a taxi to the station.

b. To indicate promise or determination on the part of the speaker, **will** is used in the first person and **shall** in the second and third persons.

> I **will wait** for you if you hurry.
> They **shall** not **leave** until the work is finished.

3. These distinctions between **shall** and **will** are fast disappearing in modern English, especially in conversation and informal writing. In the United States, for example, **will** is commonly used in all persons, to express either simple future or determination. In conversation, too, a form of **be going to** (see page 49) or the contraction **'ll** is often used to replace **shall** or **will**.

4. The contraction **'ll** makes the choice between **shall** and **will** unnecessary. The negative contractions are **shan't** and **won't**.

> **I'll see** you tomorrow.
> **You'll be** there, **won't** you?
> Mr. Miller says he**'ll get** the tickets.
> We**'ll be** looking for you.

5. **Shall** is used in questions *in the first person* to express the idea **Do you want me (us) to . . . ?**

> **Shall I wait** for you?
> **Shall** we **meet** you there?

Note: The simple future idea is indicated in the sentence **Will I see you tomorrow?**

6. **Will** sometimes has the meaning of **want to** or **be willing to**. In this case, it is used to translate the present tense of **querer,** and in the negative it is equivalent **to refuse to**.

> **Will** you **wait** for me?
> (¿Quiere Vd. esperarme?)
>
> If you **will wait,** I will go with you.
> (Si Vd. quiere esperar, iré con Vd.)
>
> He **won't go** with us.
> (No quiere ir con nosotros.)

*Practice repeating the following sentences, (1) filling the blanks with **will**, except in the last three sentences, which require **shall**, and (2) using a contraction of **will**, where possible.*

1. What time ——— they arrive?
2. If the train isn't late, they ——— be here for dinner.
3. We ——— take a taxi to the station.
4. I ——— be glad to see them.
5. He ——— not be able to play tennis today.
6. She ——— meet us in front of the theater.
7. I ——— see you in class tomorrow.
8. The doctor says he ——— be busy until noon.
9. We ——— not have a class tomorrow.
10. He ——— not receive his degree until next year.
11. They ——— not be home by six o'clock.
12. No, I ——— not leave the office before six.
13. When ——— I call you up?
14. ——— I read the next sentence?
15. ——— we wait for them?

B. The future perfect tense is formed by using the future tense of **have** with the past participle of the principal verb.

> **I will (shall) have finished** the letter when he comes. (habré terminado)

C. **Should** and **would** are auxiliary verbs, used to form the conditional tense.

> 1. These auxiliaries are used with the simple form of the principal verb. The conditional tense thus formed is equivalent to the Spanish *postpretérito* or *potencial*.
>
> 2. According to formal rules, **should** is used with the first person, and **would** is used with the second and third persons, as **shall** and **will** are used in the future. However, in conversation and informal writing **would** is used in all three persons, singular and plural. The phrase **I should like to** . . . is an exception, since it is commonly used in informal as well as formal English.

> > **Would** you like to visit Miami?
> > Yes, **I would like** to see it sometime.
> > Yes, **I would like** to go there some day.
> > He said (that) he **would like** a new car.

3. The affirmative contraction of both **should** and **would** is **'d,** added to the subject pronoun. The negative contractions are **shouldn't** and **wouldn't.**

I'd like to go, but I am very busy now.
He said that he **wouldn't be** there.

4. **Would** is sometimes used instead of the phrase **used to** to express habit in the past. (See page 75.)

As a child, he **would get up** early every morning. (se levantaba)
He **would study** before going to school. (estudiaba)
He **would** always **come** to class early. (venía)

5. **Would** sometimes has the meaning of **want to** or **be willing to** and is used to translate the past tenses of **querer** (**quería, quise, querría, quisiera**). (See the similar use of **will**, page 158.)

Would you **help** me, please?
(¿ Quisiera [Querría] ayudarme?)
He **wouldn't come** with us because it was late.
(No quiso venir con nosotros porque era tarde.)

Note: **He wouldn't come** is equivalent to **he refused to come** in this sentence.

6. In modern English **should** is commonly used in all persons to indicate obligation and is the equivalent of **debería** or **debiera.** (See Lesson XV.)

We **should go** now if we want to be on time. (deberíamos ir)
You **should study** this lesson carefully. (deberían estudiar)

7. For the use of **should** and **would** in conditional sentences, see Lesson XXI.

D. The conditional perfect is formed by using the **conditional** tense of **have** with the past participle of the principal verb.

I **would have sent** it to her, but I didn't know her address.
(habría o hubiera enviado)

Practice answering these questions in complete sentences.
1. Would you like to speak English well?
2. Would you like to dance?
3. Would she like to read that book?
4. Would they like to live in Miami Beach?
5. Would you like to review this lesson?
6. Would they like to go for a walk with us?
7. Did you say that you would have time to see me now?
8. Would many people like to go to Florida in the winter?
9. Did he tell you that he would cross the causeway?
10. Would it be interesting to visit an Indian village?
11. If you don't feel well, do you think it would be a good idea to call a doctor?
12. Why did he say that he wouldn't be able to come to the party tomorrow?
13. Wouldn't he go with you yesterday? (¿ no quiso ir ?)
14. Wouldn't she wait for you? (¿ no quiso esperar ?)
15. Wouldn't they take a taxi? (¿ no quisieron tomar ?)
16. Do you think that we should wait for them?
17. What time should we be there?
18. Should I send the letter by air mail?
19. Shouldn't you make your reservation now?
20. Should we write these sentences for tomorrow?

Fairchild Aerial Surveys

LESSON XIV

An Air View of Washington, D. C.

WASHINGTON, D. C.

The beautiful city of Washington, the nation's capital, is situated on the Potomac River in the District of Columbia. The terms **Washington** and **District of Columbia** are practically synonymous. This federal district is a piece of land ten miles square; it is neither north nor south, and it does not belong to any one state, but to all the states. For that reason, the government of Washington is unique: the inhabitants of the District do not have the right to vote; on the contrary, it is Congress, elected by the people of all the states, which makes the laws for the District.

The capital owes a great deal to the nation's first president, George Washington. It was Washington who selected the site for the District. It was Washington who chose a young French engineer in the American Revolutionary Army, Major Pierre l'Enfant, to make plans for the new city. It was Washington who laid the cornerstone of the Capitol Building, where Congress meets. Although he also laid the cornerstone of the White House, he is the only president who has not lived in it. Certainly it is very appropriate for the city to be called Washington, and for the lofty monument of white marble built in his memory to dominate every view in the city.

At the beginning of the nineteenth century, the new capital was called the "Wilderness City" and the "City of Streets without Houses." In one hundred and fifty years it has developed, according to the original plan of L'Enfant, into a beautiful city with wide avenues, numerous parks, stately monuments, and imposing government buildings. It is not the largest city in the United States, for it cannot compare in size with cities like New York, Chicago, Philadelphia, Detroit, and Los Angeles, which have more than a million inhabitants. In the political sense, however, it is the center of the Republic and the most important city in the United States.

Besides the Washington Monument, visitors may also see the Jefferson and Lincoln Memorials in the capital. These are classical structures of white marble; one is dedicated to the memory of Thomas Jefferson, the third President, who was also a great statesman and political philosopher; the other is dedicated to the memory of Abraham Lincoln, the sixteenth President, who saved the Union and freed the slaves.

There are other interesting places to visit in the capital, such as the Pan American Union, the Library of Congress, the Supreme Court Building, and the National Gallery of Art. Thousands of visitors also go to Washington to see its famous cherry trees in bloom in the spring. Across the Potomac River stretches a wide bridge to Arlington, Virginia, and the Arlington National Cemetery, where many distinguished soldiers and sailors are buried. There lies the body of L'Enfant, and there also is the Tomb of the Unknown Soldier, with its permanent guard of honor, day and night. While in Washington, we should certainly take a day to visit Mount Vernon, the lovely colonial home and tobacco plantation of George Washington. Mount Vernon is located on the Potomac River about twenty miles from Washington. Today it is a national shrine and holds the tomb of the man who was "first in war, first in peace, and first in the hearts of his countrymen."

VOCABULARY

according to	según	marble	mármol
although	aunque	to meet	reunirse
appropriate	apropiado	memorial	monumento
army	ejército	neither ... nor	ni ... ni
bridge	puente	peace	paz
to bury	enterrar	plantation	plantación
century	siglo	right	derecho
certainly	por cierto, sin duda	sailor	marinero
cherry tree	cerezo	to save	salvar
cornerstone	primera piedra	sense	sentido
countryman	compatriota	shrine	lugar sagrado
to elect	elegir	site	sitio
for	porque, pues	slave	esclavo
to free	libertar	soldier	soldado
government	gobierno	stately	majestuoso
to hold	contener	statesman	estadista
imposing	imponente	to stretch	extenderse
law	ley	structure	construcción
to lie	yacer	unique	distinto, especial
located	situado	view	vista
lofty	muy alto	wilderness	tierra silvestre
lovely	hermoso		

IDIOMS

in bloom	en flor
on the contrary	al contrario
we should take	deberíamos tomar

CONVERSATION

Answer the following questions in complete sentences.
1. Where is Washington located? 2. Is Washington in the North or the South? 3. What is the District of Columbia? 4. Why is the government of Washington unique? 5. Who selected the site for the capital? 6. Who laid the cornerstone of the Capitol Building and of the White House? 7. How is the Capitol Building used? 8. Who lives in the White House? 9. Who was Pierre l'Enfant? 10. What was the city of Washington called at the beginning of the nineteenth century? 11. Why is Washington a beautiful city? 12. How does it compare in size with New York and Chicago? 13. What are the principal monuments in the city? 14. What places would you like to visit in the city? 15. When are the cherry trees in bloom? 16. Where is the Tomb of the Unknown Soldier? 17. Do other countries have a memorial to the Unknown Soldier? 18. What is Mount Vernon? Where is it located? 19. What words are often used to describe George Washington? 20. Who was Thomas Jefferson? Abraham Lincoln? 21. Is the capital of your country older than Washington? 22. What are some of the places to visit in your capital? 23. Does your city have beautiful parks and monuments? 24. Is your city located on a river?

PRONUNCIATION

[st] **st**ate, **st**ately, **st**atesman, **st**reet, **st**retch
[ə] famous, numerous, various, synonymous, country, nation, government, lovely, statesman, federal, memorial, monument, president, colonial, such, thus, hundred, unknown, Columbia, republic
[tʃ] century, nature, lecture, agriculture
[yu] you, union, use (n.), use (v.), view, usually, university
[aɪ] site, wide, mile, shrine, library
[m] from, home, bloom, tomb, supreme, imposing, important, compare

GRAMMAR   Section 1

I. The Formation of the Past Perfect Tense.

The past perfect is formed from the past tense of the auxiliary verb **have** (haber) and the past participle of the principal

165

verb. It corresponds to the *ante-copretérito* or *pluscuamperfecto* in Spanish.

	Long Forms	Contracted Forms
Affirmative:	I had waited you had waited he had waited we had waited you had waited they had waited	I'd waited you'd waited he'd waited we'd waited you'd waited they'd waited
Negative:	I had not waited etc.	I hadn't waited etc.
Interrogative:	had I waited? etc.	
Negative Interrogative:	had I not waited? etc.	hadn't I waited? etc.

Note: The contracted forms of the negative interrogative are much more common in conversation than the long forms.

II. Uses of the Past Perfect Tense.

A. The past perfect is used to indicate an action which was completed before another action in the past occurred. Therefore, in the sentence with the past perfect there is usually another verb in the simple past tense.

> They **had gone** when we arrived.
> We arrived after they **had gone.**

Note: The past perfect with **just** is equivalent to **acababa de** with an infinitive.

> They **had just gone** when I telephoned.

Practice reading the following sentences using the past perfect tense of the verb indicated.

1. They didn't know where Mr. Miller ——— (go).
2. They said that he ——— not ——— (be) at the office.
3. I ——— (write) the letter before I received yours.
4. I ——— (make) my plans before I knew that they were coming.

5. I ——— not ——— (realize) that until you told me.
6. The mailman ——— not ——— (come) when I left the house.
7. I soon realized that I ——— (dial) the wrong number.
8. They ——— (be) in Washington a few days when I arrived.
9. After I ——— (finish) breakfast, I sat down to read the paper.
10. I didn't leave until I ——— (read) the newspaper.

B. The past perfect is also used to indicate an action which continued until a certain time in the past. The **ing** form (**had been** with the **ing** form of the principal verb) is often used to emphasize the action of the verb.

> I **had been reading** for an hour when I remembered that I had an engagement. (Hacía una hora que leía cuando recordé que tenía un compromiso.)
> I **had thought** of going there until you advised me differently. (Había pensado ir allá hasta que me aconsejó Vd. otra cosa.)

*Practice using the past perfect with **ing** in these sentences.*

1. We ——— (talk) for an hour when Virginia said she had to leave.
2. I ——— (write) letters for two hours when they came.
3. She ——— (wait) for him for an hour when he phoned her.
4. They ——— (play) tennis for an hour when it began to rain.
5. We ——— (speak) Spanish until Mrs. Miller came in.

Section 2

III. The Auxiliary Verbs <u>can</u>, <u>could</u>; <u>may</u>, <u>might</u>.

A. These auxiliaries are used with the simple form of the principal verb. The same form is used for all persons.

> 1. **Can** (*present*) expresses *ability, mental* or *physical*. In other words, it expresses the idea of *know how to* do something, *be able physically* to do it, or the idea that the circumstances will permit an action. **Can** also expresses permission. The negative form of **can** is **cannot** or the contraction **can't**.

Can he **swim** well? (¿ sabe nadar?)
He **can go** swimming at Miami Beach. (puede bañarse)
Can I go with him?

2. **Could** is the past tense and the conditional tense of **can.** The negative form is **could not** or **couldn't.**

Past

He **could** not **swim** last year. (no sabía nadar)
He **could** not **go** yesterday. (no pudo ir)

Conditional

I thought (that) I **could go.** (podría ir)
I **could go** if I had the money. (podría ir)
I **could have gone** if I had had the money. (hubiera podido ir)

Note: The verb **can** is defective. It lacks the infinitive, the past participle, the future tense, and three perfect tenses. In these cases, the corresponding forms of the verb **be able** are used. The conditional perfect tense is formed by using **could have** with the past participle of the principal verb. A simple outline of **can go** and **be able to go** follows.

Present:	I can go	*or*	I am able to go
Past:	I could go	*or*	I was able to go
Future:	...		I will be able to go
Conditional:	I could go	*or*	I would be able to go
Present Perfect:	...		I have been able to go
Past Perfect:	...		I had been able to go
Future Perfect:	...		I will have been able to go
Conditional Perfect:	I could have gone	*or*	I would have been able to go

3. **May** (*present*) expresses either *permission* or *possibility.* There is usually no contraction in the negative.

Permission

May I borrow your book? (Puedo pedir su libro prestado?)
Of course you **may borrow** it. (puede pedirlo prestado)

Possibility

I **may see** her tomorrow. (posiblemente la vea)
He **may have gone out,** because his hat isn't here. (posiblemente haya salido)

4. **Might** is the past tense and the conditional tense of **may.** It also indicates future time. Although **might** sometimes has the idea of permission, it is used especially to express a slight possibility in the future. The negative form is **might not.**

Permission

My mother said (that) I **might go.** (podía ir, podría ir)

Possibility

I said (that) I **might see** her tomorrow. (que podría verla)
I **might see** her tomorrow, but I am not sure. (posiblemente la vea)
He thought that they **might have left,** but he didn't know. (posiblemente hubieran salido)
She **might have gone** with us if we had waited. (posiblemente hubiera ido)

Note: Since **may,** like **can,** is a defective verb, the present perfect tense is formed by using **may have** and the past participle of the principal verb. The past perfect and conditional perfect are formed by using **might have** with the past participle of the principal verb.

Present: He **may leave.**
Present Perfect: He **may have left** already.
Past or Conditional: I thought he **might leave** any minute.
Past Perfect or
   Conditional Perfect: I thought he **might have left** before it rained.

Practice using these auxiliaries as indicated.

*A. Ability: **can, could.***

     1. ―――― we finish the book this year? (podemos)
     2. Who ―――― translate that sentence? (puede)
     3. No one ―――― translate that sentence. (podía)
     4. He says (that) he ―――― wait for us. (no puede)
     5. He said (that) he ―――― wait for us. (no podía)
     6. You ―――― see the Washington Monument from **here.** (puede)
     7. She said (that) she ―――― be there by noon. (podría)
     8. You ―――― travel by plane or by train. (puede)
     9. ―――― you tell me where she is? (puede)
   10. I ―――― come to the last class. (no pude)

11. I ——— have sent it by air mail. (pude)
12. We ——— have come earlier. (podríamos)

B. *Permission:* **may, might.**
1. ——— I borrow your pencil? (puedo)
2. Certainly you ——— use it. (puede)
3. You ——— enter this class if you already know some English. (puede)
4. Her mother says (that) she ——— go. (puede)
5. Her mother said (that) she ——— go. (podría)

C. *Possibility:* **may, might.** (*Be careful to translate the entire Spanish expression.*)
1. I ——— with them if I have time. (posiblemente vaya)
2. We ——— the book this year. (posiblemente no terminemos)
3. They ——— a little late today. (posiblemente lleguen)
4. We ——— swimming on Saturday. (posiblemente vayamos)
5. I think it ——— this afternoon. (posiblemente llueva)
6. You ——— wait for them. (posiblemente tenga que)
7. I thought I ——— go swimming, but it rained. (podría)
8. He said he ——— go to the United States soon. (podría)
9. I said I ——— go, but I wasn't sure. (podría)
10. She thought that the lecture ——— be good. (podría)
11. It ———, but I didn't know it. (posiblemente haya llovido)
12. They ——— while we were downtown. (posiblemente hubieran venido)
13. We are late; she ——— already. (posiblemente haya salido)
14. He ——— English, but he can't speak it. (posiblemente haya estudiado)
15. She ——— there, but we didn't see her. (posiblemente hubiera estado)

Philip Gendreau, N.Y.

LESSON XV

Independence Hall

PHILADELPHIA, PENNSYLVANIA

Halfway between Washington and New York is the city of Philadelphia, an old city of great historical interest to the visitor. It was founded in 1683 by the Quakers, under the leadership of William Penn. Persecuted in England for their religion, a group of Quakers came to America to establish

171

a colony where they might live together in peace. The colony became the state of Pennsylvania, or "Penn's Woods," and the largest city was named Philadelphia, which means "City of Brotherly Love."

From the beginning, the city was a prosperous settlement; at the time of the American Revolution, a hundred years later, it was a political center and one of the large American cities, just as it is today. No other American city except Boston contains so many buildings of historical interest. On July 4, 1776, the Declaration of Independence was signed in the now famous Independence Hall. There we can also see the Liberty Bell, which was rung on that memorable occasion, and the room where the Constitution of the United States was adopted. The city was once the headquarters of the Revolution, and from 1790 to 1800 it was the capital of the new Republic. We can visit Congress Hall, where the first Congress of the new nation met; the Betsy Ross House, where Betsy Ross made the first flag of the United States; and also the home of William Penn.

Philadelphia contains many reminders of another illustrious citizen, Benjamin Franklin. He went there from Boston as a young man, and there he lived until his death. First he became famous as a printer, then as an author, later as a scientist (inventor of the lightning rod) and as a diplomat. At the same time, he made many contributions to American life. In Philadelphia, he helped to create the University of Pennsylvania, the first hospital, the first fire insurance company, and the first public library in America. As a diplomat, Benjamin Franklin represented the colonies in London and later in Paris, where he won the friendship and the financial aid of France during the Revolution against England. He also helped to write both the Declaration of Independence and the Constitution of the United States. When Benjamin Franklin died in 1790, he was a distinguished citizen of the New World, second only to George Washington.

Today Philadelphia, a metropolis with a population of a little more than two million inhabitants, is one of the world's busiest industrial cities. Although it is almost a hundred miles up the Delaware River from the Atlantic Ocean, it is both a river port and a seaport. It is an important railroad, industrial, and shipbuilding center. It has oil refineries and sugar refineries, textile mills, tanneries, rug factories, and ironworks for the construction of streetcars, locomotives, and bridges. With the abundance of coal in the state, Philadelphia has become the principal center for its distribution.

Last but not least, the city is also an important cultural center. It has many institutions of learning: several professional schools of law, dentistry, and medicine; art schools and music schools; and, of course, the big University of Pennsylvania. The city also possesses one of the great symphony orchestras of the country. Altogether, there is a feeling of contentment in the life of this old city, which is commonly known to its citizens and neighbors as "Philly."

VOCABULARY

aid	ayuda	**headquarters**	cuartel general
altogether	del todo	**ironworks**	fundición de hierro
bell	campana	**leadership**	dirección
brotherly	fraternal	**learning**	estudio; educación
citizen	ciudadano	**lightning rod**	pararrayos
coal	carbón (de piedra)	**oil**	aceite
to contain	contener	**to persecute**	perseguir
contentment	regocijo	**to possess**	poseer
to create	crear	**printer**	impresor
death	muerte	**Quakers**	cuáqueros
distinguished	distinguido	**reminder**	recuerdo
to establish	establecer	**scientist**	hombre de ciencia
factory	fábrica	**seaport**	puerto de mar
feeling	sentimiento	**settlement**	colonia
fire insurance	seguro contra incendio	**tannery**	tenería, curtiduría
flag	bandera	**textile mill**	fábrica de tejidos
to found	fundar	**together**	juntos
friendship	amistad	**woods**	bosque(s)

IDIOMS

a hundred miles up the river	a cien millas de la desembocadura
both ... and	a la vez; tanto ... como
halfway between	a mitad del camino entre
last, but not least	lo último pero no lo menos importante
to make contributions to	contribuir a enriquecer

CONVERSATION

Answer the following questions in complete sentences.
1. Where is Philadelphia located? 2. Is it a port? 3. What does the name of the city mean? 4. When was it founded? By whom? 5. What do you know about the Quakers? 6. What does Pennsylvania mean? 7. When did Philadelphia become a prosperous settlement? 8. Why is it an interesting city? 9. Why is Independence Hall famous? 10. Where did the first Congress of the United States meet? 11. Who was Betsy Ross? 12. Why was Benjamin Franklin the second citizen of the New World? 13. What are the three largest cities of the United States? 14. What are some of the industries of Philadelphia? 15. Is there much coal in the state of Pennsylvania? 16. Why is Philadelphia considered an important cultural center? 17. What are some of the schools there? 18. Which symphony orchestras of the United States are the best? 19. What do the inhabitants of Pennsylvania call Philadelphia?

PRONUNCIATION

[ə]   much, rug, rung, under, culture, cultural, abundance, public, republic, construction, industrial, hundred
[yu]   distribution, contribution, persecute, persecution
[ŋ]   beginning, feeling, building, learning, lightning, containing
[kw]   Quakers, quart, quarter, headquarters, quite, quiet, quick, quickly, quality, quantity, question, equivalent
[ɛks]   except, exception, express, expect, explain, explanation, extend, extensive, expensive, expenses, export

GRAMMAR   Section 1

I. The Passive Voice: be (ser) and the Past Participle.

A. The passive voice is used more often in English than in Spanish. It is formed with different tenses of the auxiliary verb **be** and the *past participle* of the principal verb. In the passive voice the subject receives the action; in other words, it is acted upon *by* someone or something, known as the *agent.* The preposition **by** always precedes the agent.

Note: The auxiliary and the past participle are separated in the negative by the word **not,** in the interrogative by the subject, and in the negative interrogative by the subject and **not.** The adverbs of frequency (see Lesson IV, page 42) may also separate the auxiliary and past participle.

ACTIVE

	Statement	Interrogative
Present:	Everybody **understands** him.	**Does** everybody **understand** him?
Future:	Everybody **will understand** him.	**Will** everybody **understand** him?
Past:	Everybody **understood** him.	**Did** everybody **understand** him?
Present Perfect:	Everybody **has understood** him.	**Has** everybody **understood** him?

PASSIVE

Present:	He **is understood** by everybody.	**Is** he **understood** by everybody?
Future:	He **will be understood** by everybody.	**Will** he **be understood** by everybody?
Past:	He **was understood** by everybody.	**Was** he **understood** by everybody?
Present Perfect:	He **has been understood** by everybody.	**Has** he **been understood** by everybody?

Practice changing these verbs from the active to the passive voice. Be sure to keep the same tense.

1. The Quakers **founded** the city.

   The city was founded by the Quakers.
2. Benjamin Franklin **created** the first public library.
3. Franklin also **laid** the foundations for the University of Pennsylvania.
4. Eugene Ormandy **conducts** the Philadelphia Orchestra.
5. Betsy Ross **made** the first American flag in Philadelphia.
6. The people **choose** the President of the United States.
7. The people also **elect** the senators, representatives, governors, and mayors.

8. George Washington **selected** the site for the District of Columbia.
9. Washington also **laid** the cornerstone for the Capitol Building.
10. Pierre l'Enfant **made** the plans for the city of Washington.

B. The *agent* is not always expressed. It is usually not expressed when it is a pronoun.

1. The peace treaty **will be signed** in the very near future.
2. The Declaration of Independence **was signed** in Philadelphia.

Practice using the passive voice in these sentences.

1. Philadelphia ——— (know) as the "City of Brotherly Love."
2. Those locomotives and streetcars ——— (make) in Philadelphia. (*past*)
3. Philadelphia ——— (found) in 1683.
4. The Quakers ——— (persecute) in England for their religion.
5. Pennsylvania ——— (name) for William Penn. (*past*)
6. The Liberty Bell ——— (ring) when the Declaration of Independence ——— (sign).
7. The Constitution ——— (adopt) in Independence Hall.
8. Financial aid ——— (receive) from France during the Revolution.

C. The passive voice is often used in English to translate the Spanish reflexive verb with an indefinite subject.

Portuguese **is spoken** in Brazil. (se habla)

Practice repeating and answering these questions in complete sentences.

1. Is the passive **used** very much in English? (se usa)
2. Is the subject always **expressed** in English? (se expresa)
3. Is this sentence **translated** literally? (se traduce)
4. **Are** notebooks and pencils **sold** here? (se venden)
5. Isn't that name **used** in English? (se usa)
6. Is much coffee **exported** from Colombia? (se exporta)
7. **Are** rugs **made** in Philadelphia? (se hacen)
8. What **is made** in that factory? (se hace)
9. Is much coal **mined** in Pennsylvania? (se extrae)
10. What languages **are spoken** in Switzerland? (se hablan)

D. The English passive is often used to translate verbs which, in Spanish, are in the active voice and have as their subject the indefinite pronoun **ellos,** understood.

>I **was told** that he had left. (me dijeron)
>I **have been told** that she is back. (me han dicho)
>He **was taken** home from the hospital. (lo llevaron)
>The piano **was taken away.** (se llevaron)
>It **has** always **been called** the "City of Brotherly Love." (la han llamado)

II. The Use of be (estar) with the Past Participle.

The auxiliary **be** with the past participle is also used to describe a condition, a state of mind, or the result of an action. Here the past participle is used as an adjective after the verb **be.** This is not a passive construction.

>The city **is located** on a river. (está situada)
>She **is interested** in her work. (está interesada)
>The doors **are closed** now. (están cerradas)
>The letter **is written** in English. (está escrita)

Section 2

III. The Auxiliaries of Obligation.

A. **Have to** (tener que) expresses *necessity*. It is followed by the simple form of the principal verb. The past tense of **have to** is **had to,** and the future tense is **will have to.** A form of the auxiliary verb **do** is always used in the negative and interrogative of the present and past tenses.

Practice reading these sentences (1) in the interrogative, (2) in the negative.

1. We have to write this exercise.

   Do we have to write this exercise?
   No, we don't have to write this exercise.

2. They have to learn the new words.
3. He has to leave home early tomorrow.
4. They have to go now.
5. The teacher has to explain it again.
6. You had to wait for a bus.

7. Virginia had to see the doctor.
8. Robert had to call her up.
9. She had to write some letters.
10. We had to ask the driver for change.
11. We will have to be on time.
12. You will have to see her before class.
13. They will have to take a train at six o'clock.
14. You will have to get up early.
15. We will have to pay for it immediately.

B. **Must** (deber) expresses *necessity* or *probability*.

1. When **must** is used to express necessity, it is equivalent to **have to**. **Must** is used in all persons of the present tense, followed by the simple form of the principal verb. The negative form, **must not** or **mustn't**, expresses a prohibition. **Must** has no past or future tenses; therefore **had to** is used in the past and **will have to** in the future. In questions and negations in the present, only the auxiliary **must** is used; **do** and **does** are not used.

Statement	Interrogative
You **must study** now.	**Must** you **study** now?
You **had to study** last night.	**Did** you **have to study** last night?
You **will have to study** tonight.	**Will** you **have to study** tonight?

Negative

You **mustn't study** now. (*prohibition — present*)
You **don't have to study** now. (*no necessity — present*)
You **didn't have to study** last night. (*no necessity — past*)
You **won't have to study** tonight. (*no necessity — future*)

Read the following sentences with the auxiliary **must;** *then change them to past and future time.*

1. Virginia **must** go to see the doctor.
   Virginia had to go to see the doctor.
   Virginia will have to go to see the doctor.
2. She ——— go on a light diet.
3. She ——— take some tonic, too.
4. She ——— stand up in the crowded bus.
5. They ——— go to Washington by train.
6. ——— we learn these words?
7. ——— you wait for them?

8. ——— we make reservations?
9. ——— they take a taxi to see the city?
10. ——— they stop in Philadelphia?

2. **Must** sometimes indicates probability. In this case, the past tense form is **must have** followed by the past participle of the principal verb.

Philadelphia **must be** an interesting city. (*It seems probable.*)

They **must have visited** Independence Hall while they were there. (*It seems probable.*)

*Practice using **must** or **must have**, as required, in the following sentences.*

1. It ——— be time for dinner.
2. It ——— been two o'clock when I saw them.
3. Virginia ——— speak English well by this time.
4. He ——— left, because his hat and coat are not here.
5. I ——— called you about two o'clock.
6. Have you finished the book already? You ——— read it very fast.
7. Mr. Miller hasn't arrived yet; he ——— be working late.
8. You ——— had a wonderful vacation.
9. It ——— been a fine trip.
10. You ——— be tired after your long trip.

C. **Should** (deber) implies *moral obligation*, but not *necessity*.

1. Although **should** may be used in the first person of the conditional tense, it is used much more often in all persons to translate **debería**. (See Lesson XIII.) The negative form is **should not** or the contraction **shouldn't**.

I **should write** some letters, but I don't have time today.
I **shouldn't go** out today; I have a bad cold.

*Practice using **should** in these sentences.*

1. We ——— study our English a little every day.
2. We ——— go to English lectures in order to train our ear.
3. We ——— always speak English in class.
4. We ——— come to class regularly.
5. She ——— not talk so much.
6. He ——— not drive so fast; it is dangerous.

7. I ——— answer this letter immediately.
8. I ——— call her up and tell her about our plans.
9. You ——— not forget your book.
10. You ——— realize that New York is not the United States.

2. The past tense form in this case is **should have** followed by the past participle of the principal verb.

    I **should have written** some letters, but I didn't have time.

Practice using this past tense of **should** *in the following sentences.*

1. You ——— (come) a little earlier today.
2. You ——— (wait) for them.
3. You ——— (go) to that movie with us.
4. I ——— (send) it by air mail.
5. I ——— (answer) her letter immediately.
6. I ——— (call) her up yesterday.
7. We ——— (ask) her to go with us.
8. We ——— (talk) with him about the work.
9. She ——— (stay) at home and rested.
10. She ——— (take) a taxi.

D. Ought to (debería) also expresses *moral obligation* and is equivalent to **should**. **Ought to** is used in all three persons, singular and plural. Its past tense form is **ought to have** followed by the past participle of the principal verb. There is seldom a negative contraction.

                         Present

You **should come** early tomorrow.   (shouldn't)
You **ought to come** early tomorrow.   (ought not to)

                            Past

You **should have come** early yesterday.   (shouldn't have)
You **ought to have come** early yesterday. (ought not to have)

Practice using the correct form of **ought to** *in the sentences of* **C,** *sections 1 and 2.*

REVIEW LESSON V

I. Practice using the correct auxiliaries.

A. Review the following auxiliaries.

Habit (past):	used to (would)
Future:	be going to, shall, shall have, will, will have
Questions (I, we):	shall (¿ quiere que yo, nosotros . . . ?)
Willingness:	will, would
Conditional:	(should), would
Ability:	can, could, could have
Permission:	may, might, can
Possibility:	may, may have, might, might have
Necessity:	must, have to
No necessity:	have to (*negative*)
Prohibition:	must not (mustn't) (*present*)
Probability:	must, must have
Obligation:	should, should have, ought to, ought to have

B. Translate the words in parentheses, using an auxiliary.

1. I ——— go now, but I promised to wait for Virginia. (debería)
2. ——— I wait for her? (debo)
3. He ——— drink so much coffee. (no debe)
4. I ——— write a letter, but I ——— find my pen. (tengo que, no puedo)
5. He said that he ——— me his. (prestaría)
6. I ——— go home before coming here. (tuve que)
7. ——— they write English? (saben)
8. They said that they ——— understand English. (no podían)
9. They said that they ——— come tomorrow. (podrían)

181

10. If I ——— speak English, I ——— to go to the United States. (pudiera, me gustaría)
11. ——— I borrow your book for a moment? (puedo)
12. I think that she ——— be in Washington. (va a)
13. He says that he ——— here next month. (no estará)
14. We ——— you on Tuesday at five o'clock. (veremos)
15. ——— we write the sentence? (¿quiere que?)
16. Virginia ——— play the piano every day. (acostumbraba)
17. We ——— to the movies on Saturday. (posiblemente vayamos)
18. Who knows? We ——— go to the United States some day. (podríamos)
19. He has left the office. It ——— after five o'clock. (deben ser)
20. He ———. (debe [de] haber salido)
21. You ——— up earlier. (debería haber llamado)
22. I ——— to play tennis, but it rained. (podría haber ido)
23. I hope that we ——— this book by the end of the year. (habremos terminado)
24. They ——— there, but I didn't see them. (tal vez hayan estado)

C. *Complete these sentences with an appropriate auxiliary. Where several are possible, notice the difference in meaning.*

1. He thinks that he ——— leave tomorrow.
2. She thought that we ——— like to go.
3. We hoped that you ——— return early.
4. I know that he ——— have a good time.
5. I thought that you ——— gone.
6. I knew that they ——— be interested in it.
7. Did you think that I ——— forgotten you?
8. She promised that she ——— be here.
9. They think that they ——— go with us.
10. He said that the program ——— begin at seven.
11. He says that he ——— meet us.
12. I thought that it ——— rain today.
13. He told us that they ——— living in Washington.
14. Where did you say he ——— going?
15. I didn't realize that he ——— speak English.
16. They said that they ——— stay a week or more.
17. She said that she ——— like to see the picture.
18. Do you know where she ——— gone?
19. She asked me what time we ——— leaving.
20. He said that he ——— not get any tickets.

182

II. Give the principal parts of these irregular verbs.

begin	eat	go	read	shake
break	fall	hear	ride	sleep
buy	feel	know	ring	speak
come	fly	lend	run	take
cost	forget	mean	see	teach
do	give	meet	sell	write

III. Practice completing these exercises on <u>for</u>, <u>since</u>, and <u>ago</u>.

A. *Choose the correct word: for, since, or ago.*

1. The Quakers founded the city of Philadelphia many years ———.
2. The present city of Miami has developed ——— 1896.
3. He has been in Washington ——— a year now.
4. What have you been doing ——— the last time I saw you?
5. How long ——— did you see them?
6. I haven't seen them ——— a month.
7. I haven't seen them ——— last month.
8. It has been two years ——— I was there.
9. I met my teacher a year ———.
10. I have known him (her) ——— a year.

B. *Fill each blank with the correct verb form.*

1. They ——— (come) to South America one year ago.
2. They ——— (live) in South America for a year. (*todavía están*)
3. They ——— (live) in South America since last year. (*todavía están*)
4. She ——— (begin) to study English several years ago.
5. She ——— (study) English for several years. (*todavía estudia*)
6. She ——— (study) English since she was in school. (*todavía estudia*)
7. We ——— (arrive) half an hour ago.
8. We ——— (wait) here for half an hour. (*todavía esperamos*)
9. We ——— (wait) here since nine o'clock. (*todavía esperamos*)
10. Washington ——— (be) the capital since 1800. (*todavía es*)

IV. Fill the blanks with a form of say or tell, as required. Use the present or the past tense as indicated.

1. People ——— (that) Washington is a beautiful city. (*present*)
2. The teacher ——— us about Mount Vernon. (*past*)
3. He ——— (that) we should visit Mount Vernon. (*past*)
4. He ——— (that) it isn't far from Washington. (*present*)
5. Will you please ——— me why the Washingtonians can't vote?
6. Did you ——— (that) Washington is not the largest city in the United States?
7. Where did you ——— us to go?
8. She ——— to me, "I'll surely be there by two o'clock." (*past*)
9. She ——— (that) it might rain. (*past*)
10. They ——— us (that) they were leaving soon. (*past*)

V. Change the following sentences to questions.

1. Philadelphia is halfway between Washington and New York.
2. Philadelphia means "City of Brotherly Love."
3. You can see the Liberty Bell there.
4. Philadelphia contains many reminders of Benjamin Franklin.
5. He lived there most of his life.
6. It is a busy industrial city.
7. They will arrive there at noon.
8. They should spend a few days there.
9. They want to stay at one of the main hotels.
10. You would like to hear the Philadelphia Orchestra.

VI. Fill each blank with a reflexive pronoun ending in self or selves, as required, and read the sentences aloud.

1. Virginia made the trip by ———.
2. Virginia bought ——— a new hat.
3. She went to sun ——— on the beach.
4. They will enjoy ——— in Washington.
5. George Washington ——— selected the site.
6. Look at ——— in the mirror.
7. God helps them that help ———.

8. Benjamin Franklin studied arithmetic by ———.
9. We entertained ——— during the afternoon.
10. This record player changes the records ———.

VII. Fill each blank with <u>some</u>, <u>any</u>, or <u>no</u>, as required.

1. I didn't have ——— breakfast this morning.
2. Virginia has ——— friends in Philadelphia. (*affirmative*)
3. Miami has ——— historical buildings. (*negative*)
4. I found ——— gloves on the table in the hall. (*affirmative*)
5. I don't need to buy ——— bread today.
6. Does Robert have ——— money in his pocket?
7. There isn't ——— good hotel there.
8. I met ——— friends while I was waiting. (*affirmative*)
9. Do you have ——— questions to ask about this?
10. There is ——— snow in Miami in the winter. (*negative*)

VIII. Choose the correct word of the two in parentheses.

1. The people in the room (is, are) very quiet.
2. (Much, Many) people (was, were) in the park.
3. The people in Washington (doesn't, don't) have the right to vote.
4. (Is, Are) there any important news in the paper today?
5. The news about the vacation (is, are) good news.

IX. <u>Comparisons</u>. Translate the Spanish expressions, and read the sentences aloud.

1. Washington is not ——— Philadelphia. (tan grande como)
2. New York is ——— Philadelphia. (más grande que)
3. New York is ——— city in the United States. (la más grande)
4. Philadelphia is a ——— city ——— Miami. (más histórica, que)
5. It ——— in Miami ——— in Philadelphia. (hace más calor, que)
6. Benjamin Franklin was ——— a scientist ——— he was a diplomat. (tan famoso, como)
7. There are ——— factories in Washington ——— in Philadelphia. (menos, que)
8. There are ——— hotels in Miami ——— in other cities of its size. (más, que)

185

9. There are ——— people in Miami in the summer ——— in the winter. (menos, que)
10. New York is not ——— North American city. (la más típica)
11. There is much ——— coal in Florida ——— in Pennsylvania. (menos, que)
12. Philadelphia is one of ——— industrial cities in the world. (las más animadas)
13. Washington is not ——— Philadelphia. (tan vieja como)
14. This hotel is ——— that one. (más barato que)
15. That is ——— meal we have had. (la peor)

X. *Arrange each sentence in the correct order.*

1. Remember to put { the direct object / after the verb }
2. The expression of time { follows / the adverb of place / always }
3. Virginia bought { yesterday / her ticket }
4. She enjoyed { very much / the concert }
5. I returned { very promptly / to her / the book }
6. Miami attracts { in the winter / many tourists }
7. It is { in the winter / never / there / cold }
8. They visited { Independence Hall / in Philadelphia }
9. They were also { two weeks / in Washington }
10. They returned { a month ago / here }
11. Is Mr. Miller going to be { next week / in New York }

12. He has been { three times / there

13. The postman did not bring { this morning / any letters / us

14. They had { yesterday / their dinner / at the hotel

15. We had { there / a good time / last Saturday

16. I { see / there / my friends / often

17. I wanted to invite { the Millers / next week / for dinner

18. She served { sandwiches / her guests / for tea / today

19. I'll be { at six o'clock / there

20. I had { this morning / in bed / my breakfast

New York Convention and Visitors Bureau, Inc.

LESSON XVI

Times Square, New York, at Night

NEW YORK, NEW YORK

Here we are in New York, the incredible city where all the languages of the world are spoken, and where people live on the ground, travel under the ground, and work in the sky. New York makes a profound impression on all visitors because of its many lofty buildings, its gigantic department stores, its immense theaters, museums, and hotels, its magnificent bridges, and its exclusive shops with their fabulous prices.

The first permanent white settlers came to New York from Holland in 1626. Seeing the city today, we find it hard to imagine that these Dutch settlers bought all of Manhattan Island from the Indians for the equivalent of twenty-four dollars (U.S.), while today some of this land is worth a million dollars an acre. This island is the heart of the city; it is connected by six long suspension bridges, as well as by tunnels and ferries, with the other four boroughs that constitute New York City, and with the state of New Jersey across the Hudson River.

New York is the largest city in the United States. Today there are more people living in New York City than in Venezuela, Iraq, or Sweden. There are people from every state, from every Canadian province, and from every country in the world. Among the seven million New Yorkers, there are two million who were born in foreign countries. Of these the Italians, the Russians, and the Germans form the largest groups. To these many foreigners, now Americans, the Statue of Liberty in the harbor has always symbolized the ideal of freedom in the New World.

For transportation New York depends mainly on buses, subways, taxis, and ferries. The buses are slow because of the crowded streets, whereas the subway trains go as fast as railroad trains, sometimes stopping only at the most important stations. We may ride all day on the subway for fifteen cents, if we change trains but do not go out of the stations.

New York moves vertically as well as horizontally, taking its citizens by elevator to their offices on the fortieth, sixtieth, or eightieth floor. Here is the tallest building in the world, the Empire State Building, with its 102 stories that are served by sixty-three passenger elevators. The Chrysler Building (77 stories), the RCA Building (70 stories), and the Woolworth Building (60 stories) also reach into the clouds; and many other skyscrapers have from 40 to 71 floors.

New York is the richest and the poorest, the most modern and the most old-fashioned of cities. It is the home of exclusive hotels and cheap boardinghouses; the home of great symphonies and popular jazz, of cathedrals and night clubs; the home of the famous Metropolitan Opera, the Metropolitan Museum of Art, and the American Museum of Natural History; the home of many of the publishing houses of the United States and of the biggest newspapers. On Fifth Avenue there are many exclusive stores of international fame, but around the corner one may find little shops where imitation diamonds and cheap souvenirs are sold. New York is a city of immense beauty and immense ugliness, a place where everyone is in a hurry and where no one seems to have time to live.

Bright, noisy, spectacular, and impersonal — that is New York. It would take years for one person to see everything that is important in New York. It is a mixture of all that is the United States, but it is not like any other American city.

VOCABULARY

as well as	así como	ground	tierra
to be born	nacer	harbor	puerto
to be worth	valer	Irish (*pl.*)	irlandeses
beauty	belleza	island	isla
boardinghouse	pensión	jazz	música popular sincopada
borough	distrito municipal	mainly	principalmente
bright	brillante	mixture	mezcla
cloud	nube	night club	cabaret
department store	(gran) almacén	noisy	ruidoso
		old-fashioned	a la antigua, anticuado
diamond	diamante		
Dutch	holandés	passenger	pasajero
elevator	ascensor	profound	profundo
exclusive	exclusivo, de primera	publishing house	casa editorial
fame	fama	settler	colono
ferry	barco de transporte a corta distancia	shop	tienda
		sky	cielo
		skyscraper	rascacielo
freedom	libertad	souvenir	recuerdo
German	alemán	statue	estatua
gigantic	gigantesco	story	piso

subway	ferrocarril subterráneo	Sweden	Suecia
suspension *(adj.)*	colgante	to symbolize	simbolizar
		ugliness	fealdad
		while	mientras que

IDIOMS

around the corner   a la vuelta de la esquina
to be in a hurry   tener prisa
to change trains   cambiar de trenes

CONVERSATION

Answer the following questions in complete sentences.

1. Why is New York called the incredible city? 2. Who were the first permanent white settlers? 3. Where did they come from? 4. How much did they pay for Manhattan Island? 5. How many different boroughs constitute New York City? 6. How are they connected today? 7. What river separates Manhattan Island from New Jersey? 8. How many people live in New York? 9. Where do the inhabitants of New York come from? 10. What are the largest foreign groups? 11. Where is the Statue of Liberty? 12. How can one reach it? Can one go inside it? 13. What are the principal means of transportation in New York? 14. Why do so many people prefer the subway? 15. What is the fare on the subway? 16. What is the highest building in the world? How many stories does it have? 17. Are there many other skyscrapers? 18. What are some contrasts which exist in New York? 19. What adjectives characterize the city best? 20. Why isn't New York the most typical North American city? 21. What would you especially like to see there? 22. How long would it take for one person really to know New York? 23. Do you think that you would like to live in New York? 24. Has your country had much immigration in the last hundred years?

PRONUNCIATION

[ɑɪ]   ride, bright, find, five, driver, prices, diamond, gigantic, symbolize, Empire, Irish, island, sky, Chrysler [ə] from, other, country, club, buses, under, ugly, ugliness, hundred, Hudson, Dutch, subway, tunnel, publishing, industrial

[ɚ] first, third, work, world, worth, serve, certain, impersonal, hurry

[dʒɪz] languages, bridges, changes, villages, pages

[´] Canádian, Washingtónian, Miámian, Philadélphian, Bostónian, Colómbian, Perúvian, Chílean, Bolívian, Brazílian, Argentínian, Panamánian, Guatemálan

GRAMMAR

I. The Auxiliaries had better, would rather.

A. **Had better** (sería mejor que) is a two-word auxiliary, followed by the simple form of the principal verb. It indicates the advisability of the action expressed by the following infinitive and may also indicate slight obligation. It refers to present or future time.

> We **had better go** early in order to get good seats.
> We **had better not wait** for her. She may be very late.
> **Had** we **better go** early?
> **Hadn't** we **better go** a little early?

Contractions

Affirmative: **I'd better go, you'd better go,** etc.
Negative: **I'd better not go** or **I hadn't better go,** etc.
Negative Interrogative: **hadn't I better go?** etc.

*Practice using (1) the expression **had better**, (2) the contracted form of **had better** (in the first ten sentences only).*

1. You ——— see the doctor if you don't feel well.
2. You ——— study this lesson again.
3. We ——— wait a few minutes more.
4. You ——— make your reservation today.
5. He ——— go to bed early if he is going to get up at six.
6. You ——— not go without an umbrella.
7. We ——— not visit the museum until tomorrow.
8. He ——— not walk to the top of the Empire State Building.
9. She ——— not spend too much time there.

Charles Phelps Cushing   **The New York Skyline from Bedloe's Island**

10. They ——— not try to see all of New York in a week.
11. ——— we ——— review the vocabulary?
12. ——— you ——— sell your car?
13. ——— she ——— take a coat with her?
14. ——— you ——— eat something before leaving?
15. ——— we ——— take a taxi?

B. **Would rather** (preferiría) is also a two-word auxiliary, followed by the simple form of the principal verb. It indicates present or future time.

        Would you **rather walk** or (than) **ride?**
        I would rather ride.
        I would rather not walk.
        Wouldn't you **rather walk?** It's a nice day.

Contractions

Affirmative: **I'd rather go**, **you'd rather go**, etc.
Negative: **I'd rather not go**, etc.
Negative Interrogative: **wouldn't I rather go?** etc.

Practice answering these questions.
1. Would you rather have tea or (than) coffee?
2. Would you rather stay in New York or (than) in Philadelphia?
3. Would you rather ride on a bus or (than) the subway?
4. Would you rather have a class at six o'clock or (than) at seven?
5. Would you rather spend your vacation here or (than) in the country?
6. Wouldn't you rather spend more time in Washington than in Miami?
7. Wouldn't you rather meet me in front of the theater?
8. Wouldn't you rather sit on the main floor than in the balcony?
9. Wouldn't you rather speak English in class than Spanish?
10. Wouldn't you rather learn English than Chinese?

II. <u>Used to, be used to, get used to</u>.

A. **Used to** serves as an auxiliary to express habit in the past. It is followed by the simple form of the principal verb (see Lesson VII). The negative form of **used to** is **did not use to** or (contracted) **didn't use to**. The interrogative is **did . . . use to.**

    He **used to** live around the corner from us.
    He **didn't use to** talk much.
    Did he **use to** play tennis?
    Didn't he **use to** write poetry?

B. **Be used to** is the equivalent of **be accustomed to** or **estar acostumbrado a.** This expression is followed by a noun or by a gerund (**ing** form of a verb).

She **is used to** cold weather.	I **am** not **used to** getting up at six o'clock.
She **was used to** cold weather.	I **was** not **used to** getting up at six o'clock.

Practice using the expression **be used to** *in the present tense.*
1. He ——— reading the newspaper every morning.
2. North Americans ——— drinking their coffee with their meals.
3. Although he writes badly, I ——— reading his writing.

4. She ——— speaking English now.
5. I ——— going to bed early.
6. I ——— not ——— reading in bed.
7. We ——— not ——— his way of speaking.
8. ——— you ——— having tea every day?
9. ——— you ——— having dinner at noon or at night?
10. New Yorkers ——— spending a great deal of time on the subway.
11. They ——— living in New York and don't want to leave.
12. She ——— not ——— the noise of the big city.
13. Latin Americans ——— not ——— the cold winters of New York.
14. They ——— not ——— the heavy traffic in New York.
15. They ——— not ——— so many high buildings.

C. **Get used to** is the equivalent of **get accustomed to or acostumbrarse a.** It is followed by a noun or by a gerund (**ing** form of a verb).

Present: You **are getting used to** the subway now, aren't you?
Past: He **got used to** the cold when he lived in New York.
Future: I think you **will get used to** the city after a while.

*Practice using the expression **get used to** in these sentences.*

1. You ——— hurrying if you live in New York. (*future*)
2. You ——— hearing rapid English in the United States. (*future*)
3. You ——— the traffic and the noise there. (*present*)
4. He ——— the food after a while. (*past*)
5. He ——— writing letters in English. (*past*)

III. Still, any more, any longer.

A. **Still** (todavía), as an adverb of time, indicates the continuation of an action. Except in the present perfect tense, it occupies the same position in a sentence as the adverb **always**: before the principal verb, after auxiliary verbs, and after the verb **be**. It is not used in the present perfect tense except in a negative statement, where it precedes the auxiliary **have**.

Are they **still** in New York?   Yes, they are **still** there.
Does he **still** walk to school?   Yes, he **still** walks to school.
Have you finished this lesson?   No, we **still** have a little to do.
We **still** haven't finished it.

195

B. Any more and **any longer** are used in negative sentences. With **not** they are the equivalent of the Spanish **no . . . más**. **Any longer** is more formal than **any more** and stresses the idea of time.

> They aren't living there **any more** (**any longer**).
> I'm sorry, but I can't wait for them **any longer**.

*Practice using **still, any more,** or **any longer,** as required, in the blanks.*

1. He is ——— studying English.
2. He ——— makes the same mistakes.
3. He doesn't make the same mistakes ———.
4. Is there ——— time to go to the movie?
5. Have they left? No, they are ——— here.
6. They aren't living in New York ———.
7. After twenty years he is ——— working for the same company.
8. Is it ——— raining? No, it isn't raining ———.
9. Do you ——— like to play tennis?
10. He doesn't smoke ———.

IV. Already and yet.

A. Already (ya) is used in affirmative statements and in questions. It occupies the same position in a sentence as the adverb **always,** except that it may follow the principal verb in questions to indicate surprise.

> It is **already** noon, and they haven't come.
> Has the class **already** begun?
> Has the class begun **already**? (*surprise*)

B. Yet (todavía) is used in negative sentences and in questions, often with the present perfect tense. It has the position of an adverb of time, at the end of the sentence.

> Has the class begun **yet**? No, **not yet**. (todavía no)
> The teacher isn't here **yet**.
> He hasn't come **yet**.

*Practice using **already** or **yet,** as required, in these sentences.*

1. Has your brother left? No, he hasn't left ———.
2. Have they visited Washington ———? Yes, they have ——— been there.

3. Have you bought your ticket ———? No, I haven't bought it ———.
4. They weren't going to come early, but they are ——— here.
5. I haven't decided what to do ———.
6. Has he finished it ———? No, he hasn't finished it ———.
7. We have ——— studied this lesson, haven't we?
8. Is it time to go ———? No, ———. (todavía no)
9. Is he a citizen ———? No, he has to wait two years more.
10. Does he have his new car ———? Yes, he has ——— had it for a week.

Philip Gendreau, N.Y.

LESSON XVII

The Old North Church and the Paul Revere Monument

BOSTON, MASSACHUSETTS

And this is good old Boston,
The home of the bean and the cod,
Where the Lowells talk only to Cabots
And the Cabots talk only to God.

Boston, the largest city in New England, is more than three hundred years old. Downtown, it has many narrow, crooked streets, but there are wide avenues in the newer parts of the city. In Boston today, there is a tendency to worship the old; Boston loves tradition, and Bostonians love their city. A well-known colonial judge once dreamed that Jesus Christ came to live in Boston; he wrote in his diary that he "admired the wisdom of Christ in coming hither."

Although there are still Lowells and Cabots in Boston, today they share the charms of the city with the more numerous Irish, Italians, Jews, and others who have come to live there more recently. Boston is a city of about 800,000 people, a majority of whom are Catholic.

In and near Boston there are many spots of historical interest. Not far from the city is Plymouth, where the Pilgrims founded the first English settlement in New England in 1620. North Americans think of Boston as the site of the "Boston Tea Party." During the years before the Revolutionary War, the King of England and the English Parliament levied various taxes on the colonies in America, without the consent of the colonists. One of these was the tax on tea. In December, 1773, three ships loaded with tea arrived in the harbor of Boston. The colonists wanted "no taxation without representation" in the English Parliament; so they would not buy the tea. One night a group of angry Bostonians, dressed like Indians, went down to the harbor, boarded the ships, and threw all the tea into the water. The British never found out exactly who had done it. This incident is known as the Boston Tea Party.

Americans also remember the Old North Church in Boston, and the famous midnight ride of the patriot, Paul Revere. One night in April, 1775, at a signal from the steeple of this church, Paul Revere went on horseback to several of the neighboring villages to warn the people that the British were coming. As a result, the British soldiers under General Gage found neither the important men nor the munitions for which they were looking, and the first battles of the American Revolution at Concord and Lexington were American victories.

After New York, the port of Boston is the busiest one on the Atlantic coast. It has commerce with all parts of the world, and it is also an important fishing center. The little fishing boats bring in many kinds of sea food, for which Boston is famous. And, by the way, what American doesn't like Boston's delicious baked beans, too?

Modern Boston also has its industrial aspect. It is in the heart of an important manufacturing region, as there are many different factories in the city and its suburbs. It is one of the leading cities in the nation in the manufacture of shoes, textiles, firearms, pianos, and paper.

Besides being an historical, commercial, and industrial city, Boston is also one of the great intellectual, musical, and artistic centers in the country. It is proud of its excellent Museum of Fine Arts, its Opera House, its Conservatory of Music, its Symphony Hall, and its world-famous symphony orchestra. There are many educational institutions in the city itself; and across the Charles River in the suburb of Cambridge are Harvard University, the oldest in the United States, and the Massachusetts Institute of Technology, commonly called M.I.T.

The old city has a unique place in the affections of the American people. Its patriots and statesmen, its educators and men of letters, have helped to shape the history of America and enrich its cultural life.

VOCABULARY

affection	afecto	**to dream**	soñar
angry	enojado	**to enrich**	enriquecer
to bake	cocer al horno, hornear	**to find out**	averiguar, descubrir
battle	batalla	**Fine Arts**	Bellas Artes
bean	habichuela, fríjol	**firearm**	arma de fuego
to board	abordar	**hither**	acá
British (*noun*)	británicos	**Jew**	judío
Cabots	los Cabot (*familia linajuda*)	**judge**	juez
		leading	principal
charm	encanto	**to levy** (*taxes*)	imponer, fijar
cod	bacalao	**loaded with**	cargado de
crooked	torcido	**Lowells**	los Lowell (*familia linajuda*)
delicious (*of food*)	delicioso		
		man of letters	literato

midnight	media noche	**steeple**	campanario
narrow	angosto	**suburb**	suburbio, pueblo contiguo a la ciudad
neighboring	cercano, adyacente		
Pilgrims	peregrinos	**tax**	impuesto
proud	orgulloso	**victory**	victoria
to shape	formar	**to warn**	prevenir
to share	compartir	**wisdom**	sabiduría
signal	señal	**to worship**	adorar

IDIOMS

as a result	como resultado
by the way	a propósito
on horseback	a caballo

CONVERSATION

Answer the following questions in complete sentences.

1. In what section of the country is Boston located? 2. What states are included in this region? 3. How old is the city? 4. How large is it? 5. Are all the streets wide? 6. What does Boston worship? 7. What was the judge's dream? 8. What did he write in his diary? 9. Who are the Lowells and the Cabots? 10. What different nationality groups have come to live in Boston more recently? 11. Are many of the Bostonians Catholic? 12. Why is Plymouth, Massachusetts, famous? 13. What happened at the Boston Tea Party? 14. Why were the Bostonians angry? 15. Who was Paul Revere? 16. What happened at Concord and Lexington? 17. Is Boston a busy seaport? 18. Can one get good sea food there? 19. For what other food is Boston famous? 20. What are the leading industries of this region? 21. Why is Boston considered a great musical center? 22. What is the oldest university in the United States? 23. What school is especially good for engineering?

PRONUNCIATION

[o] old, cold, home, loaded, boat, although, know, known, throw, narrow

[ə] England, American, Indian, colonial, musical, social, Jesus, museum, Boston, wisdom, patriot, Cabot, Lowell, Plymouth, famous, delicious

[ɚ] newer, never, hither, center, letter, modern, commerce, paper, other, per cent, educator, neighbor, neighboring, harbor, suburb

[z] wisdom, busy, represent, representation, because, reservation, thousand, Charles, Americans, Bostonians, Italians, Pilgrims, Jews, Indians, always, charms, avenues, beans, pianos, shoes, affections

[r] region, recently, wrote, history, historical, factory, American, Irish, numerous, narrow, art, heart, charm, warn, year, where, fire

GRAMMAR

I. Shortened Sentences with be, have, and the Auxiliaries.

A. In conversation the answer to a question is often a short sentence including only the subject and a verb form.

1. If the verb in the question has an auxiliary, the auxiliary is repeated in the answer without the principal verb. If the verb in the question is a form of **be**, a form of **be** is used in the answer. If the verb in the question is in the present or simple past tense, the proper form of the auxiliary **do** is used in the answer. If the verb in the question is a form of **have** in the present tense, that form or the proper form of the auxiliary **do** is used in the answer.

2. If the short sentence is negative, the contraction is usually used. **Yes** and **no** often begin the short sentence.

> **Did** they have a good time? Yes, they **did.**
> Who **studies** very hard? Virginia **does.**
> **Have** you a pencil? Yes, I **have.**
> **Do** you have a pencil? No, I **don't.**
> Who **is** hungry? I **am.**
> **Are** you used to the city? Yes, I **am.**
> **Do** you understand that? Yes, I **do.**
> Who **opened** the window? I **did.**
> **Can** she speak English? No, she **can't.**

Will you be here at two o'clock? Yes, I **will**.
Would you like to go with us? Yes, I **would**.
Must you leave now? Yes, I **must**.
Should we wait for them any longer? No, we **shouldn't**.
May they have their lunch early? Yes, they **may**.
Could she go if we waited for her? Yes, she **could**.

3. If the subject in the question is a noun, the proper pronoun usually replaces it in the short answer.

Does **John** know Mrs. White? No, **he** doesn't.
Can **your sister** play the piano? Yes, **she** can.
Would **the children** like some ice cream? Yes, **they** would.

Practice answering the following questions with this short conversational form.

1. Is Boston the largest city in New England?
2. Does Boston have some narrow streets?
3. Do Bostonians love tradition?
4. Are there many Irish in Boston?
5. Was Boston an important city in Revolutionary days?
6. Would the colonists buy the tea?
7. Did the British find out who threw the tea into the harbor?
8. Is Boston a great educational center?
9. Do you like sea food?
10. Can one study music in Boston?
11. Have you ever known a Bostonian?
12. Is Boston an important manufacturing region?

B. This short form occurs in the translation of ¿ **no es verdad?** (See Lesson IX.) If the first verb is a form of **be** or if an auxiliary verb is used, that form is repeated in the short question. If the first verb is in the present or the simple past tense, it is necessary to use the correct form of the auxiliary **do** in the short question. If the first verb is the principal verb **have** in the present tense, that form of **have** or the correct form of the auxiliary **do** may be used in the short question. If the subject of the first verb is a noun, it is changed to the proper pronoun in the short question. If the main part of the sentence is affirmative, the short question is negative, and vice versa.

She is visiting some friends in Boston, **isn't she?**
She spent a week in Boston, **didn't she?**

Virginia can hear good music in Boston, **can't she?**
The teachers have too many students, **don't (haven't) they?**
We couldn't hear the speaker very well, **could we?**

Practice completing the following sentences with the translation of ¿ no es verdad?

1. Boston is an old city, ———?
2. Some streets are narrow, ———?
3. Bostonians have a tendency to worship the old, ———?
4. Boston isn't so large as New York, ———?
5. There are many Irish and Italians in Boston, ———?
6. Americans think of Boston as an historical city, ———?
7. Some angry Bostonians threw the tea into the harbor, ———?
8. They were dressed like Indians, ———?
9. They wouldn't pay the tax on tea, ———?
10. Paul Revere was an American patriot, ———?
11. You can get excellent sea food in Boston, ———?
12. Boston has commerce with all parts of the world, ———?
13. You would like to hear the Boston Symphony Orchestra, ———?
14. Boston can't compare in size with New York, ———?
15. You don't have any friends in Boston, ———?
16. You will spend a few days in Boston, ———?
17. Harvard was the first university in the United States, ———?
18. It is not in Boston itself, ———?
19. Bostonians are proud of their culture, ———?
20. There are many private schools in New England, ———?

C. This short form also occurs in the second part of a sentence, where the subject often changes and the idea expressed is in direct contrast to the idea in the first part. Then if the first part of the sentence is negative, the short form is affirmative; if the first part is affirmative, the short form is negative.

They **are not** tired, but we **are.**
I **am** ready, but he **isn't.**
Charles **can't** come today, but Robert **can.**
Paul **went** to the game, but Robert **didn't.**
I **need** a new hat, but Virginia **doesn't.**
Virginia **has** a class now, but Robert **doesn't (hasn't).**

She **had** a good time, but her sister **didn't**.
I'll come with you, but he **won't**.

Practice using this short form.
1. Mr. Miller isn't ill, but Mrs. Miller ———.
2. There were many students absent yesterday, **but today there** ———.
3. Charles has his book, but Paul ———.
4. I haven't been sleeping, but my sister ———.
5. Virginia knew her lesson, but I ———.
6. Robert couldn't come, but Charles ———.
7. He said it might rain yesterday, but it ———.
8. We are going swimming, but Paul ———.
9. She knows how to ride horseback, but I ———.
10. Virginia isn't going to the party, but I ———.
11. Mary can't go tonight, but Virginia ———.
12. Mr. Miller didn't go to the lecture, but Mr. Smith ———.
13. She had an engagement, but I ———.
14. She probably won't go, but I ———.
15. You have met Mrs. Miller, but I ———.
16. She says she doesn't understand, but I think she ———.
17. I thought the Millers would stay, but I thought Virginia ———.
18. My sister wants to live in the country, but I ———.
19. At first, I said I couldn't learn it, but now I think I ———.
20. They didn't like the class at first, but now they ———.

D. This short form occurs with **too** and **so**. To translate **yo también, tu también,** etc., a verb must be used in English. If a form of the verb **be** or an auxiliary occurs in the preceding sentence, the proper form of **be** or the auxiliary is used with **too** or **so**. If the first verb is in the present or past tense, the correct form of the auxiliary **do** is used. If a present tense form of the verb **have** occurs, the proper form of **have** or of the auxiliary **do** is used with **too** or **so**. The two forms with **too** and **so** differ only in order.

They **are** tired.	I **am** too.	So **am** I.
Charles **was** absent.	I **was** too.	So **was** I.
Robert **likes** Mary.	I **do** too.	So **do** I.
She **saw** that movie.	I **did** too.	So **did** I.
She **has** seen that movie.	I **have** too.	So **have** I.
They **have** a new car.	I **have (do)** too.	So **have (do)** I.

He **can** come early.	I **can** too.	So **can** I.
He **could** understand it.	I **could** too.	So **could** I.
He **will** be ready.	I **will** too.	So **will** I.
They **would** like to go.	I **would** too.	So **would** I.
He **must** study his English.	I **must** too.	So **must** I.
He **should** leave early.	I **should** too.	So **should** I.
They **may** go to the States.	I **may** too.	So **may** I.
They **might** go to the States.	I **might** too.	So **might** I.

Note: As in Spanish, the two sentences may be combined into one. **And** is then used between them. The form with **so** is more usual.

They would like to go, **and so would I.**
They would like to go, **and I would too.**

Practice repeating these and the other short forms above with all the personal subjects.

1. I **am** too, you **are** too, he **is** too, we **are** too, you **are** too, they **are** too. I **was** too, you **were** too, he **was** too, etc.
2. So **am** I, so **are** you, so **is** he, so **are** we, so **are** you, so **are** they. So **was** I, so **were** you, so **was** he, etc.

Translate the Spanish phrases, and practice reading the sentences.

1. He is in a hurry. *Yo también.*
2. We are going. *Ella también.*
3. You can wait. *Yo también.*
4. She is leaving. *Nosotros también.*
5. He understands English. *Su esposa también.*
6. They visited Boston. *Virginia también.*
7. Robert will be late. *Yo también.*
8. Virginia would like to travel. *Yo también.*
9. Mr. Miller has gone to New York. *Mrs. Miller también.*
10. I like a good movie. *Mi hermana también.*
11. Paul went to the concert. *Robert también.*
12. Virginia should be here now. *Mary también.*
13. They are studying English. *Nosotros también.*
14. They took a taxi there. *Ella también.*
15. This bus will take you downtown. *Ese también.*
16. The bus costs fifteen cents. *El tranvía también.*
17. He is a North American. *Ella también.*
18. The Boston Symphony Orchestra is excellent. *La New York Philharmonic también.*
19. New York has an opera house. *Boston también.*
20. Detroit has more than a million inhabitants. *Philadelphia también.*

E. This short form also occurs with **either** and **neither to** translate **ni . . . tampoco**. **Either** follows a negative verb, and **neither** precedes an affirmative verb because of the **rule in English** requiring a single negative.

They **aren't** tired.	I **am not** either.	Neither **am** I.
Charles **wasn't** absent.	I **wasn't** either.	Neither **was** I.
Robert **doesn't** like Mary.	I **don't** either.	Neither **do** I.
She **didn't** see that movie.	I **didn't** either.	Neither **did** I.

Note: If the two sentences are combined into one, the word **and** must be used between them. The form with **neither** is more usual.

    She didn't see that movie, **and neither did I.**
    She didn't see that movie, **and I didn't either.**

Continue changing the examples under D to the negative form.

II. Shortened Sentences with Other Verbs.

Certain verbs are often used with **to** in shortened sentences when the complete idea which precedes is not repeated. Some of these verbs are **hope, expect, want, intend, need, like, have, plan, be able,** and **know how.**

    I can't speak English well yet, but **I want to.** (speak it well)
    I wrote the letter, because **I had to.** (write the letter)
    Mr. Miller hasn't made a reservation yet, but he **expects to.** (make it)
    She hasn't seen New York. **Would** she **like to?** (see it)

Complete these sentences with the correct form of the verb in parentheses and to.

1. I can't go now, but I ———— later. (hope)
2. He wants to meet her, and he ————. (intend)
3. They have not visited Boston yet, but they ————. (expect)
4. He told me to read this book, but I don't ————. (want)
5. We don't want to buy the book. Do we ————? (need)
6. She can't stay in New York, but I ————. (plan)
7. You may come with us. Would you ————? (like)
8. She wanted to wait for you, but she ———— not ————. (be able)
9. I don't want to type this letter, but I will ————. (have)
10. I like to play bridge because I ————. (know how)

Gates from F. Lewis

LESSON XVIII

The Merchandise Mart in Chicago, One of the Largest Buildings in the World

FROM BOSTON, MASSACHUSETTS, TO CHICAGO, ILLINOIS

Now we are going to leave the cities on the eastern coast and travel westward from Boston to Chicago. This is a distance of approximately one thousand miles, which will take us twenty hours on a comfortable fast train.

On the way, we should certainly stop to see Niagara Falls.

the beautiful falls of the Niagara River, which flows from Lake Erie to Lake Ontario. The falls are divided into two parts by an island: the American Falls, and the Horseshoe Falls on the Canadian side. The Indians named the falls Niagara, meaning "thunder of waters." They are not the highest falls in the world (they are 167 feet high), but they are very wide; and the immense volume of water furnishes electric light and power for many cities and factories in the vicinity. Incidentally, Niagara Falls is also a favorite spot for honeymoons.

Going from Niagara Falls to Chicago, we travel through a part of Canada and enter the United States again at Detroit, Michigan. This metropolis, with about two million inhabitants, is another one of the leading commercial and industrial centers in the country, its specialty being automobiles. From there come the Fords, Mercurys, Lincolns, Chevrolets, Pontiacs, Oldsmobiles, Buicks, Cadillacs, Plymouths, Dodges, De Sotos, and Chryslers.

Continuing our trip across southern Michigan by train, we reach Chicago five hours later. Chicago, the "Windy City," is only a hundred years old; but in that time it has become the second largest city in the United States, with a population of about four million. Located at the southern end of Lake Michigan, it is the principal city of the Middle West and the chief city between the industrial East and the agricultural West. Consequently, it is the greatest railroad center in the country.

Chicago is also an important inland port. Although boats can travel on the Great Lakes only seven months of the year because these lakes are more or less frozen during the winter, the volume of freight carried in the warm months is tremendous. The freight boats, loaded with wheat, iron, and lumber, go from Duluth on Lake Superior to Chicago, Detroit, Cleveland, and Buffalo. They return with coal and manufactured articles from these industrial centers. In July and August, many people of this lake region take trips on the modern passenger boats which stop at different points of interest on the Great Lakes; or they spend their vacations and week ends at the many excellent beaches along the shores.

With coal, iron, and lumber easy to get and with excellent means of transportation, Chicago has naturally become a great industrial city. There the Pullman Company makes dining cars and sleeping cars, usually called Pullmans; the National Harvester Company manufactures agricultural machinery; from the lumber a great deal of furniture is made in the city; and near it large steel mills produce a quantity of steel second only to that of Pittsburgh, Pennsylvania.

Chicago's largest industry, however, is meat packing. In order to appreciate its size and importance, we should spend some time visiting the enormous stockyards. Every day cattle, sheep, and hogs are brought there in freight cars by the thousand; they are killed, prepared for market, and examined by a government inspector. From the parts of the animals which cannot be used for meat a number of products are made, such as leather, buttons, combs, soap, glycerin, candles, glue, fertilizer, and lard.

Chicago is not only an industrial and commercial center but also a beautiful city with many cultural advantages. It has parks and fine boulevards, an attractive lake front, and magnificent stores. It has plenty of skyscrapers, but they are not so high as those in New York. It has a fine symphony orchestra, a large art gallery, several interesting museums, numerous theaters and educational facilities. Among the latter, the University of Chicago and Northwestern University are outstanding. Chicago is very cosmopolitan, too, because there are many nationalities represented in its population, the largest groups being the Poles and the Germans. Like New York and most other large cities, Chicago seems noisy and bustling, impersonal but exciting to the stranger.

VOCABULARY

advantage	ventaja	**comfortable**	cómodo
bustling	muy animado	**consequently**	por consiguiente
candle	vela	**dining car**	coche comedor
cattle	ganado	**exciting**	emocionante
chief	principal	**falls**	salto, catarata
comb	peine, peinilla	**fertilizer**	abono

to flow	fluir, correr	outstanding	destacado
freight	carga	plenty of	mucho(s)
to furnish	suministrar	Pole	polonés
furniture	muebles	power	energía (eléctrica)
glue	cola	shore	orilla
harvester	segadora	sleeping car	coche dormitorio
hog	cerdo	soap	jabón
honeymoon	luna de miel	specialty	especialidad
horseshoe	herradura	steel mill	fábrica de acero
inland	del interior	stockyard	corral de ganado; matadero
to kill	matar		
lake front	orilla del lago	to stop	detenerse
lard	manteca	stranger	forastero, extranjero
latter	éstos	thunder	trueno
leather	cuero	vicinity	vecindad
lumber	madera para construcción	westward	hacia el oeste
		wheat	trigo
machinery	maquinaria	windy	ventoso
means	medios		
meat packing	empacadora de carne		

IDIOMS

by the thousand   por millares
not only ... but also   no solamente ... sino también

CONVERSATION

Answer the following questions in complete sentences.

1. How far is it from Boston to Chicago? 2. Is Chicago east of Boston and New York? 3. Where is Niagara Falls? 4. How high are the falls? 5. What are the names of the two parts of the falls? How are they divided? 6. What is the meaning of **Niagara?** 7. Why did the Indians give the falls that name? 8. Why is Niagara Falls so famous? 9. What city is the automobile center of the country? 10. Where is it located? 11. In what section of the country is Chicago? 12. On what lake is it located? 13. How many inhabitants does Chicago have? 14. What are the names of the five Great Lakes? 15. When can boats travel on the Great Lakes? 16. What do the freight

boats carry to Chicago and Buffalo? With what do they return to Duluth? 17. Why has Chicago become a big industrial city? 18. What articles are manufactured in Chicago? 19. What is a Pullman car? 20. What is a harvester? 21. What is the principal industry of Chicago? 22. Describe what is done in the stockyards. 23. What are some of the products of the meat-packing industry besides meat? 24. What are some of the cultural advantages of Chicago? 25. Why is it a very cosmopolitan city? 26. Is Chicago a beautiful city? 27. How is Chicago like the eastern cities?

PRONUNCIATION

[tʃ] culture, cultural, agriculture, agricultural, furniture
[θ] thousand, theater, thunder, north, northwestern, month, Duluth
[ʃ] Chicago, Michigan, machine, machinery, shall, sheep, should, horseshoe, furnish, nation, national, nationality, location, station, population
[d] during, distance, dining, industry, tremendous, product, candle, hundred, end, inland, second, lard, boulevard, road, would, world
[ɪ] since, city, begin, English, liberty, distance, trip, minute, winter, within, million, inland, impersonal, industrial, busy, symphony

The sound of **able** [′ebl̩] changes to [əbl̩] in longer words because the accent is no longer on the **a**.

[əbl̩] cómfortable, fórmidable, próbable, cápable, deplórable, wáshable, unforgéttable, végetable, bréakable, unbréakable

GRAMMAR Section 1

I. Clauses.

A clause is a group of words, a sentence or part of one, having a subject and a predicate. A clause may be the principal or the subordinate clause of a sentence. A principal clause is complete in itself; a subordinate clause depends on the principal clause to complete its meaning. A subordinate clause may be a noun clause, an adjective clause, or an adverbial clause. In all clauses, principal and subordinate, the subject generally precedes the predicate.

II. Noun Clauses Used as Direct Objects.

A. A noun clause is a subordinate clause used as a noun. For example, a noun clause is often the direct object of a verb.

> I think **(that) Niagara Falls must be beautiful.** (*noun clause*)
>
> He says **(that) he has never seen Niagara Falls.** (*noun clause*)

Note: The conjunction **that** is usually not expressed in English conversation.

Practice completing these sentences with facts about Chicago, as indicated by the suggestions at the right.

1. The lesson explains (that) Chicago **is located** ———. (*location*)
2. It says (that) Chicago ———. (*population*)
3. It says (that) Chicago ———. (*age*)
4. It says (that) the Great Lakes ———. (*condition*)
5. It says (that) the freight boats ———. (*use*)
6. It tells us (that) ———. (*industries*)
7. It tells us (that) ———. (*trips*)
8. It tells us (that) ———. (*culture*)
9. It tells us (that) ———. (*education*)
10. I think (that) Chicago ———. (*comparison with New York*)

Note: If the verb in the principal clause is in the simple past tense, the verb in the subordinate clause must also be in one of the past tenses.

> I **thought** (that) Niagara Falls **was** much higher than that.
> He **said** (that) he **had** never **seen** Niagara Falls.

Practice changing the sentences in A to the past tense.

1. The lesson **explained** (that) Chicago **was located** ———. (etc.)

B. The word **so** is often used after certain verbs to replace a noun clause used as a direct object and introduced by **that**.

Do you think (that) it will rain? Yes, I think **so**. (that it will rain)
Is Virginia going with us? No, I don't think **so**. (that she is going)

Answer these questions, replacing the noun clauses with **so**.

1. Does the lesson say (that) Chicago is cosmopolitan?
2. Does it tell us (that) Chicago has many foreigners?
3. Did you say (that) Chicago was a quiet city?
4. Do you believe (that) it is only a city of gangsters?
5. Do you suppose (that) all the gangsters could live in Chicago?
6. Do you hope (that) you can go to the United States some day?
7. Do you imagine (that) you will like New York?
8. Do you think (that) you will be surprised by the size of the buildings?

C. A noun clause used as the direct object often begins with an interrogative word such as **who, whom, whose, which, where, when, why,** or **how.** This type of sentence is called an indirect question.

Direct Questions
- What time is it?
- When did she leave?
- Where was she going?
- Who is going to the party?

Indirect Questions
- You always ask **what time it is.**
- I don't remember **when she left.**
- I don't know **where she was going.**
- We know **who is going to the party.**

Note: In indirect questions, the subject precedes the verb in the noun clause. When **who** or **what** is the subject of the noun clause, the order is the same in the indirect question as in the direct question.

Who is going to the party? Do you know **who is going**?
What is in the box? Do you know **what is** in the box?

But: In the following sentences **who** and **what** are not the subjects. The subjects are **that girl** and **the lesson.**

Who is **that girl**? I don't know who **that girl is.**
What is **the lesson**? I don't know what **the lesson is.**

Lass from F. Lewis

Niagara Falls

Practice using (1) ***Do you know,*** *(2)* ***I don't know*** *before each question. Make the necessary changes in the word order.*

    1. When does the class begin?

        Do you know when the class begins?
        No, I don't know when the class begins.

    2. What does that mean?
    3. How much is it?

4. How far is it from Boston to Chicago?
5. What is her address?
6. Which bus should I take?
7. Whom are they going to see?
8. Whose house is that?
9. Who is her teacher?
10. Why doesn't she like it?
11. Who wrote that letter?

Complete the following sentences with indirect questions based on the direct questions that precede them.

Remember: If the verb of the principal clause is in the simple past tense, then the verb in the noun clause must also be in a past tense.

1. Who is the author of that book? She didn't know who **the author of that book was.**
2. Where are they going? They didn't know exactly where ———.
3. What is the meaning of **Niagara?** She asked me what ———.
4. Where is Niagara Falls? He didn't know where ———.
5. What do the freight boats carry from Duluth? I couldn't remember what ———.
6. When did they make their Pullman reservations? They didn't tell me when ———.
7. What is the name of that boulevard? They told us what ———, but I have forgotten it.
8. What are the most important industries in Chicago? The lesson mentioned what ———.
9. How much did the trip cost? They didn't tell me how much ———.
10. What time was it when we left? She asked me what time ———.
11. Which book is she studying? He knew which book ———.

D. Sometimes there is no interrogative word to introduce the indirect question. In this case, the conjunction **whether** is used to connect the two parts of the sentence, and the words **or not** are often used at the end of the sentence. In colloquial English **if** is often heard instead of **whether.**

Will they be here?
I don't know **whether** they will be here **or not.**

She asked me **whether** they would be here **or not.**
I don't know **if** they will be here **or not.**
She asked me **if** they would be here **or not.**

Note: The words **or not** are not always expressed, but they are understood, nevertheless.

Complete these sentences with noun clauses based on the direct questions that precede them.

1. Can she understand English? Do you know whether ———?
2. Will he wait for us? Do you know whether ———?
3. Is the house rented? I don't know whether ———.
4. Have they left yet? I don't know whether ———.
5. Does the bus stop here? Ask him whether ———.
6. Do they live on Sixth Avenue? I don't remember whether ———.
7. Did she take her camera? I don't remember whether ———.
8. Did he make his reservation? I wonder whether ———.
9. Should we take this bus? I wonder whether ———.
10. Would they like to go? I wonder whether ———.

Section 2

III. Infinitive and Participial Constructions Used after Verbs of the Senses and Certain Other Verbs.

When the principal verb is **see, hear, watch, make, have, let,** or **help,** the sentence is often completed by a noun or pronoun followed by the simple form (infinitive without **to**) of another verb. With verbs of the senses (**see, hear, watch,** etc.) the second verb may also be used in the **ing** form. The only difference in meaning is that the participle (**ing** form) implies description, while the infinitive indicates a fact, or completed action. With the verb **help,** the second verb may be in the simple form or the infinitive with **to.**

I **saw him get (getting)** on the bus.
Have you **heard him play (playing)** the piano?
We **watched the cars pass (passing)** by.

He **made us wait** for half an hour. (*caused us to wait*)
They **let me enter** the class. (*permitted me to enter*)

This book **will help you learn (to learn)** English.

217

Use an infinitive or a participle (the ing form of a verb), as required, to complete these sentences.

1. We saw you ———. (*infinitive or participle*)
2. We heard her ———. (*infinitive or participle*)
3. We watched the girls ———. (*infinitive or participle*)
4. The boy's father made him ———.
5. She let the children ———.
6. Will you please help me ——— ?

IV. The Direct Object Followed by a Noun.

After the verbs **call, name, elect, appoint, consider,** and **make,** the direct object is often followed by a noun, an objective complement.

> In English we call that **machine** a **harvester.**
> His parents named **him Charles** for his father.

Practice using a noun to complete these sentences.

1. William Penn named the new city ———.
2. People call Philadelphia ———.
3. At first people called Washington ———.
4. The Indians named the falls ———.
5. People consider Boston ———.
6. People consider New York ———.
7. The location of Chicago makes it ———.
8. The many foreigners make Chicago ———.
9. The people elected him ———.
10. The President appointed him ———.

V. The Direct Object Followed by an Adjective or a Past Participle.

A verb sometimes requires an adjective or a past participle after the direct object to answer the question **what?** or **how?**

> She made the room very **attractive.** (**What** did she make the room? **Attractive.**)
> They kept their books **closed.** (**How** did they keep their books? **Closed.**)

Practice answering these questions in complete sentences.

1. Do you like your steak well done, medium, or rare?
2. Do you like your eggs fried, boiled, or scrambled?

3. Do you like your coffee black or with milk?
4. Did she make her skirt longer?
5. Does it make you happy to speak English?
6. Did the tailor make your suit too big?
7. Does a lot of exercise make you thin?
8. Did she cut the bread thick or thin?
9. Does your work keep you busy?
10. What color did you paint the walls?

REVIEW LESSON VI

I. Write and pronounce the past tense of these verbs.

live	start	create	persecute
travel	reach	warn	manufacture
include	seem	found	represent
arrive	carry	help	possess
follow	connect	explain	prepare
describe	worship	move	contain
work	dream	cause	kill
depend	admire	flow	furnish
stop	share	extend	constitute
change	adopt	develop	distinguish

II. Arrange these sentences in the correct word order.

Remember: Subject, verb, indirect and direct objects, adverbs (except adverbs of frequency).

Remember: A verb and its objects are never separated by an adverb.

1. I am reading
   now
   in English
   a book

2. must speak
   always
   we
   in class
   English

3. there are
   near Chicago
   mills

4. to a movie
   he goes
   sometimes

5. in Chicago
to his office
a train
he has to take
every day

6. Chicago
a great industrial city
has become
in a short time

7. along the lake front
is
the boulevard
very beautiful

8. is
Chicago
an inland port
also

9. of Chicago
meat packing
an important industry
is

10. on ships
are carried
wheat and lumber

III. Change the following sentences (1) to questions, (2) to the negative form.

1. The streets are always crowded.
2. People always walk fast in New York.
3. He likes to ride on the subway.
4. The boardinghouse was full when he arrived.
5. They took a ferry from New York to New Jersey.
6. They were able to get a hotel room easily.
7. They have already seen the suspension bridges.
8. It would take a year to see that city.
9. They should plan to stay in New York longer.
10. We will be there by noon, if we leave now.

IV. Review the use of *for, since,* and *ago.*

A. Use the correct one of the above words in the following sentences.

1. Boston was founded more than three hundred years ―――.
2. There have been Cabots and Lowells in Boston ――― the early days.
3. Boston was the principal cultural center ――― many years.
4. Boston has had a university ――― 1636.
5. The Boston harbor has been important ――― three hundred years.

221

6. They arrived in Boston a month ———.
7. They have been there ——— last month.
8. They have been there ——— a month.
9. They think that they will stay there ——— six months.
10. They began to study English five years ———.

B. *Use the correct tense of the verb in these sentences.*

Remember: The present perfect tense is used with **for** and **since** if the action is still going on; the simple past tense is used with **ago**.

1. I ——— (wait) for ten minutes. (*I am still waiting.*)
2. They ——— (come) a week ago.
3. She ——— (leave) a month ago.
4. I ——— (see) her since she returned. (*negative*)
5. He ——— (be) in class since last Tuesday. (*negative*)
6. I ——— (talk) with him for a week. (*negative*)
7. He ——— (call) you up about an hour ago.
8. I ——— (take) a vacation for two years. (*negative*)
9. I ——— (live) here since 1945.
10. I ——— (study) English for two years.

V. Practice using shortened sentences.

A. *Translate the words in italics in two ways.*

1. New York is a large city, *y Chicago también.*
2. Philadelphia has its industrial aspect, *y Boston también.*
3. Boston is a cultural center, *y New York, Philadelphia, y Chicago también.*
4. The English love tradition, *y los habitantes de Boston también.*
5. Boston was founded in the seventeenth century, *y New York y Philadelphia también.*
6. Miami doesn't have any subway, *ni Washington tampoco.*
7. He couldn't speak English last year, *ni yo tampoco.*
8. Miami isn't an old city, *ni Chicago tampoco.*
9. She didn't realize that, *ni yo tampoco.*
10. We can't get reservations, *ni Vds. tampoco.*

B. *Translate the words in italics.*

1. Mr. Miller is going to New York, *¿ no es cierto?* Does Mrs. Miller want to go, too? Yes, she *quiere ir*, but she *no puede* now. She *tiene planes para ir* later.

2. My sister isn't leaving until next week, *ni mi cuñado tampoco*. She doesn't like to travel by plane, *ni él tampoco*, but they *tienen que hacerlo*.
3. Did you attend the lecture last night? No, I *no asistí, ni mi esposa tampoco*.
4. Can you translate these sentences into English? Yes, I *creo que sí*. I know that I *puedo* if you help me, and *mi esposo también*.
5. They haven't arrived yet, ¿ *no es verdad* ? We should wait a little longer, ¿ *no es cierto* ? I *supongo que sí*, but I *no quiero hacerlo*.
6. He hasn't come yet. He told me that he *vendría* if he *pudiera*. Perhaps he *no pudo* at the last minute.
7. Do you like to write letters? No, *no me gusta*, but sometimes I *tengo que hacerlo*.
8. Do you expect to have a vacation soon? Yes, I *espero que sí*. Are you going out of town? Yes, *me gustaría*, but perhaps I *no pueda*.
9. Is he studying English before going to the States? He certainly *necesita hacerlo*. He won't understand very well at first, ¿ *no es cierto* ? He should know English better, ¿ *no es verdad* ?
10. Did you come to the last class? No, I *no vine* because I *no pude*. 1 *quería venir*, but I was very busy. I *espero venir* next week, however. I certainly *vendré* if I *puedo*.

VI. Use these expressions in original sentences.

easier than	different from	you'd better
fewer than	as cold as	hadn't we better?
similar to	not as large as	would you rather?
alike	**be** used to	I'd rather not
like	**get** used to	She has just ——— (*verb*).

VII. Fill the blanks with <u>still</u>, <u>any more</u>, <u>any longer</u>, <u>already</u>, or <u>yet</u>, as required.

1. Is he used to the subways ———? (todavía)
2. Yes, he is ——— used to them. (ya)
3. Virginia isn't used to speaking English ———. (todavía)
4. Virginia ——— speaks Spanish very often. (todavía)
5. She doesn't sing ———. (no más)
6. They aren't ready to leave ———. (todavía)

7. Robert is ——— writing a letter. (todavía)
8. They don't live in their new house ———. (todavía)
9. They don't live in their old house ———. (no más)
10. She hasn't left the city ———. (todavía)
11. She is ——— staying with some friends. (todavía)
12. She has ——— sent her trunk. (ya)
13. This week I haven't received a letter ———. (todavía)
14. Do you ——— plan to go on Saturday? (todavía)
15. I ——— have my ticket, but I ——— have to do many things. (ya, todavía)

VIII. Indirect Questions. Translate the words in italics into English.

1. I don't know *cuándo pasó eso.*
2. Do you know *quién es ese señor?*
3. I don't know *quién pueda ser.*
4. I don't remember *cuál es su apellido.*
5. Do you know *cuál es su nacionalidad?*
6. Can you tell me *qué hora es?*
7. Do you know *de quién es esta pluma?*
8. Who knows *(en) dónde están mis guantes?*
9. I can't remember *(en) dónde los puse.*
10. Do you know *cuánto tiempo vivieron ellos en Boston?*
11. I have forgotten *cuánto costó el viaje.*
12. Do you know *cuáles son las industrias principales de Chicago?*
13. Do you know *dónde están las cataratas del Niágara?*
14. Do you know *en qué parte de Chicago están los corrales de ganado?*
15. Do you remember *lo que significa la palabra "old-fashioned"?*
16. Can you tell me *en qué calle está el teatro Paramount?*
17. Do you know *cuál es el edificio más alto del mundo?*
18. I don't know exactly *cuántos habitantes tiene Chicago.*
19. I don't remember *cuál es el nombre del río entre New York y New Jersey.*
20. Do you remember *cuáles son los nombres de los cinco Grandes Lagos?*
21. The dentist told you *a qué hora sería la cita.*
22. She brought me a package. I couldn't imagine *cuál era.*
23. Do you know *lo que llevan los buques de carga?*
24. I don't know *lo que él les dijo.*
25. I don't know *lo que ella va a decir.*

Link from F. Lewis

LESSON XIX

A View of the French Quarter and the Cathedral of St. Louis, New Orleans

THE MISSISSIPPI VALLEY AND NEW ORLEANS, LOUISIANA

The fertile valley of the Mississippi River is in the heart of the United States. This great river cuts the nation in two from north to south; and with all its tributaries it flows through rich farm lands, which extend from east to west for more than a thousand miles across the country. Between

Chicago and St. Louis, to the north, we see well-cultivated fields of wheat, corn, oats, and rye; while between St. Louis and New Orleans, to the south, the principal crop on both sides of the river is cotton.

Before the days of the railroads, when the Mississippi River was the principal highway through the interior of the country, the steamboats carried statesmen and slaves, food, cotton, and lumber. Abraham Lincoln, as a young man, made several business trips down the river to New Orleans from his home in Illinois; and for the first time in his life he saw Negroes being sold in the slave markets of the South. Samuel L. Clemens (Mark Twain), whose life was closely associated with the river, described it in several of his books, such as *The Adventures of Tom Sawyer*, *The Adventures of Huckleberry Finn*, and *Life on the Mississippi*. Even the name that Clemens used as an author — Mark Twain — was derived from a river term meaning "two fathoms," which indicated that the river ahead was safe for navigation.

St. Louis, Missouri, with about a million inhabitants, is one of the leading cities in the United States. It is an important railroad, industrial, and commercial center in the Middle West. However, let us continue our journey to New Orleans, since that is perhaps a more interesting city in which to stay.

New Orleans is the largest city in the South and one of the principal North American ports. It is located on the Mississippi River, which flows into the Gulf of Mexico a hundred miles to the south. The highest parts of New Orleans are less than fifteen feet above sea level. During the spring, when it rains a great deal and the snow in the north melts, the Mississippi rises very high. For this reason, huge levees were built on both sides of the river to protect the city and the surrounding country from floods. At the numerous wharves, we can see the loading and unloading of large quantities of cotton, rice, sugar, oysters, shrimp, bananas, coffee, and lumber. In fact, New Orleans is the natural center of distribution for the products of the Mississippi Valley and for the imports from the Latin-American countries to the south.

Because of its early history, it is one of the most distinctive cities in the United States. The oldest section is the

French Quarter, where Bienville founded the city of **New Orleans** in 1718. The little settlement grew as the **capital** of the French colony of Louisiana. Later the colony belonged to Spain for thirty years, and then again to France. Nevertheless, the atmosphere in New Orleans and the country south and west of the city remained definitely French, even after 1803, when Napoleon sold the colony to the United States for fifteen million dollars.

In the old part of the city, the narrow streets and the houses with their patios, balconies, and iron railings remind us of Europe. Special points of interest are the French Market, the Cabildo, which is now a museum, and the Cathedral of St. Louis. French and Spanish are still spoken by many people, and famous restaurants offer delicious French cooking.

The most picturesque tradition of the city is the celebration of Mardi Gras (Fat Tuesday). This is the last day of the carnival period, the next day being Ash Wednesday, or the beginning of Lent. During carnival there are masked balls, elaborate dinners, and colorful parades, in which a great many of the inhabitants take part. On Mardi Gras, business is completely suspended. Another interesting event is the annual spring fiesta in April. At this time, some of the old homes in the French Quarter are open to the public. There is an outdoor art exhibit where hundreds of pictures by local artists are hung on the walls of the gray Cabildo and on the iron fence in the shadow of the old cathedral.

New Orleans is like a lady of many moods, but she is more often gay than serious, for she laughs a great deal. "She is not a Puritan mother nor a hardy Western pioneeress ... She is, on the contrary, simply a Parisian who came two centuries ago to the banks of the Mississippi ... and who has never cared to return to her mother country."[1]

VOCABULARY

ahead	adelante	**atmosphere**	ambiente
Ash Wednesday	Miércoles de Ceniza	**bank** (*river*)	orilla
		closely	estrechamente

[1] From Grace King, *New Orleans*, copyright 1928 by The Macmillan Company and used with their permission.

cooking	cocina	nevertheless	sin embargo
corn	maíz	oats	avena
cotton	algodón	oyster	ostra
crop	cosecha	parade	desfile
distinctive	distintivo	picturesque	pintoresco
elaborate	elaborado, elegante	pioneeress	colonizadora, exploradora
even	aún	to protect	proteger
event	acontecimiento	quarter	barrio
farm	hacienda	railing	barandilla
fathom	braza	to remain	quedarse
fence	cerca	rice	arroz
flood	inundación	rye	centeno
food	alimento	safe	seguro
hardy	fuerte	sea level	nivel del mar
highway	carretera	shadow	sombra
huge	enorme	shrimp	camarón (camarones)
journey	viaje largo		
Lent	Cuaresma	simply	solamente, sencillamente
levee	dique		
loading	cargue	steamboat	vapor
Mardi Gras	Martes de Carnaval	surrounding	que rodea
		tributary	afluente, tributario
masked ball	baile de máscaras		
		unloading	descargue
to melt	derretirse	wharf	
mood	disposición de ánimo	(*pl.*: **wharves**)	muelle
		whose	cuyo
mother country	patria		

IDIOMS

to care to	querer, tener deseo de
down the river	río abajo
He saw Negroes being sold.	Vió que los negros eran vendidos.
to remind someone of something	recordar a alguien algo
to the north	hacia el norte
to the south	hacia el sur

CONVERSATION

Answer the following questions in complete sentences.

1. Why is the Mississippi Valley so important to the United States? 2. How large is it? 3. Does the Mississippi

River have several large tributaries? What are they? 4. Why was the river especially important in the early years of the country's history? 5. What are the crops that one sees between Chicago and St. Louis? between St. Louis and New Orleans? 6. What do you know about Abraham Lincoln? about Mark Twain? 7. In what state is Chicago? St Louis? New Orleans? 8. What is the importance of St. Louis? 9. Where is New Orleans located? 10. In which direction is it from Chicago? 11. Why was it necessary to build levees on both sides of the river? 12. What is the chief export of New Orleans? 13. Where can one see the loading and unloading of the boats? 14. What are the principal cargoes? 15. When was the city of New Orleans founded? 16. When and how did it become a part of the United States? 17. Why is New Orleans a picturesque and interesting city? 18. Describe the French Quarter. 19. What does *Mardi Gras* mean in English? 20. When is Mardi Gras? 21. How do the people celebrate it? 22. With whom is the city sometimes compared?

PRONUNCIATION

[b] banana, ball, business, balcony, describe, celebration, Abraham
[v] valley, visitor, volume, variety, river, travel, never, cover, wharves, cultivate, several, carnival, discover, develop, boulevard
[ʊ] could, would, should, book, foot, cooking, crooked, full, colorful, Puritan [yʊ]
[yu] huge, museum, beauty, beautiful, useful, usually
[ə] but, cut, gulf, hundred, cultivate, custom, lumber, industrial, young, country, flood, flooded, tributary, popular, population, occupation

GRAMMAR

I. Adjective Clauses.

A clause that follows and modifies a noun or a pronoun is commonly called an adjective clause. An adjective clause begins with **who, which, that, whom, whose, when,** or **where**. **Who** (*subject*) and **whom** (*object*) refer only to people. **Which** refers to things and animals. **That** refers to people, **things, and animals. Whose** (cuyo) usually refers to people.

1. **Who, which,** and **that** are used as subjects of adjective clauses.

> The pupil **who (that)** studies will learn rapidly.
> The book **which (that)** is on the table is mine.

2. **Whom, which, that, when,** and **where** are used as complements in adjective clauses.

> Abraham Lincoln is a man **whom (that)** we all admire.
> Children like the books **which (that)** Mark Twain wrote.
> The horse **which (that)** he rides is black.
> The day **that (when)** she came was very warm.
> The office **in which (where)** I work is next to Mr. Miller's.

Note: The words **which, that,** and **when** used as complements may be omitted in colloquial English.

3. **Whose,** meaning **of whom, of which,** modifies a noun which is used as the subject, the object, or the object of a preposition in the adjective clause.

> The teacher **whose** class meets at eleven is Miss Smith.
> The person **whose** keys I found must be worried.
> I know the man from **whose** son you bought the car.

*Practice completing the following sentences with **who, which, that, whom, whose, when,** or **where,** as required. Notice in which sentences it is possible to omit the connecting word.*

1. The lesson ——— we are studying is easy.
2. I remember the morning ——— they left the city.
3. The boy ——— she met was Robert Anderson.
4. The house ——— is on the corner is very old.
5. The street ——— I live is near here.
6. The teacher ——— speaks most clearly is Miss Smith.
7. I know a man ——— home is in Chile.
8. Is he the waiter ——— took our order?
9. There is the girl ——— you wanted to see.
10. Many tributaries ——— flow into the Mississippi are large.
11. The fields of wheat ——— you see near Chicago are characteristic of the Middle West.
12. The river boats ——— go up and down the Mississippi carry a variety of products.

13. Mark Twain, ——— book *Life on the Mississippi* describes the river boats, lived in Hannibal, Missouri.
14. New Orleans is a city ——— I would like to visit.
15. The part ——— he likes best is the Cabildo.
16. The wharves ——— the boats are being loaded are interesting.
17. Mardi Gras is the day ——— precedes Lent.
18. Shall we visit the French Quarter, ——— there are some good French restaurants?
19. The French Quarter includes the spot ——— the first settlement was made.
20. New Orleans is like a Parisian lady ——— came to the banks of the Mississippi and ——— has never cared to return to Paris.

II. Prepositions at the End of Adjective Clauses.

A. The following construction with a preposition before **whom, which,** and **whose** at the beginning of a clause is formal in English.

> The teacher **with whom** I studied last year was Miss Smith.
> This is the street **on which (where)** I live.
> The teacher **in whose class** I am learning the most is Mr. Jones.

Note: **In which** and **on which** are often replaced by **where.**

B. In adjective clauses introduced by a prepositional phrase like the examples in A, the preposition is often separated from its pronoun object and placed after the verb. The first word in the clause is then **whom, which, whose,** or **that.** In fact, the preposition cannot precede the word **that.** This use of the preposition after the verb in the adjective clause is especially frequent in English conversation.

> The teacher **whom** I studied **with** last year was Miss Smith.
> The teacher **that** I studied **with** last year was Miss Smith.
> This is the street **which** I live **on.**
> This is the street **that** I live **on.**

Note: If there is a direct object or an adjective complement in the adjective clause, the preposition follows the direct object or the adjective complement.

The teacher **whose** class I am learning the **most in** is Mr. Jones.
That is the dog **which** she is afraid **of.**

Practice reading the following sentences (1) with the preposition after the verb, direct object, or adjective complement, (2) with the preposition after the verb, direct object, or adjective complement and with the word **that** *instead of* **which** *or* **whom.**

1. This is the book *about which* I was talking.
   This is the book which I was talking about.
   This is the book that I was talking about.
2. The people *with whom* Virginia lives are Mr. and Mrs. Miller.
3. The city *about which* we are studying is New Orleans.
4. The person *for whom* I am waiting is my sister.
5. The house *at which* we were looking is on Twenty-first Street.
6. Is that the house *in which* she lives?
7. The person *from whom* I borrowed this book has left.
8. The sport *in which* I am most interested is swimming.
9. The girl *to whom* he spoke is his secretary.
10. The country *from which* he comes is Ecuador.
11. The port *from which* we will sail is New Orleans.
12. This is the sentence *with which* I had so much difficulty.
13. That is the French restaurant *to which* we went.
14. He is a person *with whom* you can talk frankly.
15. This is the chair *in which* he likes to sit.
16. He is the waiter *to whom* I gave the order.
17. Mr. Miller is the man *for whom* he works now.
18. The friend *from whom* I received the letter is in St. Louis.
19. The book *for which* I asked is not in the library.
20. The thing *about which* I often dream is a trip to the United States.

C. When the preposition is at the end of the clause, the words **which, whom,** and **that** are often omitted in conversation.

This is the street I live **on.**
The teacher I studied **with** was Miss Smith.
That is the dog she is afraid **of.**

Practice reading the sentences in B with the preposition after the verb, direct object, or adjective complement, and without the words **which** *or* **whom.**

Snider from F. Lewis **Binding Wheat on an Illinois Farm**

III. Prepositions at the End of Questions.

In spoken English, the separation of the preposition and the interrogative word often occurs in questions.

        Formal: **With what** do you write?
        Conversational: **What** do you write **with**?

Practice repeating these questions and giving original answers to them.

1. **What** were you talking **about**?
2. **Whom** were you thinking **about** a moment ago?
3. **Whom** were you speaking **to** on the telephone?
4. **What** magazine do you like to look **at**?
5. **What** kind of suit are you looking **for**?
6. **Where** are you **from**?
7. **What** city were you born **in**?
8. **What** street do you live **on**?
9. **Whom** do you correspond **with** in English?
10. **Whom** are you waiting **for**?

IV. Indefinite Pronouns.

A. In English the pronouns **one** and **they** are used as in Spanish to indicate people in general. In addition, **you is** often used instead of **one** in informal conversation.

> Where does **one** pay the bill?
> Where do **you** pay the bill? (*informal*)
> **They** grow a great deal of cotton in Louisiana. (*indefinite*)

Note: The forms of the pronoun **he** are usually used to refer to **one.**

> **One** can take out a book if **he** has a library card.
> **One** should try to be on time for **his** class.

*Practice reading these sentences (1) with **one**, (2) with **you**.*

Remember: Some of the verb forms will be different with **you.**

1. ——— can go to New Orleans by plane or by train.
2. If ——— is not in a hurry, ——— might take a trip down the river.
3. In the North, ——— sees fields of wheat, corn, oats, and rye.
4. ——— should spend some time on the wharves of New Orleans.
5. There ——— can see many ships loaded with cotton.
6. The narrow streets in the French Quarter remind ——— of Europe.
7. ——— can enjoy some delicious French cooking, too.
8. ——— is fascinated by the shops in the French Quarter.
9. ——— should go to New Orleans for Mardi Gras.
10. After Mardi Gras, ——— is usually very tired.

Practice reading these sentences with the indefinite pronoun ***they.***

1. ——— take life easy in the South, don't ———?
2. ——— say that New Orleans is a picturesque city.
3. ——— still speak French in the French Quarter.
4. ——— have many parades and parties during Mardi Gras.
5. ——— say that it is very warm there in the summer.

B. The compound indefinite pronouns are:

1. **Everyone** or **everybody** (todos), and **everything** (todo). When used as subject, they all take singular verbs.

Everyone is here today.
They sent everybody in the office an invitation.
We like everything about the house except the price.

2. No one or nobody (nadie), and nothing (nada). These pronouns are the opposites of everyone, everybody, and everything.

No one wrote his name clearly.
Nobody finished the examination on time.
Nothing makes me angrier than that.

Note: The word not must never be used in the same clause with one of these negative pronouns, since English, unlike Spanish, does not allow double negatives.

There was no one in the room.
I saw nobody that I knew.
She said nothing about the letter.

3. Someone or somebody (alguien), and something (algo). Like some, these pronouns are used in affirmative and interrogative sentences.

Is there someone here who can speak English? (*I think there is.*)
Yes, there is someone here who can speak English.

Can somebody help you with that?
Yes, somebody can help me.

Is there something that I can do for you?
Yes, there is something that you can do for me.

4. Anyone or anybody (alguien, nadie), and anything (algo, nada). Like any, these pronouns are used in interrogative sentences and in negative sentences with not.

Is there anyone here who can speak English? (*I have no idea.*)
No, there isn't anyone here who can speak English.
But: No, there is no one here who can speak English.

Did anybody help you with that?
No, there wasn't anybody who could help me.
But: No, there was nobody who could help me.

Is there anything that I can do for you?
No, there isn't anything that you can do for me.
But: No, there is nothing that you can do for me.

235

Note: Because there is no double negative in English, two indefinite negative pronouns cannot be used in one sentence. **Anyone, anybody,** or **anything** must be used as the second pronoun instead.

>**Nobody** said **anything** at first.
>**Nothing** was said to **anyone** about it.

5. **Anyone, anybody,** and **anything** may also be used in affirmative statements to translate **cualquiera** or **cualquier cosa.**

>**Anyone** in the office will help you. (cualquiera)
>**Anybody** can do this; it is so easy. (cualquiera)
>I will like **anything** that you choose. (cualquier cosa)

Note: **That** (never **which**) is always used in adjective clauses to refer to **everything, nothing, something,** and **anything. That** is often omitted in conversation when it is the direct object or the object of a preposition.

>I will get **everything that** you need.
>I will get **everything** you need.

>He liked **nothing that** he looked at.
>He liked **nothing** he looked at.

Complete the following sentences with the indefinite pronouns which translate the Spanish.

1. ——— understands your English. (todos)
2. ——— understands your English. (nadie)
3. Did ——— tell you that I couldn't come? (alguien)
4. ——— told me ———. (nadie, nada)
5. There is ——— in the waiting room now. (nadie)
6. There isn't ——— in the waiting room now. (nadie)
7. They told me about ——— they saw. (todo)
8. ——— can see ——— in the dark. (nadie, nada)
9. Do you understand ——— that I say? (todo)
10. There was ——— that I wanted to see. (algo)
11. ——— has arrived yet; it is still early. (nadie)
12. ——— in the room can explain it to you. (cualquiera)
13. There is ——— at home now. (nadie)
14. There isn't ——— at home now. (nadie)
15. Virginia ate ——— that we gave her for breakfast. (todo)
16. Virginia didn't eat ——— for breakfast. (nada)
17. ——— needs an umbrella in the tropics. (todos)
18. ——— closed the windows. (alguien)

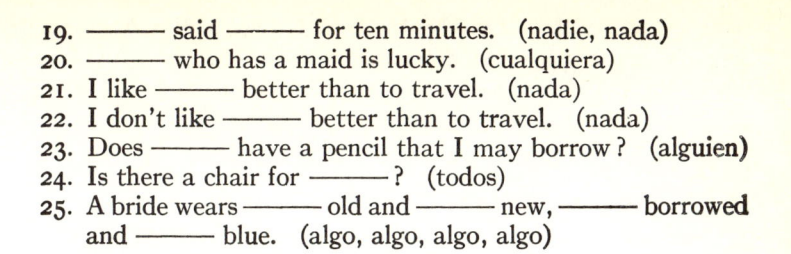

19. ——— said ——— for ten minutes. (nadie, nada)
20. ——— who has a maid is lucky. (cualquiera)
21. I like ——— better than to travel. (nada)
22. I don't like ——— better than to travel. (nada)
23. Does ——— have a pencil that I may borrow? (alguien)
24. Is there a chair for ———? (todos)
25. A bride wears ——— old and ——— new, ——— borrowed and ——— blue. (algo, algo, algo, algo)

Titcomb from Black Star

LESSON XX

Oil Wells in Texas

FROM TEXAS TO DENVER, COLORADO

It takes more than 24 hours to go from New Orleans to Denver by train, since we spend a long time crossing the state of Texas, second in size only to Alaska. It is difficult to realize that one state extends almost eight hundred miles from east to west and also from north to south. In the north-

238

eastern section of Texas is the prosperous city of **Dallas,** surrounded by land that produces both cotton and oil in abundance. In the southern part are the important cities of Houston and San Antonio. Houston, near the Gulf of Mexico, is a thriving modern city, one of the principal ports of the United States. Going south from Houston toward the Mexican border, one can visit the largest ranch in the world, the King Ranch, which contains a million acres. San Antonio, on the other hand, is a leisurely old Spanish city full of historical interest, where the Texans fought a significant battle in their revolution against Mexico. After winning its independence, the Republic of Texas was a separate nation for nine years (1836–1845) until it asked to be annexed to the United States.

In the western part of the state we cross the broad plains where thousands of cattle are raised; this is cowboy country. These plains extend across the western part of the state of Oklahoma into the state of Colorado; but as we approach Denver, we see the Rocky Mountains in the distance.

The capital of Colorado is the modern industrial city of Denver. It is called the "Mile High City," because it is located on a plain one mile above sea level near the eastern slopes of the mountains. On a clear day, the lofty peaks of the Colorado Rockies are visible in all their grandeur, including Pikes Peak (14,108 feet) and Longs Peak (14,255 feet).

Denver was founded in 1858 by miners. They were attracted by the rich deposits of gold and silver, while today people are attracted by the city's dry, cool, mountain air. Denver has grown from a rough mining town to the largest city in the Rocky Mountain region, with a population of over 400,000. In spite of the fact that New York is two thousand miles to the east and San Francisco more than a thousand miles to the west, fast trains and airplanes connect the city with all parts of the country.

Although mining is still important, the leading occupation in the surrounding country is agriculture. There are also numerous sheep and cattle ranches in this region. Among other things, the city manufactures mining machinery, tools, and dynamite. Its meat-packing plants compete with those of Chicago. **Denver is the principal city of the western plains** and also the chief commercial center for the mining districts in the mountains.

The city is a gateway to the magnificent national parks of the West. Although there are national parks in all parts of the country, those of the West are especially beautiful. The idea of establishing a system of parks originated in the United States when the national government decided that the outstanding beauty spots of the country should be set aside and preserved for the enjoyment of all the people. A variety of hotels, cabins, and camps have been provided for the millions of visitors; and in the parks one can take trips on foot, on horseback, or by automobile.

Fifty miles from Denver we visit the Rocky Mountain National Park, whose mountains tower 14,000 feet into the clouds. Then, taking a train to the northwestern corner of the state of Wyoming, we arrive at Yellowstone Park, the oldest (1872) and largest of all the parks. It is famous for its ten thousand geysers, its strange mud volcanoes, and its hot springs, which flow over colored terraces of rock. Among the most beautiful spectacles in the park are Yellowstone Lake, the canyon of the Yellowstone River, and Yellowstone Falls, which is considerably higher than Niagara Falls. The park owes its name to the dominant color, yellow, in the rocks of the canyon.

It would be difficult to find more magnificent scenery than that in Yellowstone Park, Glacier Park (Montana), Yosemite Park (California), and the Grand Canyon (Arizona). However, it is true that distances in the United States are so great that one must often travel far to enjoy these beauties of nature.

VOCABULARY

acre	acre (*4,840 varas cuadradas*)	**cowboy**	vaquero
to approach	acercarse a	**to cross**	cruzar, atravesar
as	a medida que; según	**dry**	seco
border	frontera	**enjoyment**	goce
broad	ancho	**to fight**	combatir, luchar
canyon	cañon	**glacier**	ventisquero
		gold	oro

grandeur	grandeza	**rocky**	rocoso
hot spring	aguas termales	**rough**	rudo
leisurely	pausado	**scenery**	paisaje
miner	minero	**to set aside**	apartar
mining	minería	**silver**	plata
mud	barro, lodo	**slope**	pendiente
nature	naturaleza	**strange**	extraño
peak	pico	**terrace**	terraza
to preserve	conservar	**Texan**	tejano
to provide	proveer	**thriving**	próspero
to raise	criar	**tool**	herramienta
ranch	hacienda, hato de ganado	**to tower**	elevarse
		to win	ganar

IDIOMS

a long time — mucho tiempo
in spite of (the fact that) — a pesar de (que)
on the other hand — de otra parte

CONVERSATION

Answer the following questions in complete sentences.

1. How long does it take to go from New Orleans to Denver by train? 2. Why does it take so long to cross the state of Texas? 3. What is the principal crop in the eastern part of Texas? 4. What are the principal cities in Texas? Tell something about each one. 5. Where is the largest ranch in the world? 6. How large is it, and what is its name? 7. How long was Texas an independent nation? 8. How and when did it become a part of the United States? 9. How is the western part of Texas different from the eastern part? 10. What is Denver often called? Why? 11. Who founded the city? 12. What attracted the founders to this spot? 13. Why are people attracted to Denver today? 14. How far is Denver from New York? from San Francisco? 15. What is the population of Denver? 16. What are the leading occupations in the surrounding region? 17. What articles are manufactured in the city? 18. Why did the government establish the system of national parks? 19. Which one is the oldest? 20. Why is it so interesting to visit? 21. How

did it get its name? 22. Name some of the other parks in the West, and tell where they are located. 23. Where can visitors stay in the parks? 24. What can they do in the parks? 25. What makes it difficult for some people to visit these parks? 26. Are there any national parks in your country?

PRONUNCIATION

[aʊ] out, south, mouth, proud, found, hour, cloud, thousand, mountain, surrounding, town, tower, however, cowboy, flower

[aɪ] side, rice, while, high, higher, remind, climate, mine, miner, mining, mile, refinery, realize, decide, provide, dry, sky, geyser

[e] lady, native, famous, parade, occasion, plane, nation, strange, state, same, great, greatest, wait, train, plain, raise, railroad

[ŋ] packing, mining, crossing, farming, growing, leading, taking, cutting, waiting, loading, unloading, railing, cooking, extending, interesting

[ɪd] located, attracted, connected, originated, cultivated, selected, visited, competed, decided, provided, flooded, surrounded

[d] raised, arrived, owed, entered, called, saved, carried, discovered, traveled, belonged, described, preserved

GRAMMAR

I. Adverbial Clauses of Time.

A. Adverbial clauses of time which begin with the conjunctions **when, as soon as, after, before, until,** or **since** indicate a definite time. If the idea is present or future, the simple present tense is used after these conjunctions. If the idea is past, the simple past tense is used.

He always leaves **when** the postman **comes.** (cuando)
He will leave **when** the postman **comes.**
He left **when** the postman **came.**
He was leaving **when** the postman **came.**

He will leave **as soon as** the postman **comes.** (tan pronto como)
He left **as soon as** the postman **came.**

He will leave **after** the postman **comes.** (después de que)
He left **after** the postman **came.**

> He won't leave **until** the postman **comes**. (hasta **que**)
> He didn't leave **until** the postman **came**.
>
> He won't leave **before** the postman **comes**. (antes de **que**)
> He didn't leave **before** the postman **came**.
>
> He has been reading his mail **since** the (desde **que**)
> postman **came**.

Translate the Spanish in the following sentences.

1. I want to be here *cuando llegue el cartero.*
2. The program won't begin *hasta que llegue el presidente.*
3. Let me know *tan pronto como él le escriba a Vd.*
4. Please don't leave *antes de que él lo llame a Vd.*
5. We'll see each other *después de que yo vuelva.*
6. We'll eat *en cuanto venga mi hermana.*
7. I haven't seen him *desde que volvió.*
8. I was leaving the house *cuando me llamó Vd.*
9. *Cuando entremos en Colorado*, we shall still be on the plains.
10. *Cuando estemos cerca de Denver*, we'll see the mountains.
11. *Cuando Vd. vaya a Denver*, you must visit the Rocky Mountain National Park.
12. *Cuando salgamos de Denver*, we are going north.
13. *Cuando Denver fué fundado*, it was a rough mining town.
14. We didn't see the mountains *hasta que nos acercamos a Denver.*
15. The scenery was beautiful *antes de que empezara a llover.*
16. We found a hotel room *en cuanto llegamos.*

B. The conjunction **while** indicates *duration of time* and sometimes an action simultaneous with another action. The simple present, the simple past, or the forms with **ing** may be used after this conjunction.

> **While** she **reads** (**is reading**), I am going to write a letter.
> She read **while** I **wrote** (**was writing**) a letter.
> She was reading **while** I **wrote** (**was writing**) a letter.

*Practice reading these sentences using **when** or **while**, as required.*

1. ―――― you are doing that, I'll make a telephone call.
2. ―――― Virginia was in class, Robert was studying at the library.
3. Robert was singing ―――― he took a bath.
4. The others listened ―――― I read the paragraph.

5. I couldn't read ——— they were talking.
6. ——— we were waiting for them, the telephone rang.
7. He didn't go to Denver ——— he was traveling in the United States.
8. ——— he arrived, he couldn't speak English.
9. He had no hotel reservation ——— he reached Chicago.
10. I had to leave ——— Mr. Taylor began to speak.
11. They were dancing ——— we arrived.
12. They were living in Chicago ——— I met them.

Note: The word **while** is sometimes used in the sense of **whereas** (**mien**tras que) when contrasting ideas are expressed.

> The buses in New York are slow, **while** the subways go as fast as railroad trains.
> On Fifth Avenue there are many expensive shops, **while** around the corner there are little shops where cheap souvenirs are sold.
> Boston has narrow, crooked streets downtown, **while** in the newer parts of the city there are wide avenues.
> Between Chicago and St. Louis one sees wheat fields and cornfields, **while** south of St. Louis the principal crop is cotton.
> The miners were attracted to Denver by the rich deposits of gold, **while** today people are attracted by the city's climate.

II. Adverbial Clauses of Concession.

Adverbial clauses of concession usually begin with **although** or **though** (aunque). There is no difference in the meaning of these two conjunctions, but **although** is more often used at the beginning of a sentence.

> **Although** she doesn't speak English well, she reads it easily.
> She likes it there, **though** it is very cold in winter.

Practice completing these sentences.

1. I like to go to English lectures, **though** ———.
2. I am taking my umbrella with me **though** ———.
3. I can never sleep in the daytime **though** ———.
4. He prefers to live in New York **although** ———.
5. The leading occupation is agriculture, **although** ———.
6. **Although** there are many national parks, ———.

Philip Gendreau, N.Y.   **The Lower Falls of the Yellowstone River**

    7. **Although** New Orleans is a typical American city, ―――.
    8. **Although** Chicago is only a hundred years old, ―――.
    9. **Although** Boston was founded by the English, ―――.
  10. **Although** Bogotá is situated near the equator, ―――.

III. Adverbial Clauses of Cause or Reason.

Adverbial clauses of cause or reason begin with **because, since, as,** or **for.** A clause that begins with **for** always comes

245

at the end of the sentence; the others may be used at the beginning or the end of the sentence. **Because** and **since** are used more often than **as** and **for**.

>He didn't come, **because** he was ill. (porque)
>**Since** he was ill, he didn't come. (puesto que)
>He didn't come, **as** he was ill. (como)
>He didn't come, **for** he was ill. (porque)

Practice using these causal conjunctions in answering the following questions.

1. Why does it take so long to cross the state of Texas?
2. Why are there so many cowboys in western Texas?
3. Why is Denver called the "Mile High City"?
4. Why were miners attracted to the region around Denver?
5. Why is Denver an important city?
6. Why is Denver a popular health resort?
7. Why was the system of national parks established?
8. Why do so many people visit the parks every summer?
9. Why is it difficult for some people to do this?
10. Why do you want to go to the United States?

IV. Adverbial Clauses of Purpose.

Adverbial clauses of purpose (propósito) usually begin with **so that** or **in order that** (para que). If the principal clause is in present or future time, the auxiliaries **will, can,** and **may** are used in the adverbial clause. If the principal clause is in past time, the auxiliaries **would, could,** and **might** are used.

>They are going by train { **so that** / **in order that** } they **will (can, may)** see more of the country.

>He went by bus { **so that** / **in order that** } he **would (could, might)** see more of the country.

Note: Expressions with **to** and **in order to** are often used instead of clauses of purpose. (See Lesson IX.)

Practice completing these sentences with clauses of purpose.

1. He is going to the university **so that** ———.
2. I am studying English **so that** ———.
3. I study hard **so that** ———.

4. I go to American movies **so that** ———.
5. I have to go now **so that** ———.
6. I am going to bed early **so that** ———.
7. She wears glasses **in order that** ———.
8. I got up early this morning **in order that** ———.
9. We waited for them **in order that** ———.
10. She lent me some money **in order that** ———.
11. I took my umbrella **so that** ———.
12. The bus stopped **so that** ———.
13. He bought a newspaper **so that** ———.
14. I turned on the light **so that** ———.
15. I turned off the radio **so that** ———.

V. Adverbial Clauses of Result.

An adverbial clause of result usually begins with **so, so ... that,** or **such ... that.** The second part of the sentence is the result of the first.

1. **So.**

   I couldn't get a taxi, **so** I had to come by bus.
   We went to Denver by train, **so** we saw much more of the country.

Practice completing these sentences.

1. The seats were all occupied, **so** I ———.
2. It was a beautiful day, **so** we ———.
3. The radio was too expensive, **so** we ———.
4. He has lived in the United States for several years, **so** he ———.
5. The train was late, **so** we ———.
6. There wasn't a room in that hotel, **so** I ———.
7. She likes books, **so** I ———.
8. The child was hungry, **so** I ———.
9. Virginia preferred to sit downstairs, **so** they ———.
10. The dominant color in the rocks is yellow, **so** ———.

2. **So ...** (*adjective or adverb*) **that.**

   This coffee is **so hot that** I can't drink it. (tan ... que)
   He came **so early that** no one was ready. (tan ... que)
   They had **so much** rain **that** the fields were flooded. (tanta ... que)
   There are **so many** students **that** the classes are crowded. (tantos ... que)

Practice completing these sentences with clauses of result.

1. He spoke so fast that ———.
2. He worked so hard that ———.
3. Distances are so great that ———.
4. Texas is so large that ———.
5. The mountains are so high that ———.
6. That movie was so good that ———.
7. It is so warm today that ———.
8. That book is so interesting that ———.
9. I have so many things to do that ———.
10. There is so much noise here that ———.

3. Such or such a ... (*noun*) that.

There are **such** large **states** in the West **that** an Easterner cannot get used to the idea.

Texas is **such a** large **state that** it takes two days to cross it by car.

Colorado has **such** magnificent **scenery that** you should not miss it.

He drives with **such speed that** I don't like to ride with him.

Note: If the noun is singular, but has a plural form, **such a** is used. If the noun is singular and has no plural form, **such** is used. With all plurals, **such** is used.

Practice completing these sentences.

1. This is such a heavy package that ———.
2. It is such a warm day that ———.
3. That was such a good movie that ———.
4. We had such a good time that ———.
5. She is such a busy person that ———.
6. This is such a noisy street that ———.
7. This is such a difficult lesson that ———.
8. Texas is such a large state that ———.
9. This is such an exciting book that ———.
10. This is such hot coffee that ———.
11. This is such good bread that ———.
12. He speaks with such speed that ———.
13. They are such high mountains that ———.
14. That is such good news that ———.
15. There are such great distances in the United States that

Courtesy of the Southern Pacific Company

LESSON XXI

The Railroad Bridge over Great Salt Lake

SALT LAKE CITY, UTAH

The chief commercial and manufacturing center between Denver and San Francisco is Salt Lake City, the capital and largest city (population 190,000) of Utah. It is located in a lovely green valley in the mountains and is 4,354 feet above sea level. There is so little rain that all the agriculture in

249

the valley depends on irrigation. In the mountains there are more large sheep and cattle ranches than farms, and some important mining districts are also found near by. The city is famous, however, for two things: the world headquarters of the Mormon Church, and Great Salt Lake.

The early history of Salt Lake City is similar to that of many other western cities. In 1847, under the leadership of Brigham Young, a small group of weary travelers arrived at the site of the present city. They had spent many weeks crossing the great plains and the difficult Rocky Mountains in their covered wagons. They were looking for a place to live, and they decided to build their homes there, where no white men had settled yet. The first year the crops failed, and the second year they were partly destroyed by locusts. The people soon realized that the soil would produce nothing without irrigation, so they worked to establish such a system. They had few comforts, but they survived.

These pioneers were Mormons who belonged to one of the many religious sects in the United States. Their settlement became important almost at once, because of its location on the direct route to California during the Gold Rush days of the 1850's. Now, likewise, the city is one of the principal stops on the shortest route from East to West by train or by plane. About 60 per cent of the population of Salt Lake City today are Mormons. Near the center of the city is Temple Square, which contains the sacred Mormon Temple, the big Assembly Hall, and the Tabernacle, whose organ is noted for its volume and fine tone quality.

Great Salt Lake, a few miles from the city, is one of the natural wonders of the world. It is a large shallow lake about 75 miles long and 50 miles wide; in fact, it is larger in area than the state of Rhode Island. Although it is formed by rivers of fresh water, it is a salt lake 4,000 feet above sea level. It is not connected with any sea or ocean: it is a lake with no outlet. Because of the dry air and the sunshine, there is so much evaporation that the lake never overflows; and, as a result, it is more than five times as salty as the oceans. Bathing in Great Salt Lake is a popular sport; you float in spite of yourself, for it is impossible to sink. If you want to go fishing, however, don't go there, because the water is so salty that fish cannot live in it. Commercially, the lake yields 40,000 tons of salt each year, and it is estimated that there is enough salt in the water to supply the United States indefinitely. In order to obtain the salt, the water is pumped into ponds two miles away, where it is evaporated by the heat of the sun.

Leaving Salt Lake City for San Francisco, you have another surprise when your train travels across the middle of the lake. It seems almost unbelievable that a railroad could be constructed over so many miles of water, but the fact is that it is built on a solid causeway across the shallow lake. As you ride along at sunset, you enjoy a splendid view of the sun going down over the mountains and over the great expanse of the lake.

VOCABULARY

comfort	comodidad	**pond**	estanque
deep	profundo	**to pump**	bombear
to destroy	destruir	**route**	ruta, camino
to enjoy	gozar de	**sacred**	sagrado
to estimate	calcular	**salt**	sal
expanse	extensión	**salty**	salado
fresh water	agua dulce	**shallow**	poco profundo
Gold Rush	fiebre del oro	**to sink**	hundir(se)
headquarters		**soil**	terreno
(*ecclesiastical*)	sede	**sport**	deporte
heat	calor	**stop**	escala, parada
likewise	asimismo	**sunset**	puesta del sol
locust	langosta	**to supply**	suministrar
middle	mitad, centro	**surprise**	sorpresa
near by	cerca	**to survive**	sobrevivir
noted	célebre	**ton**	tonelada
to obtain	obtener	**unbelievable**	increíble
outlet	salida	**wagon**	carreta de tracción animal
to overflow	desbordar		
partly	en parte	**weary**	muy cansado
pioneer	colonizador, explorador	**wonder**	maravilla
		to yield	producir

251

IDIOMS

at once	en seguida, inmediatamente
to go bathing	ir a bañarse
to go fishing	ir de pesca
to ride along	seguir viajando en tren
two miles away	a dos millas de distancia
75 miles long	75 millas de largo
50 miles wide	50 millas de ancho

CONVERSATION

Answer the following questions in complete sentences.

1. What state is Salt Lake City in? 2. Where did it get its name? 3. Who were the founders of the city? 4. Why did they stop at this place? 5. How did they reach this valley? 6. Did they have good luck at first? 7. Why is irrigation necessary in the West? 8. Are there many sheep and cattle ranches in the mountains? 9. Why did the settlement become important at once? 10. When was gold discovered in California? 11. For what two reasons is Salt Lake City famous? 12. How many Mormons live in the city today? 13. Is the city located on Great Salt Lake? 14. How large is Great Salt Lake? 15. Why is it a salt lake when it is formed by rivers of fresh water? 16. How salty is the lake? 17. Why is it a good place to learn to swim? 18. Is it a good place to go fishing? 19. How much salt does the lake yield annually? 20. How is the salt obtained from the water? 21. How was it possible to build a railroad across the lake?

PRONUNCIATION

[l] cat**tl**e, set**tl**e, set**tl**ement, temp**l**e, spectac**l**e, tabernac**l**e, midd**l**e, visib**l**e, possib**l**e, impossib**l**e, believab**l**e, unbelievab**l**e

[ə] commerci**a**l, commerci**a**lly, **a**long, **a**way, **a**rrive, n**a**tur**a**l, n**a**tur**a**lly, org**a**n, inh**a**bit**a**nt, **a**cross, bel**o**ng, cont**a**in, c**o**nnect, syst**e**m, c**o**nstruct, wag**o**n, purp**o**se, **o**btain, religi**ou**s

[r] **r**egion, **r**eligious, **r**eligion, **r**efinery, **r**anch, **r**ailroad, **r**ocky, **r**ide, **r**oute, **r**ush, **r**eceive, **r**esult, nea**r**, nea**r** by, yea**r**, ai**r**, the**r**e, thei**r**

[s-] sport, spite, spring, spot, spend, spectacle, Spain, Spaniard, Spanish, small, slave, slope, sky, square, strong, strange, statesman
[v] Denver, level, lovely, travel, traveler, arrive, above, leave, believe, survive, live, living, however, valley, view, volume, vegetation
[w] weary, week, wagon, world, wonder, wide, water

GRAMMAR   Section 1

I. Conditional Sentences.

Conditional sentences in English are similar to those in Spanish, with the exception that the use of the subjunctive is much more limited in English. Examples of the usual types of conditional sentences follow, with an explanation of each one below. Of course, the **if** clause may come at the end as well as at the beginning of the sentence.

> If I go, I will let you know.
> (Si voy, le avisaré.)
> If I should go, I would (will) let you know.
> (Si fuera, le avisaría.)
> If I had the money, I would buy it.
> (Si tuviera el dinero, lo compraría.)
> If I had had the money, I would have bought it.
> (Si hubiera tenido el dinero, lo habría comprado.)

1. In an **if** clause which expresses a future idea that is practical and possible, the verb is in the present tense. The auxiliary **will** is never used in the **if** clause except when it expresses the idea of willingness (querer).

> If I go, I will (shall) let you know.
> If I have time, I will (shall) read it.
> If he comes back to see us, we will (shall) write you about it.
> If you will wait a few minutes, I will (shall) go with you.
> (si quiere esperar)

Note: Although the future auxiliaries **shall** and **will** or the substitutes for the future are more common in the main clause, it is also possible to use **may, can,** or **must.** The meaning is of course different.

253

If she returns early, I **shall (will) tell** her that. (diré)
If she returns early, **shall** I **tell** her that? (¿quiere **que** diga?)
If she returns early, I **can tell** her that. (puedo decir)

If we arrive late, they **will** not **wait** for us. (no esperarán)
If we arrive late, they **may** not **wait** for us. (posiblemente no esperen)
If we arrive late, they **must** not **wait** for us. (no deben esperar)

Practice answering these questions in complete sentences.
1. If you decide to go, will you let me know?
2. If you have time, will you get the tickets?
3. If there are any tickets left, shall I get one for you?
4. If you go by the post office, will you mail this letter?
5. If it doesn't rain, are you going to take a ride?
6. If you have enough money, are you going on a vacation?
7. If we leave now, can we be back for dinner?
8. If I take the noon train, what time will I get there?
9. If I am a little late, can you wait for me?
10. If I see her, shall I ask her to go with us?

2. **If** clauses which express a future idea that is possible but not probable contain the auxiliary **should**. In this case, **should** does not imply obligation.

If I **should decide** to go, I **would (will) call** you (up).
If they **should go** to the United States, they **would (will)** not **take** their children.

Practice answering these questions in complete sentences.
1. If you should see her, would you please give her this message?
2. If you should have a toothache, whom would you go to see?
3. If it should rain, would you go anyway?
4. If you should go to Great Salt Lake, would you go bathing?
5. If you should want to go fishing, would you go there?

3. **If** clauses that express an idea contrary to fact *in the present* require the past subjunctive. However, only the verb **be** shows a difference between the past subjunctive and the simple past tense of the indicative; **were is** is used for *all* persons of **be** in the past subjunctive.

If he **had** time, he **would study** more. (*He doesn't have time.*)
If he **were** here, he **would play** the piano. (*He is not here.*)

Note: The auxiliary **would** is used after **if** only when it expresses the idea of willingness (querer). In the main clause, it is possible to use **could** or **might** in some sentences.

If you **would wait,** she **would go** too. (si quisiera esperar)
If it were not raining, I **might work** in the garden.
If I had another ticket, your sister **could go,** too.

Practice answering these questions in complete sentences.

1. Would you go if you were I (me)?
2. What would you do if you were in New York?
3. Would you go to the concert if you had a ticket?
4. Would you learn English more quickly if you spoke it every day?
5. What would you do if you had a million dollars?

4. **If** clauses that express an idea contrary to fact *in the past* require the past perfect subjunctive. However, this form of the subjunctive is the same as that of the past perfect indicative.

If I **had had** the money, I **would have bought** it. (*I didn't have the money.*)
If it **had** not **rained,** I **would have come.** (*It rained.*)

Note: Instead of **would have** in the main clause, it is sometimes possible to use **could have** or **might have.**

If I had had the money, I **could have bought** it.
If it had not rained, I **might have come.**

Practice completing these sentences.

1. If he ——— (know) that, he would have waited for you.
2. If I ——— (receive) an invitation, I would have gone.
3. If she ——— (have) time, she would have read the book.
4. If I ——— (want) a book to read, I would have borrowed one from the library.
5. If he ——— not ——— (be) ill, he would have gone with us.
6. If I had had enough money, I ——— (buy) a car.
7. If I had thought of it, I ——— (ask) her to go, too.
8. If I had seen him, I ——— (give) him your message.

9. If he had been here, he ——— (help) you.
10. If they had left early, they ——— (be) here now.

Note: The word **unless** (a menos que) is often used to replace **if ... not.**

> They will go without us **if** we don't hurry.
> They will go without us **unless** we hurry.
> I wouldn't see the doctor **if** I were **not** ill.
> I wouldn't see the doctor **unless** I were ill.

Section 2

II. Prepositions Used after Certain Verbs.

A. In some cases, an English verb with a preposition is equivalent to a simple Spanish verb.

ask for	pedir	**turn off**	apagar (*la luz*)
look for	buscar	**look at**	mirar
pay for	pagar (*una cosa*)	**listen to**	escuchar
wait for	esperar	**put on**	ponerse (*ropa*)
turn on	encender (*la luz*)	**take off**	quitarse (*ropa*)

Practice making sentences using the verbs in A.

B. In some other cases, an English verb alone is equivalent to a Spanish verb with a preposition.

play (*a game*)	jugar a	**enjoy**	gozar de
resemble	parecerse a	**change**	cambiar de
leave	salir de	**notice**	fijarse en
approach	acercarse a	**enter**	entrar en
remember	acordarse de	**marry**	casarse con
lack	carecer de		

Practice making sentences using the verbs in B.

C. In English, many basic verbs are combined with prepositions to express certain ideas, but the preposition used may differ from the one used in Spanish. It is necessary to memorize these expressions. If a verb follows a preposition, the gerund (**ing** form of the verb) is used.

arrive at   We **arrived at** the theater ten minutes early.
laugh at   What **are** they **laughing at**?
              They **are laughing at** a joke he told them.

dream about	What **did** you **dream about** last night?
	I dreamed about flying.
hear about	I am very glad to meet you, for **I have heard** many nice things **about** you.
think about	I'm not sure, but **I'll think about** it and let you know.
ask a favor of	I should like **to ask a favor of** you.
remind of	He **reminded** me **of** Mr. Smith.
think of	What **did** you **think of** that film? (*opinion*)
	I am thinking of going away next week. (pienso irme)
arrive in	He **arrived in** Miami late at night.
persist in	Why **do** children **persist in** asking questions?
succeed in	We **succeeded in** getting reservations.
agree on	They **agreed on** a plan.
depend on	Our plans for tomorrow **depend on** the weather.
insist on	He **insisted on** paying for the tickets.
be from	Where **are** you **from**? I **am from** South America.
borrow from	He **borrowed** a dollar **from** Mr. Miller.
buy from	I am going **to buy** the book **from** Virginia.
differ from	The two brothers **differ from** each other greatly.
hear from	**I haven't heard from** my sister for two months.
agree with (*a person*)	I don't **agree with** him on that.
disagree with (*a person*)	Therefore, **I disagree with** him.
correspond with	**I have corresponded with** her for a year.

Practice making other sentences using the expressions in C.

III. Prepositions Used after Certain Adjectives and Past Participles.

Some adjectives and past participles also require certain prepositions to express a particular idea. Here are a few common expressions which should be memorized. If a verb follows the preposition, the gerund (**ing** form of the verb) is used.

> interested in surrounded by
> surprised at similar to

sorry for	satisfied with
absent from	lined with
different from	ill (sick) with
covered with	fond of
angry about (*a thing*)	kind of
angry with (*a person*)	tired of
filled with	afraid of
pleased with	full of

Practice using the correct prepositions in these sentences.

1. They are very much interested ——— learning English.
2. He was ill ——— a bad cold last week.
3. Their house is similar ——— ours.
4. It was very kind ——— you to come.
5. I was surprised ——— his ability to speak English.
6. The mountains are covered ——— snow.
7. The scenery of the West is different ——— that of the East.
8. What are you angry ——— ?
9. I hope that you are not angry ——— me.
10. She is almost never absent ——— class.
11. The streets are lined ——— trees.
12. I am not afraid ——— mice.
13. We were very pleased ——— the lecture.
14. The teacher was satisfied ——— my progress in English.
15. She is very fond ——— music.
16. The city is surrounded ——— hills.
17. I feel sorry ——— her; she has to work so hard.
18. I am tired ——— reading; let's go for a walk.
19. The glasses are filled ——— wine.
20. My paper was full ——— mistakes yesterday.

REVIEW LESSON VII

I. Fill each blank with the appropriate preposition.

1. Mr. Miller is sitting ——— Mrs. Miller. (al lado de)
2. Their house is ——— the corner. (cerca de)
3. They live ——— Clark Street. What street do you live ———?
4. Their house is ——— the park. (frente a)
5. The car is ——— their house. (delante de)
6. Washington is not ——— New York. (lejos de)
7. ——— New York, they visited Boston and Chicago. (además de)
8. Is it very cold there ——— the winter?
9. My birthday is ——— June.
10. They arrived ——— the first ——— August.
11. You get ——— the bus at Fiftieth Street, and get ——— at Broadway.
12. Why do you sit ——— that chair?
13. Virginia is ——— Baton Rouge ——— Louisiana State University.
14. There were no rugs ——— the floor.
15. The room has many pictures ——— the walls.
16. Are they coming ——— the morning or ——— the afternoon?
17. The mailman is waiting ——— the door. (en)
18. They are studying English ——— the cultural center.
19. I will meet you ——— three o'clock ——— Monday.
20. It is necessary to arrive ——— the airport early.
21. When did she arrive ——— the United States?
22. Is she ——— home now?

259

23. The exercise is ——— the top of the page.
24. Although it is very warm in the daytime, it is cool ——— night.
25. The Second World War began ——— Europe ——— 1939.
26. We walked ——— Fifth Avenue to Eighth Avenue. (de)
27. I walked ——— Twenty-second Street. (hasta)
28. I went downtown ——— lunch. (antes de)
29. We danced ——— midnight. (hasta)
30. They went to the movies ——— dinner. (después de)
31. He has gone ——— the bank for a moment. ([entrar] en)
32. She found her gloves ——— the seat. (debajo de)
33. The plane flew ——— the city before landing. (encima de)
34. There were so many clouds ——— us that we could not see anything from the plane. (debajo de)
35. Would you like to walk ——— the park? (a través de)
36. We are going for a walk ——— evening. (hacia)
37. Salt Lake City is the principal city ——— Denver and San Francisco. (entre)
38. ——— other things, Yellowstone Park is famous for its geysers. (entre)
39. Mrs. Miller took the flowers ——— the table. (de)
40. I went to the movies twice ——— the week. (durante)
41. I went to the library ——— a book. (por)
42. We waited ——— them ——— half an hour.
43. It is time ——— us to go now.
44. She was able to translate the letter ——— herself. (sola)
45. Are they going ——— plane or ——— train?
46. The X bus passes ——— my house. (por)
47. Mr. Miller has gone ——— the city. ([salir] de)
48. Will he be back ——— Tuesday? (no más tarde que)
49. Shall we sit down ——— this table?
50. It has been raining ——— two hours. (durante)
51. It has been raining ——— noon. (desde)
52. The car is ——— the corner. (a la vuelta de)
53. New Yorkers always seem to be ——— a hurry.
54. ——— the way, speaking of food, what American doesn't like baked beans?
55. Paul Revere went ——— horseback to several of the neighboring villages.
56. I don't know what they are laughing ———.
57. I am thinking ——— going to the United States some day.

58. This book is different ——— that one.
59. When did he borrow that money ——— you?
60. We bought this car ——— a neighbor.
61. If you persist ——— studying these prepositions, you will learn them some day.
62. The teacher insists ——— good pronunciation.
63. I'm sorry, but I don't agree ——— you.
64. We haven't heard ——— (*received a letter*) Virginia recently.
65. Would you like to correspond ——— a North American?
66. That seems like a good suggestion, but I want to think ——— it before making a decision.
67. I've heard a great deal ——— her, but I've never met her.
68. Miss Gray, may I ask a favor ——— you?
69. I like to listen ——— records of classical music.
70. New Orleans reminds one ——— the Old World.
71. Have you paid ——— the tickets yet?
72. What are you so angry ———?
73. The valley is surrounded ——— mountains.
74. How long does it take to learn English? That depends ——— you and ——— how much time you study.
75. Now I think I will dream ——— prepositions.

II. Use who, whom, which, or that, as required, in the following sentences. Notice where the pronoun can be omitted.

1. It is the pronunciation of English ——— is the most difficult.
2. The books ——— we are going to use haven't arrived yet.
3. The girl ——— is playing the piano is my cousin.
4. The city ——— they liked best was Washington.
5. The cowboys ——— you see in western Texas wear big hats.
6. About 60 per cent of the people ——— live in Salt Lake City are Mormons.
7. There are not many cities ——— celebrate Mardi Gras as New Orleans does.
8. Even a person ——— cannot swim can float in Great Salt Lake.
9. The bears ——— you see in Yellowstone Park are very tame.
10. Abraham Lincoln, ——— everyone admires, had very little formal education.

III. *Read the following sentences with the preposition after the verb, direct object, or adjective complement of the adjective clause. Then read them with that instead of whom or which. Then read them without any pronoun.*

1. Is this the book *for which* you were looking?
    **Is this the book which you were looking for?
    Is this the book that you were looking for?
    Is this the book you were looking for?**
2. Who was that man *with whom* you were speaking?
3. What is the radio program *to which* you like to listen?
4. Is he the man *from whom* you bought your tickets?
5. Is he the waiter *to whom* we gave our order?
6. That is the young man *about whom* Virginia has told us.
7. The eighth of July is the day *on which* he was born.
8. New Orleans is the city *in which* we had such a good time.
9. Yellowstone Park is the one *through which* we drove.
10. That is the movie *at which* we laughed so much.

IV. *Change the following sentences to the passive voice. Do not express the agent when it is a pronoun. In sentence 14 change only the noun clause to the passive.*

1. Benjamin Franklin wrote that book.
2. The Mormons founded Salt Lake City.
3. The Mormons established a system of irrigation.
4. Locusts destroyed a large part of their crops.
5. One finds many sheep and cattle ranches near Salt Lake City.
6. Rivers of fresh water form Great Salt Lake.
7. They have built a railroad across Great Salt Lake.
8. Miners founded the city of Denver.
9. The excellent climate attracts people to Denver.
10. Fast trains and airplanes connect the city with other parts of the country.
11. They grow a lot of cotton in the South.
12. They raise thousands of cattle in Texas.
13. In the national parks, the government has provided hotels, cabins, and camps for the visitors.
14. The government thought that it should preserve these beauty spots for the enjoyment of all the people.
15. From Denver one can see the lofty peaks of the Colorado Rockies.

V. Use the following expressions in original sentences.

so tired that	such a beautiful day that
so sleepy that	such a good movie that
so cold that	such a big hat that
so fast that	such good news that
so slowly that	such interesting work that

VI. Use the proper verb forms in the conditional sentences of the following exercises.

A. Give the four conditional forms of these sentences.

1. If I ——— (have) time, I ——— (write) to him.
   If I have time, I will write to him.
   If I should have time, I would (will) write to him.
   If I had time, I would write to him.
   If I had had time, I would have written to him.
2. If I ——— (be) sick, I ——— (call) the doctor.
3. If it ——— (be) very cold in Chicago, you ——— (need) a heavier coat.
4. If they ——— (go) to New Orleans, they ——— (visit) the French Quarter.
5. If he ——— (like) Denver, he ——— (stay) there a while.

B. Answer these questions with complete sentences.

1. What are you going to do next Friday if we have a holiday?
2. Will you go with me if I get a ticket for you?
3. Where would you go on Sunday if you had a car?
4. How would you spend your time if you didn't have to work?
5. If a telegram should come for me, would you let me know?
6. If it should rain, would you go?
7. Would you have gone to the beach if it had rained?
8. Would you have lent me the money if I had asked you for it?

C. Complete the following conditional sentences.

1. If I mail it today, ———.
2. If I come to class early, ———.
3. If I can go tomorrow, ———.
4. If I were you, ———.
5. If she were here, ———.
6. If it were not late, ———.

7. If you should see her, ———.
8. If I should finish my work early, ———.
9. If I had been ready, ———.
10. If I had been able to speak English, ———.

VII. Use the present tense in these sentences, although the idea is future.

1. I'll be ready as soon as I ——— (finish) this letter.
2. We can do that after we ——— (get) there.
3. When you ——— (see) her, please say "hello" for me.
4. Please let me know when he ——— (arrive).
5. I can't begin the work until he ——— (tell) me just what to do.
6. When she ——— (call), I want to talk with her.
7. Let's go now before it ——— (rain).
8. We can't go until we ——— (get) some gasoline.
9. Will you be here when I ——— (return)?
10. As soon as she ——— (feel) better, we'll take her to the country.

VIII. Fill each blank with the indirect form of the direct question, as indicated.

1. Where is Denver? Do you know **where Denver is?**
2. Where did they go? I don't know ———.
3. What time is it? Can you tell me ———?
4. What is the name of the book? Do you remember ———?
5. How much did he pay for it? I don't know ———.
6. How many students are there? Do you know ———?
7. What does he mean? I'll ask him ———.
8. When is she leaving? She doesn't know yet ———.
9. Where did you meet them? I don't remember ———.
10. Does he understand English? I don't know ———.
11. Are they at home today? Do you know ———?
12. Did the Millers leave? Can you tell me ———?

IX. Complete the following sentences, using an auxiliary or a form of the verb be.

1. They prefer to go by car, and so ——— we.
2. Salt Lake City is located in the West, and so ——— Denver.
3. Texas produces many oranges, and Florida ——— too.

4. There are large cattle ranches near Denver, and so ——— there near Salt Lake City.
5. The Rocky Mountain National Park has some magnificent scenery, and Yellowstone Park ——— too.
6. They didn't spend much time in Yellowstone Park, and neither ——— we.
7. The geysers are very interesting, and the mud volcanoes ——— too.
8. She doesn't have a car, and I ——— either.
9. St. Louis is on the Mississippi River, and so ——— New Orleans.
10. He hasn't visited New Orleans, and I ——— either.
11. Virginia didn't go swimming in Great Salt Lake, but I ———.
12. Great Salt Lake is saltier than the oceans, ———?
13. At first she didn't like Denver, but now she ———.
14. Have you read about New Orleans? Yes, I ———.
15. Would you like to go down the Mississippi by boat? Yes, I ———.
16. Does he expect to spend some time in New Orleans? Yes, he ———.
17. The scenery in the West differs from that in the East, ———?
18. We should write about that in our diaries, ———?
19. You will often think about this trip, ———?
20. We have learned a lot of English on this trip, ———?

265

A.P.S. from Black Star

LESSON XXII

An Arizona Desert Scene with a Saguaro Cactus in front of the Superstition Mountai

THE SOUTHWEST

Instead of proceeding directly from Salt Lake City to San Francisco, let us take a long but interesting way through the Southwest. This is the land of sunshine, of old Indian villages, of great irrigation projects, and of one of the world's greatest wonders, the Grand Canyon.

The history of the Southwest began with the Spanish explorations. In 1540, Francisco Vásquez de Coronado started out from Mexico with a group of Spaniards and Indians to look for the seven cities of fabulous wealth of which he had heard; but after two years of futile search in the states which are now Arizona, New Mexico, Texas, Colorado, and Kansas, he returned to Mexico, a disillusioned man. Through the years, however, the Spanish influence in most of this region has predominated to such an extent that newspapers, plays, and moving pictures are often in Spanish, and many of the inhabitants are bilingual.

There are about 344,000 Indians in the United States. Many of them live on large reservations established by the national government for their exclusive use. Although Indians may live anywhere in the United States, as other citizens do, the reservation lands are given to them; and there they may have their tribal villages. On the plateaus of Arizona and New Mexico there are several of these reservations, where the Indians make their living by farming, by raising cattle, and by selling wool, hides, and silver jewelry. Of the various tribes, the Pueblos and the Navajos are the best known; the Pueblos are skilled in making fine pottery, while the Navajos are especially known for their beautiful blankets.

The principal river of the Southwest is the Colorado River, which forms the boundary between Arizona and southern California and gives life to the Great American Desert. This is not a flat desert of sand dunes like the Sahara Desert in Africa: in some places there are steep mountains of rock, and there is some vegetation as well as deposits of minerals.

As in almost all the Far West, however, agriculture depends mainly on irrigation. This has been made possible by the construction of several dams, of which Hoover Dam on the Colorado River is the largest. It is four times as high as Niagara Falls; the lake formed by it is one of the largest artificial lakes in the world, more than a hundred miles long and in some parts eight miles wide. Below the dam is the powerhouse which generates electricity for this region and for much of southern California, even as far away as Los Angeles, a distance of 256 miles. Thus, with the development of irrigation projects, the worthless desert has become fertile farm land and brought prosperity to thousands of people. The most magnificent sight in the Southwest is the Grand Canyon of the Colorado River in the northern part of Arizona. It is an enormous gorge, more than a mile deep in places, about two hundred miles long, and from eight to ten miles wide.[1] To go from one side to the other by road or by railroad, one would have to travel hundreds of miles. For thousands of years the Colorado River has been cutting its way through these rocks, so that today it looks like a narrow ribbon at the bottom of the canyon. An adventurous tourist may go down to the river by donkey in one day, stay overnight at a small hotel, and return to the top on the following day. If one gazes at the walls of the canyon, he can watch the colors change each hour of the day and imagine that he sees castles, cathedrals, and ships in the strange formations of the rocks. A visit to the Grand Canyon is truly impressive, a trip one never forgets.

VOCABULARY

anywhere	en cualquier parte	powerhouse	planta de la energía
blanket	manta, frazada	to proceed	proseguir
bottom	fondo	project	proyecto
boundary	límite, frontera	prosperity	prosperidad
castle	castillo	reservation	territorio reservado para los indios
dam	represa		
desert	desierto	ribbon	cinta
development	desarrollo	sand dune	duna de arena
donkey	burro	search	búsqueda
flat	plano	sight	vista
futile	inútil	skilled	hábil
to gaze at	contemplar	to start out	ponerse en marcha
gorge	cañon, abra	steep	muy inclinado
to hear of	oír hablar de	thus	así
hide	cuero	tribe	tribu
impressive	impresionante	to watch	observar
jewelry	joyas	wealth	riqueza(s)
plateau	altiplanicie	wool	lana
play	pieza teatral	worthless	sin valor
pottery	alfarería		

[1] Authorities differ as to the width.

Fairchild Aerial Surveys   Hoover Dam

IDIOMS

to cut its way through   labrar su camino por
to look like   parecerse a
to make one's living   ganarse la vida
to stay overnight   pasar la noche, pernoctar
to such an extent that   hasta tal punto que

CONVERSATION

Answer the following questions in complete sentences.

1. Which states are included in the Southwest? 2. Who was the first white man to explore the Southwest? 3. Where did he come from? 4. What was the purpose of his expedition? 5. How did it end? 6. How is the Spanish influence shown in this region today? 7. Is the number of Indians in the United States comparatively large or small? 8. Where do many of the Indians live? 9. What advantages do they have there? 10. How do the Indians of Arizona and New

Mexico make their living? 11. Give the names of two well-known tribes. 12. Where is the Great American Desert? 13. How does it differ from the Sahara Desert? 14. What have you learned about the Colorado River? 15. What does most agriculture depend on in the Far West? 16. Where is Hoover Dam? 17. Is it as high as Niagara Falls? 18. How large is the artificial lake formed by the dam? 19. What is the purpose of the dam? 20. Where is the Grand Canyon? 21. What are its dimensions? 22. How long has it taken for the river to form this canyon? 23. Describe the colors and the formations of the rocks. 24. If you should go to the Grand Canyon, would you like to take the trip by donkey to the bottom of the gorge? 25. Are you an adventurous tourist?

PRONUNCIATION

[θ] through, thousands, theater, cathedral, fourth, tenth, wealth, worthless, Southwest, three, thirteen, thirty, third
[ʃ] ship, sunshine, establish, Chicago, Michigan, ocean, nation, national, irrigation, exploration, reservation, construction
[tʃ] search, reach, watch, beach, which, charm, change, nature, natural, picture, agriculture, adventure, adventurous
[dʒ] jewelry, journey, project, region, village, villages, language, languages, gorge, strange, imagine, generate
[z] Arizona, Kansas, reservation, raising, desert, thousand

GRAMMAR   Section 1

I. The Formation and Use of the Present Subjunctive in English.

A. The present subjunctive has the simple form of the verb in all persons, including the third person singular.

that I come   that we come
that you come   that you come
that he **come**   that they come

B. After certain verbs the present subjunctive is used in a subordinate clause when the subject changes. The same form of the subjunctive is used, whether the main verb is in the present, past, future, or any other tense. The common verbs that require the present subjunctive are **demand, sug-**

gest, prefer, propose, and **recommend.** The verb **insist may** be followed by the subjunctive or the preposition **on with a** gerund as its object.

> I demand (demanded) that he **be** here on time.
> I would suggest that she **go** to see the doctor.
> I insist (insisted) that he **come** early.
> I insist (insisted) **on his coming** early.

Translate the Spanish in these sentences.

1. I suggest *que él escriba* the letter again.
   I suggested *que él escribiera* the letter again.
2. They insist *que él vaya* with them.
   They insisted *que él fuera* with them.
3. I propose *que ella tome* her vacation now.
   I will propose *que ella tome* her vacation next week.
   I proposed *que ella tomara* her vacation now.
4. I prefer *que ella espere* until next month.
   I preferred *que ella esperara* until next month.
   I would prefer *que ella esperara* until next month.
5. I recommend *que Vd. lea* this book.
   I recommended *que Vd. leyera* this book.
   I would recommend *que Vd. leyera* this book.
6. He suggests *que Vds. estén* here at seven o'clock.
   He suggested *que Vds. estuvieran* here at seven o'clock.
   He had suggested *que Vds. estuvieran* here at seven o'clock.

C. Many verbs that require the subjunctive in Spanish are followed by an infinitive in English. The subject of the Spanish subjunctive becomes the subject of the infinitive in English (see Lesson XI); if it is a pronoun, the object pronoun is used.

> I want John **to begin** the work on Monday.
> (Quiero **que Juan empiece** el trabajo el lunes.)
>
> I wanted **him to begin** the work on Monday.
> (Quería **que él empezara** el trabajo el lunes.)

Note: The use of the infinitive in English will not seem strange if it is remembered that the verbs **permitir, dejar, mandar,** and impersonal expressions are often followed by an infinitive in Spanish.

Permítame que vaya.   Permítame **ir.**
No es necesario que Vd. nos espere.   No le es necesario **esperarnos.**

D. After the verb **insist** and some impersonal expressions, two constructions are possible.

> They insist (insisted) **that he go** with them.
> They insist (insisted) **on his going** with them.
> It is important **that he find** those papers.
> It is important **for him to find** those papers.
> It was necessary **that he finish** it yesterday.
> It was necessary **for him to finish** it yesterday.

Practice 1. Read these sentences in English, using an infinitive in place of the Spanish verb.

Remember: After **let** the word **to** is omitted.

1. He advises me *que lea* aloud.
   He advised me *que leyera* aloud.
2. I am going to ask her *que venga* with us.
   I asked her *que viniera* with us.
3. They want us *que estemos* there on time.
   They wanted us *que estuviéramos* there on time.
4. She begs me *que le enseñe* English.
   She begged me *que le enseñara* English.
5. Tell them *que nos encuentren* at five o'clock.
   We told them *que nos encontraran* at five o'clock.
6. I'll urge her *que se quede* longer.
   I urged her *que se quedara* longer.
7. They require us *que estudiemos* English in school.
   They required us *que estudiáramos* English.
8. He will order the men *que vuelvan* to work.
   He ordered the men *que volvieran* to work.
9. She will not permit (allow) us *que salgamos*.
   She would not permit (allow) us *que saliéramos*.
10. She will not let us *que salgamos*.
    She did not let us *que saliéramos*.

Practice 2. Answer these questions in complete sentences.

1. Does he insist that we go now?
2. Did you suggest that she come with us?
3. Where did they propose that we spend our vacation?
4. Do you recommend that I stay at that hotel?

5. Do you prefer that I speak English or Spanish?
6. What book do you advise me to read?
7. Does the teacher want us to write these sentences?
8. Did she ask you to wait for her?
9. Did they urge you to go with them?
10. Do they require children to study English in the schools of your country?
11. Did you order them to send it immediately?
12. Will her mother allow her to visit us?
13. Will you let me look at your book a minute?
14. Is it difficult for her to learn English?
15. Did she insist on your going with her?

I. The Formation and Use of the Past Subjunctive.

A. The past subjunctive is the same as the past indicative, except for the verb **be**. The past subjunctive of **be** is the form **were,** which is used in all three persons, singular and plural.

B. The past subjunctive is used in a subordinate clause, which usually expresses an idea contrary to fact. The past subjunctive occurs:

1. After **if** in a conditional sentence when the idea expressed is contrary to fact in present time (see Lesson XXI).

   If I **had** the money, I would buy a new hat. (*I don't have it.*)
   If he **were** here, he would know what to do. (*He isn't here.*)

2. After the expressions **as if** and **as though** (como si).

   She **sings** as if (as though) she **enjoyed** it. (*She does or doesn't enjoy it.*)
   She **sang** as if (as though) she **enjoyed** it. (*She did or didn't enjoy it.*)
   He **speaks** English as if (as though) he **were** a North American. (*He is not a North American.*)
   He **spoke** English as if (as though) he **were** a North American. (*He was not a North American.*)

3. After the verb **wish** when the idea is contrary to fact in present time. The expression **I wish** is equivalent to **Ojalá** in Spanish.

I wish (that) I **knew** their address. (*I don't know it.*)
She wishes (that) she **were** a blonde. (*She is not a blonde.*)
They wish (that) they **understood** English better.

III. The Formation and Use of the Past Perfect Subjunctive.

The past perfect subjunctive is the same as the past perfect indicative. It is used to indicate past time in contrary-to-fact conditional clauses and after the verb **wish**; it is used to indicate time before the time of the principal clause in **as if** or **as though** clauses.

If I **had had** the money, I would have bought a new hat.
If he **had been** here, he would have known what to do.
I wish (that) I **had seen** her yesterday.
She looked as if she **had had** a good vacation.

Complete these sentences with the past or past perfect subjunctive, as required, of the verbs in parentheses.

1. I wouldn't go if I ―――― (be) you.
2. He wouldn't have said that if he ―――― (be) in my place.
3. If I ―――― (live) there, I would walk downtown.
4. If she ―――― (want) to go, she could.
5. She drives a car as if she ―――― (be) afraid.
6. He talked about Paris as if he ―――― (spend) his whole life there.
7. They spent money as if they always ―――― (have) plenty of it.
8. I wish I ―――― (can) speak English well, but I can't.
9. He wishes he ―――― (be) in your class.
10. I wish he ―――― (come) with us yesterday.

Section 2

IV. The Gerund.

A. The **ing** form of a verb when used as a noun is called a gerund. The gerund may be the subject, direct object, or predicate noun (after **be**).

Swimming is his favorite sport. (*subject*)
He likes **swimming** better than horseback **riding**. (*direct object*)
Seeing is **believing**. (*predicate noun*)

B. The gerund is the verb form used after prepositions, **where** in Spanish an infinitive is used.

>They insisted **on coming** with us.
>The child persisted **in asking** questions.
>I am thinking **of going** there on my vacation.
>Thank you **for bringing** me the flowers.
>**On arriving,** I took a taxi to the hotel.
>They are used **to having** lunch early.

Complete these sentences with the gerund of the verb indicated. Then read them using other verbs.

1. We are very much interested in ——— (learn) English.
2. One can't learn it without ——— (study).
3. One learns to speak English by ——— (practice) it.
4. If you persist in ——— (talk) English, you will learn it quickly.
5. I am not fond of ——— (write) letters.
6. He finished his work before ——— (leave).
7. After three hours of ——— (drive), I was very tired.
8. They were successful in ——— (find) an apartment.
9. They succeeded in ——— (sell) their house.
10. His illness prevented him from ——— (work).
11. I have no intention of ——— (do) that work today.
12. He insisted on ——— (walk) instead of ——— (take) a streetcar.
13. She left yesterday without ——— (say) good-bye.
14. They drove through the Southwest instead of ——— (go) directly to San Francisco.
15. I am tired of ——— (read). Let's go out for a walk.
16. She has had a great deal of experience at ——— (translate).
17. Thank you very much for ——— (call).
18. After ——— (wait) an hour, I finally had to go.
19. He came near ——— (lose) his hat.
20. He is thinking about ——— (go) to the United States.

C. The gerund, not the infinitive, is used as a direct object after certain verbs, such as **practice, finish, stop, enjoy, consider, mind,** and **avoid.**

Complete these sentences with the gerund of the verb indicated. Then read them using other verbs.

1. He finished ——— (read) that book last night.
2. It has stopped ——— (rain).

3. She stopped ——— (play) the piano when he came in.
4. I enjoy ——— (dance).
5. Do you mind ——— (turn) off the radio?
6. He avoided ——— (see) her for several days.
7. We considered ——— (go) away for the week end.

Note: Either the gerund or the infinitive may be used after some verbs, such as **begin, start, continue,** and **like.**

He began **to work (working)** at the age of fifteen.
We started **to look (looking)** for an apartment last week.
Please continue **to read (reading)**, Miss Miller.
He likes **to swim (swimming)** better than **to fish (fishing)**.

Herbert from F. Lewis

LESSON XXIII

Wilshire Boulevard, Los Angeles

CALIFORNIA: LOS ANGELES AND SAN FRANCISCO

Like Arizona and New Mexico, California has a Spanish past. The first settlements were made by Franciscan missionaries, of whom Father Serra was the best known. They founded twenty-one missions, extending along the coast from San Diego in the south to San Francisco in the north. The strong Spanish influence is still evident today in most of the place names and in the mission style of architecture, with its arches, balconies, patios, and iron-grilled windows.

One of these missions was Los Angeles, now the largest city on the Pacific Coast with about 2,500,000 inhabitants. The city has grown like a mushroom in recent years and spread over a very large area. Its people are proud of the size and advantages of their city, and there is a great deal of rivalry between Los Angeles and San Francisco. Because of its many beautiful suburbs, its subtropical climate, and its scenery, the "City of the Angels" attracts many new residents as well as visitors from the eastern states; as a matter of fact, native Californians constitute only a small percentage of the population of this region.

The principal advantage of living in Los Angeles or its environs is the climate. Both winter and summer, you can almost live outdoors: your patio is like an outdoor living room; you can swim, go sailing, or lie on the beach; you can play tennis or golf; you can attend a play in an open-air theater, or you can listen to concerts played by the Los Angeles Symphony Orchestra in the Hollywood Bowl; and in the mountains, two hours from the city, you can go climbing or skiing.

The city has developed rapidly both as a rich agricultural center and as a great commercial and industrial community. Fresh fruits and vegetables are sent out in great quantities to other parts of the country and the world. The petroleum industry and the motion-picture industry, the airplane factories and the automobile assembly plants, all have contributed to its growth. Hollywood, now included within the city limits of Los Angeles, is the movie capital of the world, principally because of the variety of natural scenery near the city and the good weather which it enjoys during all seasons of the year. However, Hollywood seems to be more important to the rest of the world than to those who live near it and who have nothing to do with the movie industry.

Five hundred miles north of Los Angeles is San Francisco, which was also a Spanish mission originally. It was a small town until 1849, when large numbers of miners went to California in search of gold. Many of the city's 800,000 inhabitants are descendants of those carefree miners of the gold-rush days, although this important commercial city is no longer a mining town. Its symphony orchestra, its theaters, its art galleries, and its opera season with stars from the Metropolitan Opera in New York make San Francisco the principal cultural center of northern California.

For beauty of location, few cities can compete with San Francisco, built on a hilly peninsula between San Francisco Bay and the Pacific Ocean. The narrow strait, one mile wide, which connects the bay with the ocean is called the Golden Gate, perhaps because of the golden sunsets which may sometimes be seen there. In the bay, which is fifty-five miles long, there are many islands; and around the bay there are several towns, of which the most important are Oakland and Berkeley. Since these two cities across the bay are connected with San Francisco by ferries and a long bridge, the three together are like one large city of more than a million inhabitants.

San Francisco is a city of hills: some of the streets are so steep that stairs are provided for pedestrians, and you must drive your car up or down in low gear. "The diminutive cable cars, which are the streetcars, hold on to the cable tenaciously like spiders and proceed to crawl up the walls, which are the streets."[1] Yet, in spite of the inconvenience of such streets, the most beautiful residential sections are situated on these hills overlooking the Pacific, the bay, or the Golden Gate. Almost in the center of the city rise two outstanding hills called Twin Peaks, through which tunnels have been built to make transportation more rapid to certain residential districts.

Like New York, three thousand miles to the east, San Francisco is a very cosmopolitan city. The Chinese form a large group in the greatly varied population of the city. They occupy one section of the city called Chinatown, where their picturesque houses, stores, restaurants, and theaters still follow the best Chinese traditions. The city also has its Spanish, Mexican, Greek, and Japanese sections.

Another interesting part of the city is the water front.

[1] From Germán Arciniegas, *Rascacielos y Zanahorias*, Bogotá, Librería Suramérica, 1945.

There you can see ships that have come from Australia, China, Japan, the Philippine Islands, and Hawaii, and ships bound for Alaska, New York, and South American ports; you can watch the great fishing fleet; and you can enjoy fresh shrimp, lobsters, crabs, and oysters at one of the restaurants near the wharves. All this activity makes you realize that San Francisco has one of the largest and best harbors in the world.

Unlike Los Angeles, San Francisco has a cool climate the year round, because of the presence of so much water and because of the fog that comes in from the ocean. For this reason, some people would rather live in the cities across the bay, such as Berkeley, where the University of California is located; while others prefer the suburbs on the peninsula south of San Francisco, such as Palo Alto, where Stanford University is situated.

People from across the bay reach San Francisco by the magnificent Bay Bridge, the longest suspension bridge in the world. It is a double-deck bridge, with six lanes for automobile traffic on the upper deck, while buses, trucks, and electric trains cross on the lower level. However, it is the graceful bridge across the Golden Gate which is the longest single-span bridge in existence. This bridge also has six lanes for automobile traffic, and giant ocean liners can pass under it easily. As the link between San Francisco and the Northwest, it saves motorists a long trip around the bay. Can you imagine the view from the city at night? Lights everywhere — on the islands, on the bridges, on the hills of Oakland and Berkeley — a fairyland which can be seen from any hill in San Francisco.

VOCABULARY

assembly plant	fábrica de montaje	**deck**	piso
carefree	despreocupado	**double-deck**	de dos pisos
Chinese	chino, chinos	**environs**	alrededores
community	centro	**fairyland**	país de hadas
cool	fresco	**fleet**	flota
crab	cangrejo	**fog**	niebla
to crawl up	trepar	**giant**	gigantesco
		Golden Gate	Puerta Dorada

graceful	gracioso	to outnumber	exceder en número
Greek	griego		
growth	crecimiento	to overlook	dominar (el océ-
hill	colina	(the ocean)	ano)
hilly	montañoso	pedestrian	peatón
to hold on	agarrarse	percentage	porcentaje
Hollywood Bowl	Hollywood Bowl (nombre de un anfiteatro)	rivalry	rivalidad
		to save	ahorrar
		single-span	de un tramo o un solo arco
iron-grilled	con reja de hierro		
		spider	araña
lane	vía	to spread	extender
level	piso	stairs	escalera
link	eslabón	star	estrella
lobster	langosta	strait	estrecho
low gear	primera (marcha)	tenaciously	tenazmente
lower (deck)	(piso) inferior	truck	camión
mushroom	hongo	twin	gemelo
ocean liner	vapor grande	unlike	diferente de
open-air (adj.)	al aire libre	upper (deck)	(piso) superior
originally	al principio	water front	tierra ribereña
outdoors (adv.)	al aire libre	yet	sin embargo

IDIOMS

bound for	rumbo a
five hundred miles north	quinientas millas al norte
for beauty of	en cuanto a la belleza de
to go climbing	hacer el alpinismo
to go sailing	hacer excursión en buque de vela
to go skiing	ir a esquiar
to have nothing to do with	no tener nada que ver con
in search of	en busca de

CONVERSATION

Answer the following questions in complete sentences.

1. Who was Father Serra? 2. How many missions were founded in California? 3. Where were they located? 4. What signs of the Spanish influence are still evident in

California today? 5. In which part of California is Los Angeles? San Francisco? 6. How do the two cities differ in size? 7. How do their climates differ? 8. What are the principal attractions of Los Angeles? 9. What activities can one enjoy outdoors there? 10. What agricultural products are sent out in great quantities? 11. What are the chief industries of this region? 12. Why is Hollywood one of the best-known cities in the world? 13. How far is San Francisco from Los Angeles? from New York? 14. What do you know about its history? 15. Describe its location. 16. Why is it difficult to drive or walk in some parts of the city? 17. What is Chinatown? What does one see there? 18. What other nationalities are well represented in the population? 19. Why is the water front an interesting section of the city? 20. What are the cultural advantages of San Francisco? 21. What is the Golden Gate? 22. How large is San Francisco Bay? 23. What cities are located across the bay from San Francisco? 24. Where is the University of California? 25. Where is Stanford University? 26. What are the names of San Francisco's two bridges? 27. Which one is the longest suspension bridge in the world? 28. Which one has the longest single span in the world? 29. Which one has a double deck? What is the purpose of each deck? 30. How does the Golden Gate Bridge help motorists? 31. How does the bay look at night from a hill in San Francisco? 32. If you went to San Francisco, would you want to see the bay at night?

PRONUNCIATION

[v] over, movie, evident, university, develop, several, advantage
[dʒ] language, percentage, advantage, disadvantage, package
[d] double, deck, diminutive, during, descendant, day, spider, pedestrian, tradition, wide, hide, hold, gold, good, spread
[ŋ] long, living, sailing, climbing, skiing, extending, beginning, overlooking, nothing, fishing, saving
[r] room, recent, recently, rapidly, rest, remain, rush, reason, residential, restaurant, missionary, factory, scenery, environs, narrow, important, north, far, star, air, year, near, carefree, grilled, grown, crop, strong, strait

Brown Brothers

The Golden Gate Bridge at San Francisco

GRAMMAR

Various Uses of the Five Common Verbs <u>do</u>, <u>make</u>, <u>have</u>, <u>get</u>, <u>take</u>.

A. The verb **do** (**do, did, done**) is used both as an auxiliary and a principal verb.

    1. As an auxiliary, **do** is used in the following ways:

        a. In questions, present and past.

            Do you speak English? **Did** you speak English?
            Does he study hard? **Did** he study hard?

        b. In negative sentences, present and past.

            I **don't** know her. I **did**n't meet her.
            He **doesn't** like it. He **didn't** like it.

        c. In shortened sentences, present and past.

            They always come early, **don't** they?

Fill the blanks in these sentences, using a form of **do.**
1. She knew her lesson, ——— she?
2. He speaks English, but his wife ———.
3. He went to the United States, but she ———.
4. Virginia didn't write to me, and Mary ——— either.
5. She speaks English, and so ——— her sister.
6. She left before I ———.
7. Do you often see her? Yes, I ———.
8. Did you go to class last Friday? No, I ———.

    d. In affirmative sentences, present and past, in order to contradict or emphasize a fact.

> He probably didn't see you. Yes, he **did** see me.
> You may not believe it, but I **did** study.
> I **do** hope that he comes.

2. As a principal verb, **do** is often confused with **make** because both verbs are equivalent to **hacer** in Spanish. Special uses of **do** are:

    a. To indicate a general activity.

> What **are** you **doing** now? I am reading.
> What **did** you **do** yesterday?
> The maid **did** everything that I told her **to do.**
> **Will** you please **do** something for me?
> What can I **do** for you?

    b. With certain nouns, as in these sentences.

> She always **does** her **work** carefully.
> **Did** you **do** your **homework** for today?
> Mrs. Miller **does** her own **housework.**
> I have **to do** my English **lesson** now.
> The maid **does** the **dishes** after each meal.
> He **did** a lot of **business** last month.
> I am going downtown **to do** some **errands.**
> **Will** you please **do** me a **favor?**

B. The verb **make** (**make, made, made**) is used with several common meanings.

    1. **Make** usually means **perform, create, form, produce, construct,** or **manufacture.**

> He is going **to make** a **speech** tonight.
> Let's **make** a **fire** in the fireplace.

> I always **make** a **list** of the things I have to do.
> Shall I **make** some **sandwiches** for the picnic?
> She **made** herself a new **dress**.
> He **made** a **diagram** to show us the way to go.
> **Streetcars** and **locomotives are made** in Philadelphia.
> They **are making plans** for an extensive trip.
> **Will** you please **make** a **copy** of this letter?
> She **didn't make** many **mistakes** in her English.

2. **Make** means **cause to** when it is followed by a noun and the simple form of a verb.

> She **made Robert wait** for half an hour.
> The teacher **made us speak** English.

3. **Make** means **cause to be** when it is followed by a noun or pronoun and an adjective.

> Women **are making** their **dresses longer** now.
> Too much chocolate always **makes her sick**.
> His work **made him** very **tired** at night.

4. **Make** is used in the following idiomatic expressions.

> How much **money does** he **make**?
> It **doesn't make** any **difference** which word you use.
> You must **make** an **effort** to speak English.
> Virginia **makes** her own **bed** every morning.
> Robert **made** a **date** with Virginia.
> She **makes friends** easily.

Practice 1. *Answer these questions, using the correct verb.*

1. Do you **do** an effort or **make** an effort?
2. Do you **do** your work or **make** your work?
3. Do you **do** an errand or **make** an errand?
4. Do you **do** a mistake or **make** a mistake?
5. Do you **do** a favor or **make** a favor?
6. Do you **do** the dishes or **make** the dishes?
7. Do you **do** a list or **make** a list?
8. Do you **do** a speech or **make** a speech?

Practice 2. *Use the correct form of* **do** *or* **make**, *as required, in translating these sentences.*

1. ¿ Por qué no cerró Vd. la puerta?
2. No se le olvide la llave.
3. ¿ Qué está Vd. haciendo?

4. ¿ Qué hizo ella anoche?
5. ¿ Qué hace Vd. los domingos?
6. Ellos vinieron temprano, ¿ no es verdad?
7. Tengo que preparar mi lección de inglés.
8. Ellos hicieron mucho dinero durante la guerra.
9. Roberto lee más que su hermana.
10. ¿ Lee novelas o biografías?
11. El tuvo que hacer un esfuerzo para hacer el trabajo.
12. Quisiera pedirle a Vd. que me hiciera un favor.
13. Ella dice que hará los emparedados.
14. Siempre hago unas faltas en mis frases.
15. No pude hacer la tarea porque estuve enfermo.
16. Voy a hacer una lista de las cosas.
17. Sí, vive en San Francisco. Estoy seguro de eso.
18. Sí, leyó ese libro. El me lo dijo.
19. Ella hizo llevar sombrero a su hija.
20. A veces las cosas pequeñas me enfurecen.

C. The verb **have** (**have, had, had**) is used both as an auxiliary and a principal verb.

1. As an auxiliary, **have** is used with the past participle of the principal verb to form:

   a. The present perfect tense.

   Has he **finished** his lunch yet?
   Yes, but he **hasn't eaten** much.
   I think that he **has lost** his appetite.
   What **have** you **been doing?**
   I have been reading.
   The children **haven't been sleeping** enough recently.

   b. The past perfect tense.

   The class **had** already **begun** when I entered.
   He said he **hadn't been listening.**
   If I **hadn't run,** I would have missed the bus.
   She said that she **hadn't been** there.

   c. The future perfect tense.

   He **will have worked** there five years at the end of this month.
   I **shall have finished** this before you go.
   You **will have eaten** supper by seven o'clock.

d. **The conditional perfect tense.**

   Everything **would have been** fine if it hadn't **rained.**
   If I had had time, **I would have gone.**

2. As a principal verb, **have** is used in the following ways:

   a. To show possession, as the equivalent of **tener.**

   Does Mr. Smith **have** his new car?
   No, he **doesn't have** it yet.
   He still **has** his old one.
   Do you **have** your book?
   No, I **don't have** it here.

   b. With **to** to show necessity, as the equivalent of **tener que.** The auxiliary **do** must be used with **have to** in the interrogative and negative forms.

   Do you **have to** study much to learn English?
   Yes, we **have to** study a little every day.
   You **don't have to** leave now, do you?
   I wrote the sentences, but I **didn't have to.**
   Did he **have to** wait for her?
   Yes, he **had to** wait almost half an hour.

   c. With names of things to eat or drink, or with the name of a meal, as the equivalent of **comer or tomar.**

   Which are you going **to have,** tea, coffee, or milk?
   Have you **had** breakfast?
   No, I am going **to have** breakfast now.
   Did you **have** a good dinner?
   Yes, we **had** an excellent dinner.

   d. To mean **ask** or **cause to,** as the equivalent of **hacer** or **pedir.**

   We **had** them **bring** the radio to the house.
   We **had** the radio **brought** to the house.

Note: In the first example, the simple form of the verb **bring is** used because **they bring the radio.** In the second example, the past participle **brought** is used because **the radio is brought** by someone not mentioned.

Practice translating these sentences, using a form of **have.**
1. El profesor nos hizo pronunciar las palabras.
2. Me hice servir el desayuno en la cama.
3. Voy a hacerme cortar el pelo.
4. Voy a hacer que Juan me corte el pelo.
5. Que lo haga Jaime.
6. Hice que el muchacho me comprara estampillas.
7. Le pediré al chófer que pare allí.
8. ¿ Dónde hace Vd. limpiar sus vestidos ?
9. Le hice lustrarme los zapatos.
10. Me hice lustrar los zapatos.
11. Tienen una casa bonita en el campo.
12. No tengo tiempo para escribirle ahora.
13. No tuve tiempo para escribir mis frases.
14. Tuvimos una clase muy interesante.
15. Tenemos que ir a conseguir los billetes.
16. Vd. no tiene que ponerse abrigo.
17. ¿ Tuvo Vd. que esperar mucho tiempo ?
18. No tuve que esperarla.
19. ¿ Qué va Vd. a tomar ? Voy a tomar cerveza.
20. Virginia no ha tomado su café.
21. Todavía no hemos conseguido los billetes.
22. Si no hubiera tenido un resfriado, habría ido.
23. Yo había escrito la carta antes de recibir la de él.
24. Hace un año que vivimos aquí.
25. Hacía veinte minutos que estaban esperando cuando llegamos.

D The verb **get** (**get, got, got** or **gotten**), like the verb **make**, has many different meanings.

1. **Get** is a popular substitute for several other verbs.

I need **to get** some information about it.	(conseguir, obtener)
She is going **to get** her dress at the cleaner's.	(recoger, buscar)
Where **did** you **get** that hat ?	(comprar)
Did you **get** a letter today ?	(recibir)
They are going **to get married** soon.	(casarse)
The Millers don't have a maid **to get** the meals.	(preparar)
When **did** you **get** here ?	(llegar)

Virginia is feeling better. I hope she
will **get well** soon.   (ponerse bien)
They **got ready** in ten minutes.   (alistarse)
I hope that you **will** not **get wet**.   (mojarse)

2. **Get** is sometimes used in conversation in place of **have** meaning **cause to**.

I am going **to get** my hair cut.
I **got** Henry to cut my hair.
Where **do** you **get** your clothes cleaned?
He **got** his shoes shined this morning.
I'll **get** him to buy me some stamps.

Note: **Have** in this meaning is used with the simple form of the verb or the past participle; **get** is used with the infinitive with **to**, or the past participle.

I **had** him **polish** my shoes. (*simple form*)
I **had** my shoes **polished**. (*past participle*)

I **got** him **to polish** my shoes. (*infinitive with to*)
I **got** my shoes **polished**. (*past participle*)

3. **Get** is used in many idioms. (See two-word verbs in Lesson XXIV.)

What time **did** you **get up** this morning?   (levantarse)
How can I **get rid of** those ants?   (deshacerse de)
I think he **will get ahead** in his new job.   (avanzar)
He had **to get a letter off** before leaving the office.   (despachar una carta)

4. **Get** has two past participles, **got** and **gotten**. North Americans use **gotten** more frequently than **got**. (See Lesson XIII, page 153.) **I've gotten** (or, more rarely, **I've got**) is equivalent to **he conseguido, he comprado, he preparado, he recibido, he llegado,** etc.

She **has gotten** lazy.
He **has** already **gotten** the tickets.
Mrs. Miller **hasn't gotten** dinner yet.
Has he **gotten** his new car yet?
I **haven't gotten** any letters this week.
My cold **has gotten** better since yesterday.

Haven't they **gotten** married yet?
We **have gotten** as far as California on our trip across the United States.

Practice using the correct form of **get** *in these sentences.*
1. I am going to ——— my suit tomorrow.
2. I have an important letter to ——— off tonight.
3. He works hard. I am sure that he will ——— ahead in his business.
4. What time do you usually ——— up?
5. When we moved, we ——— rid of many old things.
6. Shall we ——— ready to go now?
7. It rained hard; didn't you ——— wet?
8. There were so many people in the theater that we ——— very warm.
9. She usually ——— tired very easily.
10. I hope that you will ——— better soon.
11. They ——— married in a hurry, didn't they?
12. I am going to ——— a book to read.
13. She has ——— thin this summer.
14. We didn't ——— a newspaper this morning.
15. I ——— my father to play bridge.
16. She ——— a new hat yesterday.
17. When do you think they will ——— here?
18. Mrs. Miller is ——— breakfast now.

E. The verb **take**, (**take, took, taken**) also has several meanings.

    1. **Take** is sometimes equivalent to **tomar** in Spanish.

        Do you **take** cream and sugar in your coffee?
        Shall we **take** a bus or a streetcar?
        Take your books, and put them on the table.
        Have you **taken** your medicine?
        Did the army **take** many prisoners?
        She always **takes** notes on what the teacher says.

    2. **Take** is sometimes equivalent to **llevar** when it means **take something somewhere** or **take someone somewhere**.

        Aren't you going **to take your umbrella** with you?
        Get in. I'll **take you** there in my car.

    3. **Take** is used in many idioms. It is necessary to learn these expressions.

Let's **take a walk** this afternoon. (dar un paseo)
I prefer **to take a ride**. (pasear en auto)
Which road **shall** we **take**? (seguir)
I want **to take** some **pictures** with my new camera. (sacar fotografías)
They **took** a **trip** through the West. (hacer un viaje)
She **is taking** a course in history this year. (seguir)
He had **to take** an **examination** yesterday. (presentarse a examen, sufrir examen)

The lecture **will take place** tomorrow evening. (tener lugar)
How long **does** it **take** to learn English? (necesitarse)
He **took charge of** the office during my absence. (encargarse de)
Does the maid **take care of** the children? (cuidar)
She **takes after** her mother. (parecerse a)

*Practice using the correct form of **take** in these sentences.*

1. Will this bus ——— me downtown?
2. Virginia is ——— an examination now.
3. Shall we ——— the elevator or walk up?
4. Mrs. Miller always ——— sugar in her tea.
5. I ——— a walk through the park yesterday.
6. We are ——— a course in English.
7. Whom do you ——— after, your father or your mother?
8. I haven't ——— any notes on this lesson.
9. How long does it ——— to go there by train?
10. It usually ——— about four hours to go from Washington to New York by train.
11. I'll ——— you downtown and show you where to go.
12. She ——— some good pictures last week end.
13. The man was ——— to the hospital after the accident.
14. She was so cold that she ——— a bath to get warm.
15. I think you had better ——— your raincoat.
16. He has ——— care of our garden for many years.
17. The child ——— her medicine as if she liked it.
18. After they had had dinner, they ——— a ride.
19. This road will ——— us by their country house.
20. Have you ——— many trips in this country?

Charles Phelps Cushing

LESSON XXIV

Logging with a Tractor in the State of Washington

THE NORTHWEST

Going north from San Francisco, we travel through northern California into the Northwest. The forested mountains and fertile valleys of this region provide great quantities of timber and agricultural products, while its streams furnish an abundance of water power and fish.

The chief waterway of the Northwest is the Columbia River, which flows between the states of Oregon and Washington and, in fact, forms the boundary between them for many miles. It is known as one of the greatest salmon streams in the world and is equally famous for its beautiful scenery. We can drive on a paved highway, along the banks of the river, over mountains and through tunnels, for more than three hundred miles. Not only is this river navigable for five hundred miles, but it is also capable of generating more electricity than any other river in North America. For this purpose the government has built two large dams on the river: the Grand Coulee Dam and the Bonneville Dam.

Although Sir Francis Drake sailed along this coast in 1579, the first white settlers were the American and English explorers, fur traders, and missionaries, who did not arrive until the middle of the nineteenth century. By 1890, many Americans from the East had gone west to engage in farming, lumbering, fishing, mining, or shipbuilding. Today the whole Pacific Coast region, from San Diego to Seattle, is young in spirit, gay, progressive, and optimistic.

The largest city in Oregon and one of the outstanding ports in the world for the shipping of lumber is Portland. Its population is close to 450,000. It is also known as the "City of Roses," since roses and other flowers bloom outdoors in this mild climate the year round. While Portland is celebrating its annual Rose Festival in June, the snow-capped peak of Mount Hood offers a beautiful winter scene in the background.

In the northwest corner of the United States lies the city of Seattle, the largest in the state of Washington and in the Northwest (population 500,000). The city's finest homes are beautifully located on the hills surrounding Puget Sound, while high mountain ranges rise to the east and to the west of the city. Seattle has a milder climate than any other city of the United States in the same latitude because of the presence of so much water near by and because of the prevailing winds from ocean to land.

Located about a thousand miles north of San Francisco, Seattle is the principal port in the Northwest. It is one of the few deep seaports on the West Coast. Freighters bring tea, silks, and spices from the Orient and carry gold, copper, fish, and furs from Alaska; the ships go back with lumber, hides, flour, machinery, big red Washington apples, and other food products. Since Seattle is one of the largest salmon markets in the world, great quantities of that fish are packed at the city's canneries. Other important industries include the manufacture of airplanes and of various lumber products.

Now we have come a long way from Miami, Florida, to Seattle, Washington, where our imaginary journey must end. We have visited some of the old cities of the East and some of the newer cities of the West, the industrial city of Chicago in the Middle West, and the picturesque city of New Orleans in the South. We have learned a little of the history of these places, and we have gazed at some of the scenic wonders of the nation. However, we have touched only the high spots, that is to say, the principal cities and regions of the country; but we realize now that New York is only one of the many interesting places in the United States.

VOCABULARY

background	fondo	**prevailing**	predominante
to bloom	florecer	**progressive**	progresista
cannery	fábrica de conservas	**Puget Sound**	Puget Sound (*nombre de un estrecho grande*)
close (*adj.*)	cercano		
copper	cobre		
to engage in	dedicarse a	**range**	cordillera
equally	igualmente	**to sail**	navegar
flour	harina	**scenic**	pintoresco
forested	con bosques	**snow-capped**	nevado
freighter	buque de carga	**spice**	especia
fur trader	negociante en pieles	**stream**	río, corriente
furs (*pl.*)	pieles	**timber**	bosques; madera
gay	alegre	**to touch**	tocar
to go back	volver, regresar	**various**	de varias clases
lumbering	industria de maderas	**water power**	energía hidráulica
mild	suave	**waterway**	vía fluvial
paved	pavimentado	**whole**	entero

IDIOMS

to come a long way	cubrir una gran distancia
high spots	puntos importantes
that is to say	es decir

CONVERSATION

Answer the following questions in complete sentences.

1. What two states are part of the region called the Northwest? 2. What do the mountains provide? the valleys? the streams? 3. Where is the Columbia River? 4. Why is it one of the great rivers of the United States? 5. What are the names of the two large dams on the river? 6. Who first sailed along this coast? 7. Who were the first white settlers? 8. What are the occupations of the people there? 9. What kind of climate does this region have? 10. What are the principal cities of the Northwest? 11. What is Portland noted for? 12. Why is it called the "City of Roses"? 13. Where is Seattle located? 14. How far is it from San Francisco? 15. Why is it such an important port? 16. What do the freighters bring from the Orient? 17. With what products do they go back? 18. What is the purpose of the canneries in Seattle? 19. What adjectives characterize the cities of the East? the cities of the West? Chicago? New Orleans? 20. What is the meaning of **high spots**? 21. Have you enjoyed this imaginary trip across the United States? 22. Which city was the most interesting one to you? Why? 23. Would you like to study more about the cities of the United States? the history? the geography? the art and the music? the customs?

PRONUNCIATION

I. Read the following words, observing the position of the accent.

prófitable	appróximately	élevator
návigable	beáutifully	península
reásonable	horizóntally	móuntain
cómfortable	vértically	árchitecture
sítuated	ínteresting	manufácture
lócated	cathédral	machínery

situátion	democrátic	cúltivate
locátion	aristocrátic	cúlture
occupátion	demócracy	átmosphere
populátion	aristócracy	pioneér
índustry	consérvatory	réalize
indústrial	imáginary	oríginate
ágriculture	revolútionary	refínery
agricúltural	sýmphony	séttlement
cómmerce	órchestra	devélopment
commércial	muséum	góvernment

II. There is at least one silent letter in each of these words. Try to pronounce the words correctly.

comb	freight	walk	Lincoln	whole
climb	although	talk	autumn	wrong
han**d**kerchief	daughter	half	island	write
We**d**nesday	ought	should	listen	two
sign	thought	would	castle	building
foreign	knife	could	often	vegetable
foreigner	know	salmon	answer	sailed
hi**g**her	knock	palm	toward	touched

GRAMMAR

I. Two-Word Verbs.

A. The two-word verb is a phenomenon of the English language which is enough to confuse any student. Since the list of these verbs is endless, in this lesson it is possible to indicate only a few of the common ones and briefly explain their use.

B. A two-word verb is a one-syllable verb of Anglo-Saxon origin followed by a preposition or adverb which changes the usual meaning of the verb so that the two words together have a new meaning. They may be divided into two groups: those which are intransitive (inseparable) and those which are transitive (separable).

  Intransitive: I am going **to get up** early tomorrow.
  She **is getting in** (**into**) the car now.

Transitive: He **turned on** the light.
He **turned** the light **on**.
He **turned** it **on**.

Note 1: A noun object may follow or separate the transitive two-word verb. A pronoun object always separates the two-word verb. When separated, the preposition or adverb comes immediately after the object.

Note 2: There are also a few three-word intransitive verbs, such as **get along with, go back on,** and **put up with.**

C. Here are some of the common intransitive two-word verbs.

1. We are going **to call on** the Millers today. (visitar)
2. I'll **call for** you at two o'clock. (**ir** a buscar)
3. The work of a teacher **calls for a** lot of patience. (exigir)
4. When **are** you **coming over** to see me? (venir a mi casa)
5. How **are** you **getting along** in English? (marchar)
6. **Does** Paul **get along** well **with** his classmates? (simpatizar con)
7. When **did** you **get back** from your vacation? (volver)
8. He **got in (into)** the car and waited for us. (subir a)
9. I saw them as **I was getting out of** the taxi. (bajarse de)
10. The buses are so crowded at noon that it is almost impossible **to get on** or **get off.** (subir, bajarse)
11. I hope you **will get over** your cold soon. (ponerse bien)
12. What time **do** you **get through with** your work? (terminar)
13. They used **to get together** every week to play bridge. (reunirse)
14. I **don't** usually **get up** so early on Sunday. (levantarse)
15. He couldn't guess the answer, but he didn't want **to give up,** either. (darse por vencido)
16. Although she didn't want to go, she finally **gave in** and went with us. (asentir)
17. They **are going away** next week. (irse)
18. I promise to do that, and **I won't go back** on my word. (faltar a)
19. Please **go on with** what you were doing. (**continuar**)
20. I shall be glad **to go over** this letter with you. (examinar)
21. The program **went over** very **well,** didn't it? (tener éxito)
22. Who is going **to look after** the dog while you are gone? (cuidar)
23. **Look out for** the steps. (cuidado con)
24. I **put up with** the noise as long as I could. (tolerar)

25. As I was walking down the street, **I ran into (across)** an old friend. (dar con)
26. Will you have time **to see about** getting the tickets? (ocuparse de)
27. His intentions are quite obvious. It is not difficult **to see through** him. (calar)
28. The plane **took off** an hour late. (despegar)

D. Here are some of the transitive two-word verbs, which **are** separable.

1. The teacher **brought out** that point very clearly. (dar énfasis a)
2. Mrs. Miller **brought up** her children to be very polite. (criar)
3. They had **to call off** the game because of the rain. (cancelar)
4. I **called up** Mrs. Smith, but no one answered. (telefonear)
5. **Will** you please **fill out** this application blank? (llenar)
6. **Will** the teacher **give back** our papers tomorrow? (devolver)
7. He **has given up** his job with that company. (renunciar a)
8. The teacher promised **to look over** this letter for me and to correct the mistakes in English. (examinar)
9. You should **look up** Mr. Reed when you are in Chicago. (buscar)
10. **Did** you **look up** the word in a dictionary? (buscar)
11. She is going **to make over** that dress for me. (reformar)
12. We **picked out** some new records yesterday. (escoger)
13. The children **picked up** the magazines and put them on the table. (recoger)
14. Johnny always **puts away** his toys like a good little boy. (colocar en su lugar)
15. They **have put off** their trip until next month. (aplazar)
16. **Did** he **put on** his hat and coat? (ponerse)
17. It **took** them an hour **to put out** the fire. (apagar)
18. When **are** you going **to take back** those books? (devolver)
19. Don't you want **to take off** your coat? It's warm here. (quitarse)
20. She went to the library **to take out** a book. (sacar)
21. She **tried on** several hats before buying one. (probarse)
22. We **turned off** the radio, and we **turned out** the lights. (apagar)
23. Please **turn on** the radio. (encender)

298

Practice reading the sentences in D in three ways, following the example of the first one.

    1. The teacher brought out that point very clearly.

    The teacher brought that point out very clearly.
    The teacher brought it out very clearly.

II. A Few Things to Remember.

A. The following uses or forms of verbs should be noted.

1. The pronunciation of the regular past tense: **asked, lived, looked, followed, gazed, watched, developed, started, inspected, completed, visited, depended, included**
2. The people **are** and the news **is**
3. **Have** breakfast, lunch, tea, dinner, or supper
4. **Say** a thing **to** a person, or **tell** a person something
5. **Do** a favor and **make** an effort
6. She **began** to study English two years **ago**.
7. She **has studied** English **for** two years.
8. She **has studied** English **since** 1965.
9. I **haven't seen** him **yet**.
10. I wanted (asked, told) them **to come**.

B. The following expressions with prepositions are useful.

1. **Wait for** a person or thing
2. **Think of** or **about** a person or thing
3. **Think of doing** something.
4. **Dream of** or **about** a person or thing
5. **Remind** a person **of** something or **to do** something
6. **Enter** a house, a building, a room (*no preposition*)
7. **Between** two people or things; **among** several
8. **The longest** bridge **in** the world
9. **Arrive in** a country or city; **arrive at** a city or a place within a city
10. He married a **Chicago** girl. (*no preposition*)
11. **Borrow from** a person; **buy from** a person
12. **Depend on, insist on, laugh at, differ from**
13. **Get on** or **off** a streetcar, a bus, a train, a plane
14. **Get into** or **out of** a taxi, a car, a plane
15. **Put on** or **take off** clothes
16. **Turn on** or **turn off** the light, the radio

C. The following English constructions occur frequently and should be especially noted.

1. **President** Roosevelt, **Dr.** Mayo, **General** MacArthur, **Captain** Smith, Madison Avenue, Brazil, Argentina, Canada (*no article*)
2. He is **a** lawyer (**a** doctor, **a** teacher, **an** engineer).
3. **What is** the meaning of that word?
4. **Whose book** is this? (*order*)
5. I like the book **very much.** (*order*)
6. The big **one,** the big **ones,** this **one,** that **one**
7. Taller than, shorter than, colder than, warmer than, **as** tall **as,** as short **as, not so** cold **as, not so** warm **as**
8. It is **so warm** today. It is **such a warm day.**
9. **Little** English, **a little** English, few people, **a few** people
10. I didn't receive **any** letters, or I received **no** letters.
11. He looks **like** his father. I spoke to him **as I always do.** (*Like is a preposition, and as is a conjunction.*)
12. Do you know what time **it is?** (*order*)

300

REVIEW LESSON VIII

I. Pronounce the past tense of the following verbs.

proceed	generate	occur	provide	furnish
contribute	reach	attract	outnumber	sail
look	travel	play	occupy	arrive
return	flow	attend	follow	visit
predominate	found	listen	inspect	carry
establish	watch	develop	enjoy	cross
live	change	start	prefer	end
believe	imagine	include	pass	engage
form	gaze	stay	save	penetrate
depend	extend	call	stretch	touch
replace	connect	climb	compete	realize

II. Change these sentences to the interrogative form.

1. California has a Spanish past.
2. The first settlements were made by Franciscan monks.
3. The missionaries founded twenty-one missions.
4. The Spanish influence is still evident today.
5. Los Angeles attracts many visitors from the East.
6. The city has developed rapidly into an industrial center.
7. Miners went to San Francisco in search of gold.
8. Oakland and Berkeley lie across the bay from San Francisco.
9. Some people would rather live across the bay.
10. Some people prefer the warm suburbs down the peninsula.
11. The Golden Gate connects the bay with the ocean.
12. The Northwest has a mild climate.

13. Sir Francis **Drake** sailed along this coast.
14. The Columbia River flows between Oregon and Washington.
15. A paved highway follows the river for three hundred miles.
16. Seattle is the port closest to Alaska.
17. Freighters bring gold, copper, fish, and furs from Alaska.
18. Great quantities of salmon are packed at the canneries.
19. We have touched only the high spots.
20. You realize now that New York is not the United States.

III. *Change these sentences to the negative form.*

1. The Great American Desert is like the Sahara Desert.
2. Agriculture depends on irrigation.
3. We bought some Navajo blankets.
4. We will be in Los Angeles on New Year's Day.
5. We can attend the concert in the Hollywood Bowl.
6. They are going swimming this afternoon.
7. They climbed to the top of the mountain.
8. Their house has iron-grilled windows and a patio.
9. I'd rather walk up the hills in San Francisco.
10. He drove up the hills in low gear.
11. The fog comes in from the ocean every morning.
12. She could watch the ships at the water front all day.
13. He remembered the name of the street.
14. He was surprised at the distances in the West.
15. They stayed in California a month.

IV. *Answer the following questions, using* for, since, *or* ago.

1. How long have you been in this class?
2. How long have you studied English?
3. How long have you lived in this city?
4. How long have you been married?
5. How long have you worked in your present job?
6. How long has Virginia been in the United States?
7. How long have you been waiting for the bus?
8. How long has it been raining?
9. How long have you known me?
10. How long has he had his car?
11. How long ago did you begin to study English?
12. How long ago did he go to work there?
13. How long ago did he come to this country?

14. How long ago did you have something to eat?
15. How long ago was she in the United States?
16. How long ago did you see her?
17. How long ago did you talk with him?
18. How long ago did you have your hair cut?
19. How long ago did you go to the dentist?
20. How long ago did you get your tickets?

V. Use the correct form of <u>say</u> or <u>tell</u>, as required, in these sentences.

1. Please ——— me what time it is.
2. He ——— that he gets up at six o'clock.
3. Please ——— us a story.
4. She ——— me that she would look after the children.
5. He ——— "Look out for the cars!"
6. He ——— that he will get through at five-thirty.
7. They ——— us to take this streetcar, didn't they?
8. Yesterday his wife ——— to him, "Why don't you get rid of that old hat?"
9. They ——— that they were going to play bridge.
10. His mother ——— him to pick up the paper.
11. He always ———, "I'll see about it."
12. Can you ——— me how to get to the post office?
13. She ——— that she won't be here next week.
14. ——— that word again, please.
15. Do you often have your fortune ———?
16. When are you going to ——— about your trip?
17. He ——— that she was very clever.
18. Why didn't you ——— her to wait for you?
19. They ——— that the climate is very mild there.
20. The teacher always ——— us to practice our English.

VI. Practice reading these sentences with the proper auxiliary verb.

A. Habit (*past*): **used to.**

1. I ——— imagine that I saw castles in the rocks.
2. We ——— live on State Street.
3. He ——— call her up every day.
4. They often ——— call on us.
5. I never ——— realize how important it was.
6. She ——— write her family a letter on Sundays.

B. Future: **will, shall** (*first person*), **will have, shall have** (*first person*), **be going to.** Questions with the first person: **shall.**

1. ——— you be ready at six o'clock?
2. No, I ——— not be ready until six-thirty.
3. She ——— replace Miss Jones next week.
4. We ——— take the road near the river.
5. I ——— finished it when you arrive.
6. He ——— taken all his examinations by Saturday.
7. What time ——— we meet?
8. ——— I wait for you?
9. Where ——— we spend our vacation?
10. When ——— I send the package?

C. Conditional: **would, should** (*first person*), **would have, should have** (*first person*).

1. What did he say the price ——— be?
2. I thought that I ——— go to bed early.
3. If we had time, we ——— take you home in the car.
4. I ——— like to take a walk this afternoon.
5. I ——— liked to take a ride yesterday.
6. If they had insisted, we ——— gone.

D. Ability: **can, could, could have.**

1. He says that he ———'t speak English.
2. He said that he ———n't speak English.
3. She said that she ———n't go tomorrow.
4. I ———n't come to class yesterday.
5. Who ——— tell me where she lives?
6. If they ——— find a house, they would move.
7. I wish that I ——— see her.
8. I wish that I ——— seen her.

E. Permission: **may, might.**

1. ——— I ask you a question?
2. You ——— keep the book as long as you wish.
3. I said that you ——— keep the book.
4. Her mother says that she ——— go with us.
5. Her mother said that she ——— go with us.

F. Possibility: **may, might, may have, might have.**

1. Virginia ——— spend another year there.
2. I thought that it ——— rain today.

3. You ——— like the climate of San Francisco.
4. We ——— go by plane if it doesn't cost too much.
5. He ——— been there, but I didn't see him.
6. I haven't heard from her for a long time; she ——— gotten married.
7. She ——— come when I was downtown.

G. Probability: **must, must have.**

1. It ——— be twelve o'clock now.
2. He ——— be very busy.
3. You ——— been tired when you returned.
4. Since no one answers the telephone, they ——— gone out.
5. The streets are wet this morning; it ——— rained all night.

H. Necessity: **must, have to, had to.**

1. I ——— change my shoes before going out.
2. You ——— try to find it.
3. Last night we ——— take a taxi.
4. He will ——— see the doctor.
5. They said that they would ——— leave early.
6. What time did you say that you ——— go?

I. Obligation: **should, ought to, should have, ought to have, had better.**

1. I ——— write some letters, but I am tired.
2. You ——— save some of your money.
3. We ——— not believe everything that we hear.
4. She ——— gone with us last night.
5. He ——— not ——— said that.
6. I ——— not ——— waited so long to get a ticket.

VII. Fill each blank with the indirect form of the direct question, as indicated.

1. Who is Sir Francis Drake?
   Do you know **who Sir Francis Drake is?**
2. Where is the Columbia River?
   Do you know ———?
3. What are the principal products of the Northwest?
   Can you tell me ———?
4. What do the freighters bring from the Orient?
   I don't remember ———.
5. What is the name of that dam?
   He doesn't know ———.

6. Why is Great Salt Lake so salty?
   She doesn't understand ———.
7. Who are the Mormons?
   Do you know ———?
8. Why did Coronado return to Mexico after two years?
   Do you remember ———?
9. When was San Francisco founded?
   Do you know ———?
10. What are the principal attractions of Los Angeles?
    Please tell me ———.
11. What is the Golden Gate?
    Can you tell me ———?
12. How large is San Francisco Bay?
    I don't remember ———.
13. How long is the Bay Bridge?
    Do you know ———?
14. Where is the University of California?
    Please ask him ———.
15. How does the climate of San Francisco differ from that of Los Angeles?
    Do you know ———?
16. Where can one see a lot of salmon canneries?
    Do you know ———?
17. What did they say about the trip?
    Did she tell you ———?
18. Whose Indian blanket is this?
    I don't know ———.
19. What time is it now?
    Can you tell me ———?
20. Which reading lesson did you enjoy the most?
    Please tell me ———.

VIII. Idiom Review. Complete the idiomatic expressions in the following sentences.

1. Did you ——— a good time last Saturday?
2. She spends a great ——— of time in her garden.
3. They have three English classes ——— week.
4. I am so glad to ——— seen you.
5. She asked them ——— with her.
6. We sat ——— the main floor because we don't like to sit ——— the balcony.
7. He always arrives ——— time. He always arrives ——— time for class.

8. Can you make yourself ———? ([hacerse] entender)
9. You must ——— careful to dial the right number.
10. The phone is not working; it is ——— order.
11. Did you ——— him ——— that you were coming? (avisar)
12. If you walk straight ahead, you can't ——— it. (equivocarse)
13. Can the druggist ——— the prescription quickly?
14. He has worked so hard that he is very ———-down. (agotado)
15. He has a ——— throat and a fever.
16. One thing depends ——— another.
17. You must make your reservation ——— advance.
18. They live just ——— the corner.
19. ——— the way, what time is it?
20. Is he going with us? He ———. (quiere ir)
21. They have nothing to ———- with their neighbors.
22. He makes his ——— by selling cars.
23. How are we going to get ——— of these old magazines?
24. How long does it ——— to learn English?
25. Now, ——— we review this book from the beginning?

APPENDIX

I. Conjugation of the Regular Verb <u>ask</u> (preguntar, pedir).

PRINCIPAL PARTS
ask, asked, asked

ACTIVE VOICE

Present Infinitive
to ask

Perfect Infinitive
to have asked

Present Participle
asking

Perfect Participle
having asked

Past Participle
asked

INDICATIVE

Simple *Progressive*

Present

I ask	I am asking
you ask	you are asking
he (she, it) asks	he (she, it) is asking
we ask	we are asking
you ask	you are asking
they ask	they are asking

Past

I asked
you asked
he (she, it) asked
we asked
you asked
they asked

I was asking
you were asking
he (she, it) was asking
we were asking
you were asking
they were asking

Future

I will (shall) ask
you will ask
he (she, it) will ask
we will (shall) ask
you will ask
they will ask

I will (shall) be asking
you will be asking
he (she, it) will be asking
we will (shall) be asking
you will be asking
they will be asking

Conditional

I would (should) ask
you would ask
he (she, it) would ask
we would (should) ask
you would ask
they would ask

I would (should) be asking
you would be asking
he (she, it) would be asking
we would (should) be asking
you would be asking
they would be asking

Present Perfect

I have asked
you have asked
he (she, it) has asked
we have asked
you have asked
they have asked

I have been asking
you have been asking
he (she, it) has been asking
we have been asking
you have been asking
they have been asking

Past Perfect

I had asked
you had asked
he (she, it) had asked
we had asked
you had asked
they had asked

I had been asking
you had been asking
he (she, it) had been asking
we had been asking
you had been asking
they had been asking

Future Perfect

I will (shall) have asked
you will have asked
he (she, it) will have asked
we will (shall) have asked
you will have asked
they will have asked

I will (shall) have been asking
you will have been asking
he (she, it) will have been asking
we will (shall) have been asking
you will have been asking
they will have been asking

Conditional Perfect

I would (should) have asked

you would have asked
he (she, it) would have asked

we would (should) have asked

you would have asked
they would have asked

I would (should) have been asking
you would have been asking
he (she, it) would have been asking
we would (should) have been asking
you would have been asking
they would have been asking

IMPERATIVE
(second person, singular and plural)

Affirmative: ask   **Negative:** do not ask

SUBJUNCTIVE

Simple   *Progressive*

Present

that I ask
that you ask
that he (she, it) ask
that we ask
that you ask
that they ask

that I be asking
that you be asking
that he (she, it) be asking
that we be asking
that you be asking
that they be asking

Past

that I asked
that you asked
that he (she, it) asked
that we asked
that you asked
that they asked

that I were asking
that you were asking
that he (she, it) were asking
that we were asking
that you were asking
that they were asking

Past Perfect

that I had asked	that I had been asking
that you had asked	that you had been asking
that he (she, it) had asked	that he (she, it) had been asking
that we had asked	that we had been asking
that you had asked	that you had been asking
that they had asked	that they had been asking

PASSIVE VOICE

Present Infinitive	**Perfect Infinitive**
to be asked	to have been asked
Present Participle	**Perfect Participle**
being asked	having been asked

Past Participle

been asked [1]

INDICATIVE

Simple   *Progressive*

Present

I am asked	I am being asked [2]
you are asked	you are being asked
he (she, it) is asked	he (she, it) is being asked
we are asked	we are being asked
you are asked	you are being asked
they are asked	they are being asked

Past

I was asked	I was being asked [2]
you were asked	you were being asked
he (she, it) was asked	he (she, it) was being asked
we were asked	we were being asked
you were asked	you were being asked
they were asked	they were being asked

---

[1] Only in the formation of compound tenses. When used as an adjective, the past participle omits the word **been**.

[2] The progressive form (form with **ing**) is used only in the present and past indicative tenses of the passive.

Future

I will (shall) be asked
you will be asked
he (she, it) will be asked
we will (shall) be asked
you will be asked
they will be asked

Conditional

I would (should) be asked
you would be asked
he (she, it) would be asked
we would (should) be asked
you would be asked
they would be asked

Present Perfect

I have been asked
you have been asked
he (she, it) has been asked
we have been asked
you have been asked
they have been asked

Past Perfect

I had been asked
you had been asked
he (she, it) had been asked
we had been asked
you had been asked
they had been asked

Future Perfect

I will (shall) have been asked
you will have been asked
he (she, it) will have been asked
we will (shall) have been asked
you will have been asked
they will have been asked

Conditional Perfect

I would (should) have been asked
you would have been asked
he (she, it) would have been asked
we would (should) have been asked
you would have been asked
they would have been asked

IMPERATIVE
(second person, singular and plural)

Affirmative: be asked **Negative:** do not be asked

SUBJUNCTIVE

Present

that I be asked
that you be asked
that he (she, it) be asked
that we be asked
that you be asked
that they be asked

Past

that I were asked
that you were asked
that he (she, it) were asked
that we were asked
that you were asked
that they were asked

Past Perfect

that I had been asked
that you had been asked
that he (she, it) had been asked
that we had been asked
that you had been asked
that they had been asked

II. Principal Parts of Irregular Verbs.

Present	Past	Past Participle	
be	was, were	been	ser, estar
become	became	become	llegar a ser, hacerse, ponerse

begin	began	begun	empezar
break	broke	broken	romper
bring	brought	brought	traer
buy	bought	bought	comprar
catch	caught	caught	coger
choose	chose	chosen	escoger
come	came	come	venir
cost	cost	cost	costar
cut	cut	cut	cortar
die	died	died	morir
do	did	done	hacer
drink	drank	drunk	beber
drive	drove	driven	manejar (*un automóvil*)
eat	ate	eaten	comer
fall	fell	fallen	caer(se)
feel	felt	felt	sentir(se)
find	found	found	encontrar, hallar
fly	flew	flown	volar
forget	forgot	forgotten	olvidar(se)
freeze	froze	frozen	congelar
get	got	got, gotten	conseguir
give	gave	given	dar
go	went	gone	ir
grow	grew	grown	crecer
hang	hung, *hanged* [1]	hung, *hanged* [1]	colgar
have	had	had	tener, haber
hear	heard	heard	oír
hold	held	held	tener, sostener
keep	kept	kept	guardar
know	knew	known	saber, conocer
lay	laid	laid	colocar
leave	left	left	salir, dejar
lend	lent	lent	prestar
let	let	let	permitir, dejar
lie	lay	lain	estar situado
lose	lost	lost	perder
make	made	made	hacer
mean	meant	meant	significar
meet	met	met	encontrar(se), conocer
pay	paid	paid	pagar

[1] See page 153 for an explanation of these two forms.

put	put	put	poner
read [rid]	read [rɛd]	read [rɛd]	leer
ride	rode	ridden	montar, pasear en ve- hículo
ring	rang	rung	sonar, timbrar
rise	rose	risen	levantarse
run	ran	run	correr
say	said	said	decir
see	saw	seen	ver
sell	sold	sold	vender
send	sent	sent	enviar
shake	shook	shaken	sacudir
shine	shone, *shined* [1]	shone, *shined* [1]	brillar, lustrar
sing	sang	sung	cantar
sit	sat	sat	sentarse, estar sen- tado
sleep	slept	slept	dormir
speak	spoke	spoken	hablar
spend	spent	spent	gastar, pasar
stand	stood	stood	ponerse de pie, estar de pie
steal	stole	stolen	robar
swim	swam	swum	nadar
swing	swung	swung	balancear(se)
take	took	taken	tomar, llevar
teach	taught	taught	enseñar
tear	tore	torn	romper, rasgar
tell	told	told	decir, contar
think	thought	thought	pensar
throw	threw	thrown	echar, lanzar
understand	understood	understood	comprender, enten- der
wake	woke, waked	waked	despertar(se)
wear	wore	worn	usar, llevar (*ropa*)
win	won	won	ganar
write	wrote	written	escribir

III. Numerals.

Cardinals

1 one   3 three
2 two   4 four

See page 154 for an explanation of these two forms.

316

5	five	23	twenty-three
6	six	24	twenty-four
7	seven	30	thirty
8	eight	31	thirty-one
9	nine	40	forty
10	ten	50	fifty
11	eleven	60	sixty
12	twelve	70	seventy
13	thirteen	80	eighty
14	fourteen	90	ninety
15	fifteen	100	one hundred
16	sixteen	101	one hundred and **one**
17	seventeen	200	two hundred
18	eighteen	1,000	one thousand
19	nineteen	1,001	one thousand and **one**
20	twenty	2,000	two thousand
21	twenty-one	1,000,000	one million
22	twenty-two	2,000,000	two million

Ordinals

1st	first	20th	twentieth
2nd	second	21st	twenty-first
3rd	third	22nd	twenty-second
4th	fourth	23rd	twenty-third
5th	fifth	24th	twenty-fourth
6th	sixth	30th	thirtieth
7th	seventh	31st	thirty-first
8th	eighth	40th	fortieth
9th	ninth	50th	fiftieth
10th	tenth	60th	sixtieth
11th	eleventh	70th	seventieth
12th	twelfth	80th	eightieth
13th	thirteenth	90th	ninetieth
14th	fourteenth	100th	(one) hundredth
15th	fifteenth	101st	(one) hundred and **first**
16th	sixteenth	200th	two hundredth
17th	seventeenth	1,000th	(one) thousandth
18th	eighteenth	2,000th	two thousandth
19th	nineteenth	1,000,000th	(one) millionth
		2,000,000	two millionth

IV. Months, Days, and Seasons.

Months of the Year

January	May	September
February	June	October
March	July	November
April	August	December

Days of the Week

Sunday	Wednesday
Monday	Thursday
Tuesday	Friday
	Saturday

Seasons of the Year

spring	fall, autumn
summer	winter

V. The United States of America.

States	Abbreviations
Alabama	Ala.
Alaska	Alas.
Arizona	Ariz.
Arkansas	Ark.
California	Calif.
Colorado	Colo.
Connecticut	Conn.
Delaware	Del.
Florida	Fla.
Georgia	Ga.
Hawaii	Hawaii
Idaho	Idaho
Illinois	Ill.
Indiana	Ind.
Iowa	Iowa
Kansas	Kans.
Kentucky	Ky.
Louisiana	La.
Maine	Maine
Maryland	Md.
Massachusetts	Mass.
Michigan	Mich.

Minnesota	Minn.
Mississippi	Miss.
Missouri	Mo.
Montana	Mont.
Nebraska	Nebr.
Nevada	Nev.
New Hampshire	N. H.
New Jersey	N. J.
New Mexico	N. Mex.
New York	N. Y.
North Carolina	N. C.
North Dakota	N. Dak.
Ohio	Ohio
Oklahoma	Okla.
Oregon	Oreg.
Pennsylvania	Pa.
Rhode Island	R. I.
South Carolina	S. C.
South Dakota	S. Dak.
Tennessee	Tenn.
Texas	Tex.
Utah	Utah
Vermont	Vt.
Virginia	Va.
Washington	Wash.
West Virginia	W. Va.
Wisconsin	Wis.
Wyoming	Wyo.

VI. Some Rules for English Spelling.

A. The following rules determine the use of **ie** or **ei** in English spelling.

1. If the letters are pronounced [i] as in the word **see**, **i** is put before **e** except after **c**.

believe, niece, piece
ceiling, receive

Exceptions: either, neither, leisurely, seize

2. If the letters are pronounced [e] as in the word **day**, **e** is put before **i**.

eight, freight, weigh, weight

B. When a word ends in a single consonant preceded by a single vowel and the accent is on the last syllable, the consonant is doubled before a suffix beginning with a vowel. Some common suffixes are **ing, er, est, ed, en,** and **y.**

    stopping, bigger, biggest, omitted, forgotten, funny

C. If a word ends in a silent **e,** the **e** is omitted before a suffix beginning with a vowel.

    coming, bluer, bluest, lived, given

Exceptions: agreeable, pronounceable

D. After a consonant, **y** changes to **i** before any suffix except **ing.** After a vowel, **y** does not change.

    cities, libraries, universities
    cries, cried, studies, studied
    busier, busiest, easier, easiest
    crying, studying, flying

    boys, days, keys
    pays, paying, says, saying, buys, buying
    plays, playing, played, player

E. Many nouns have irregular plurals.

    1. The plural of nouns ending in **s, sh, ch,** or **x** is **es.**

        classes, dishes, churches, boxes

    2. The plural of some nouns ending in **o** preceded by a consonant is **es.**

        heroes, Negroes, potatoes, tomatoes

    3. The plural of some nouns ending in **f** or **fe** is **ves.**

        knives, wives, leaves, thieves

    4. For nouns ending in **y,** Rule D above applies.

F. An adverb formed by adding **ly** to an adjective ending in **l** is written with two **l**'s.

    carefully, generally, really, usually

G. When **all** is combined with another word to form a single word, it is written **al.** Likewise, when **full** is added to another word to form a single word, it is written **ful.**

    almost, **al**ready, **al**so, **al**though, **al**together, **al**ways
    care**ful**, color**ful**, use**ful**, wonder**ful**, hope**ful**

VII. Capitalization.

Capital letters are used more often in English than in Spanish. They are used in the following cases:
1. At the beginning of a sentence.
2. For the first person singular pronoun **I**.
3. For names of languages.
4. For names of the months.
5. For names of the days of the week.
6. For proper names.
7. For titles preceding a proper name.
8. For words in the titles of books, articles, stories, plays, etc., except for the words **a, an, the,** and short prepositions within the title.

VIII. Syllabication.

Where possible, the division of a word at the end of a line should be avoided. When it is necessary, the word is divided between syllables; both parts should be pronounceable. In doubtful cases the dictionary should be consulted.

1. Words pronounced as one syllable should never be divided.

    come, leaves, brings, asked, bought

2. A single letter may not stand alone at the end or the beginning of a line.

3. A division may be made between double consonants, except **bl, cl, fl, gl, pl, sl, br, cr, dr, fr, gr, pr, tr, ch, gh, th, sh, sp,** and **st** when they are pronounced together in the same syllable.

    let - ter   a - cross   post - man
    Ger - man   coun - try   cus - tom

4. A division may also be made between the main part of a word and its suffix or its prefix, if the suffix or prefix can be pronounced as a separate syllable.

    per - cent - **age**   **in** - side
    a - muse - **ment**   **out** - num - ber
                   bring - **ing**

VOCABULARY

ENGLISH–SPANISH

a, un(o), una
ability, capacidad
able: be able, poder
about, cerca de, (a) eso de; de, acerca de
above, encima de; arriba
absence, ausencia
absent (from), ausente (de)
abundance, abundancia
accent, acento
accept, aceptar
accident, accidente
according to, según
accustomed to, acostumbrado a
ache, dolor; doler
acre, acre (*4,840 varas cuadradas*)
across, a través de; al otro lado de; de un lado a otro
act: be acted upon by, sufrir la acción de
acting, actuación
action, acción
active, activo
activity, actividad
actress, actriz
actual, real, verdadero
actually, verdaderamente, realmente
add, añadir

address, dirección
adjective, adjetivo
admire, admirar
adopt, adoptar
adult, adulto, mayor
advance: in advance, con anticipación
advantage, ventaja
adventure, aventura
adventurous, atrevido, amigo de aventuras
adverb, adverbio
advisability, conveniencia
advise, aconsejar
affair, función, acto
affection, afecto, cariño
affectionately, cariñosamente
affirmative, afirmativo
afraid: be afraid of, tener miedo a
after, después de; **take after,** parecerse a
afternoon, tarde; **in the afternoon,** por la tarde
afterwards, después
again, otra vez
against, contra
age, edad
agent, agente

ago, hace; **a year ago,** hace un año; **how long ago?** ¿cuánto tiempo hace que...?
agree, estar de acuerdo, convenir en, concordar; **agree on,** convenir en; **agree with,** estar de acuerdo con
agreeable, agradable
agriculture, agricultura
ahead, adelante
aid, ayuda
air, aire
airplane, aeroplano
airport, aeropuerto, aeródromo
Alice, Alicia
alike, iguales
all, todos, todas; **all over,** por todas partes; **all right,** muy bien, está bien
allow, permitir, dejar
almost, casi
alone, solo
along, a lo largo de, por
aloud, en voz alta
already, ya
also, también
although, aunque
altogether, del todo
always, siempre
American, americano
among, entre
amuse, divertir; **amuse oneself,** divertirse
amusement, diversión
and, y; **and so on,** etcétera
Andrew, Andrés
Anglo-Saxon, anglosajón
angry, enojado, enfadado; **angry about,** enojado de; **angry with,** enojado con
annex, anexar
annual, anual
annually, anualmente
another, otro

answer, contestación; contestar; **answer the door,** ir a ver quién llama a la puerta
ant, hormiga
antecedent, antecedente
any (*adj.*), unos, alguno(s), ninguno(s); cualquiera; **any longer,** no más; **any more,** no más
anybody, alguien, nadie; cualquiera
anyone, alguien, nadie; cualquiera
anything, algo, nada; cualquier cosa
anywhere, en cualquier parte
apartment, apartamento
apiece, cada uno
apostrophe, apóstrofo
appetite, apetito
apple, manzana
application, solicitud; **application blank,** formulario
appoint, nombrar
appointment, cita
appreciate, apreciar
approach, acercarse a
appropriate, apropiado
approximately, aproximadamente
April, abril
arch, arco
architecture, arquitectura
aristocracy, aristocracia
aristocratic, aristocrático
arithmetic, aritmética
arm, brazo
armless, sin brazos
army, ejército
around, alrededor de; **around the corner,** a la vuelta de la esquina
arrange, arreglar
arrive, llegar; **arrive in, at,** llegar a; **on arriving,** al llegar
art, arte; **art gallery,** galería de arte
article, artículo

artist, artista; **local artist,** artista de la vecindad
artistic, artístico
as, como; a medida que, según; **as a child,** cuando niño; **as ... as, tan ...** como; **as far as,** hasta (*distancia*); **as follows,** como sigue; **as much as,** tanto como; **as soon as,** en cuanto, tan pronto como
Ash Wednesday, Miércoles de Ceniza
ask, preguntar; pedir; **ask a favor of someone,** pedirle un favor a uno; **ask a question,** hacer una pregunta; **ask for,** pedir
aspect, aspecto
assembly hall, salón de reunión
assembly plant, fábrica de montaje
associated with, relacionado con
at, a, en
Atlantic, Atlántico
atmosphere, ambiente
attend, asistir a
attract, atraer
attraction, atracción, película
attractive, atractivo
August, agosto
aunt, tía
author, autor
automobile, automóvil
autumn, otoño
auxiliary, auxiliar
avenue, avenida
average, promedio
avocado, aguacate
avoid, evitar
away, a una distancia de; **two miles away,** a una distancia de dos millas

bachelor, soltero; bachiller
back, de atrás; **be back,** estar de vuelta
background, fondo
bad, malo; **bad cold,** fuerte resfriado
badly, mal
bake, hornear, cocer al horno
balcony, balcón
ball, baile elegante
banana, banano, plátano
bank, banco; orilla de un río
base, basar
baseball, béisbol
basic, básico
basis, razón, base
bath, baño
bathing, acción de bañarse; **go bathing,** ir a bañarse
battle, batalla
bay, bahía
be, ser, estar; **be able,** poder; **be about,** tratar(se) de; **be acted upon by,** sufrir la acción de; **be cold,** tener o hacer frío; **be hot,** tener o hacer mucho calor; **be hungry,** tener hambre; **be in a hurry,** tener prisa; **be lucky,** tener suerte; **be sorry,** sentir; **be warm,** tener o hacer calor; **be worth,** valer
beach, playa
bean, frijol, habichuela; **string bean,** habichuela tierna
bear, oso
beautiful, bello, hermoso
beautifully, bellamente
beauty, belleza; **for beauty of,** en cuanto a la belleza de
because, porque; **because of,** por, a causa de
become, hacerse, ponerse; llegar a ser, convertirse en; **become impatient,** impacientarse
bed, cama
bedroom, alcoba

before, antes de; antes
beg, rogar
begin, comenzar, empezar
beginning, principio
behind, detrás de
believable, creíble
believe, creer
bell, campana
belong, pertenecer
below, debajo de; abajo
beside, al lado de
besides, además de; además
best, (el) mejor (*superlativo*)
better, mejor (*comparativo*); **had better** (*aux.*), sería mejor que
between, entre
big, grande
bilingual, bilingüe
bill, billete; cuenta
bird, pájaro
birthday, cumpleaños
black, negro
blackboard, pizarra
blank, rayita, espacio
blanket, manta, frazada
block, manzana, cuadra
blond(e), rubio (-a)
blood, sangre; **blood pressure,** tensión arterial
bloom: in bloom, en flor
blue, azul
board, alimentación; abordar
boardinghouse, pensión
boat, barco, buque
Bob, Bob (*diminutivo de Robert*)
body, cuerpo
Bolivian, boliviano
book, libro
bookcase, estante para libros
bookstore, librería
border, frontera, límite
born: be born, nacer
borough, distrito municipal
borrow, pedir prestado; **borrow from someone,** pedirle prestado a uno
both, ambos; **both ... and,** a la vez; tanto ... como
bottle, botella
bottom, fondo; **bottom of the page,** pie de la página
boulder, piedra grande
boulevard, bulevar, avenida ancha
bound for, rumbo a, con destino a
boundary, límite, frontera
box, caja
boy, muchacho
bracelet, pulsera
brackets, paréntesis cuadrados
Brazil, el Brasil
Brazilian, brasileño
bread, pan
break, romper
breakable, frágil
breakfast, desayuno; **eat (have) breakfast,** desayunarse
breath, aliento; **take a deep breath,** respirar profundo
breathe, respirar
brick, ladrillo
bride, recién casada
bridegroom, recién casado
bridge, puente; juego de cartas
brief, breve
briefly, brevemente
bright, brillante
brightly, espléndidamente, claramente
bring, traer; **bring out,** dar énfasis a; **bring up** (*children*), criar
British, británico
broad, ancho, extenso
broadcast, radiodifundir
bronchitis, bronquitis
brother, hermano
brother-in-law, cuñado
brotherly, fraternal

brown, pardo, carmelita
brunet(te), moreno (-a)
brush, cepillar
build, construir
building, edificio
bury, enterrar
bus, autobús; **bus stop,** paradero, parada
busily, diligentemente
business, negocio(s); **business letter,** carta comercial
businessman, hombre de negocios
bustling, muy animado
busy, ocupado
but, pero, sino; menos, excepto
butter, mantequilla
button, botón
buy, comprar; **buy from someone,** comprarle a uno
buzz, zumbido, sonido prolongado; zumbar
by, por

cabin, cabaña
cable car, carro que corre sobre carriles por tracción de cable
Cabots, los Cabot (*familia linajuda*)
cactus, cacto
call, llamada; llamar; **call for,** ir a buscar; exigir; **call off,** cancelar; **call on,** visitar; **call up),** telefonear, llamar
camera, cámara fotográfica
camp, campamento
campus, terrenos que rodean una universidad y le pertenecen
can, poder, saber; **can** (= be able to), poder; **can** (= know how to), saber
Canadian, canadiense
candle, vela
cannery, fábrica de conservas
canyon, cañón
capable, capaz

capital, capital; **capital letter,** letra mayúscula
capitalization, uso de las mayúsculas
Capitol, Capitolio
captain, capitán
car, automóvil; **dining car,** coche comedor; **sleeping car,** Pullman, coche dormitorio
card, tarjeta; **calling card,** tarjeta de visita
care: take care of, cuidar; **care to,** querer, tener deseo de
carefree, despreocupado
careful, cuidadoso; **be careful,** tener cuidado
carefully, cuidadosamente
cargo, carga
carnival, carnaval
carrot, zanahoria
carry, llevar
cartoon, dibujo cómico, caricatura
case, caso; **in any case,** de todos modos, de todas maneras
cash, cambiar, cobrar
castle, castillo
catch, coger
cathedral, catedral
Catholic, católico
cattle, ganado
cauliflower, coliflor
cause, causa; causar
causeway, calzada
cease, cesar
ceiling, cielo raso
celebrate, celebrar
celebration, celebración
cement, cemento
cemetery, cementerio
cent, centavo
center, centro
Central America, Centroamérica
century, siglo; **nineteenth century,** siglo diez y nueve
certain, cierto

certainly, por cierto, sin duda
chair, silla
chalk, tiza
chance, probabilidad, casualidad
change, cambio; dinero suelto o menudo; cambiar (de); **change trains,** cambiar de trenes
chaperon, acompañante de los jóvenes
characteristic, característico
characterize, caracterizar
Charles, Carlos
charm, encanto
cheap, barato
check, cheque; **check blood pressure,** tomar la tensión arterial
cherry, cereza; **cherry tree,** cerezo
chest, pecho
chief, principal
child, niño, niña
Chilean, chileno
Chinatown, barrio chino
Chinese, chino(s)
choice, preferencia, elección
choose, escoger
Christmas, Navidad
church, iglesia
cigarette, cigarrillo
circumstance, circumstancia
circus, circo
citizen, ciudadano
city, ciudad
class, clase
classical, clásico
classmate, compañero de clase
classroom, sala de clase
clause, cláusula
clean, limpio: limpiar
cleaner: at the cleaner's, en la lavandería
clear, claro
clearly, claramente
clerk, dependiente
clever, inteligente, listo, hábil

climate, clima
close [z], cerrar
close [s] to, cerca de
closely [s], estrechamente
clothes, ropa
cloud, nube
coal, carbón (de piedra)
coast, costa
coat, abrigo
coconut, coco
cod, bacalao
coeducational, coeducacional, para ambos sexos
coffee, café
Coke, Coca Cola
cold, frío; resfriado; **be cold,** tener frío; hacer frío; **have a cold,** estar con resfriado
college, facultad de una universidad; escuela al nivel universitario; **go to college,** seguir estudios universitarios
colloquial, familiar; de uso corriente
Colombian, colombiano
colonist, colono
colony, colonia
colorful, lleno de colorido
comb, peine, peinilla; peinar(se); **comb one's hair,** peinarse
combine, combinar
come, venir; **come a long way,** cubrir una gran distancia; **come along,** venir; **come back,** volver; **come in,** entrar; **come over,** venir a visitar
comfort, comodidad
comfortable, cómodo
coming, venidero
commerce, comercio
commercially, comercialmente
common, usado, común
commonly, frecuentemente
community, centro
company, compañía

comparatively, relativamente
compare, comparar
comparison, comparación
compete, competir
complain, quejarse
complement, complemento; **objective complement,** complemento atributivo
complete, completo; completar
completely, completamente
compound, compuesto
compulsory, obligatorio
concert, concierto
concession, concesión
condition, condición
conditional, condicional, postpretérito
conduct, conducir
confuse, confundir
Congress, Congreso
conjugation, conjugación
conjunction, conjunción
connect, conectar, juntar; **connected with,** relacionado con
consent, consentimiento
consequently, por consiguiente
Conservatory, Conservatorio
consider, considerar
consonant, consonante
constant, constante
constitute, constituir
constitution, constitución
construct, construir
construction, construcción
consult, consultar
contact, contacto
contain, contener
contentment, placer, satisfacción, regocijo
continent, continente
continuation, continuación
continue, continuar
continuous, continuo
contract, contraer

contraction, contracción
contradict, contradecir
contrary, contrario; **contrary to fact,** contrario a la realidad; **on the contrary,** al contrario
contrast, contraste; contrastar, oponer
contribute, contribuir
conversation, conversación
conversational, de conversación
cooking, cocina
cool, fresco
copper, cobre
copy, copia
cord: vocal cords, cuerdas vocales
corn, maíz
corner, esquina, rincón
cornerstone, primera piedra
correct, correcto
correctly, correctamente
correspond, corresponder; **correspond to,** corresponder a; **correspond with someone,** llevar correspondencia con uno
corresponding, correspondiente
cosmopolitan, cosmopolita
cost, precio; costar
cotton, algodón
cough, tos
counter, mostrador
country, país, campo; **mother country,** patria
countryman, compatriota
couple, pareja, matrimonio; **a couple of days,** un par de días
course, curso; **of course,** por supuesto; **take a course,** seguir un curso
court, corte
cousin, primo, prima
cover, cubrir; **covered with,** cubierto de
cowboy, vaquero
crab, cangrejo

crawl up, trepar
cream, crema
create, crear
crooked, torcido
crop, cosecha
cross, cruzar, atravesar
crosstown bus, autobús que corre en Nueva York de este a oeste o vice versa
crowded, concurrido
cry, llorar; gritar
Cuban, cubano
cuff, puño de camisa
cultivate, cultivar
culture, cultura
cup, taza
custom, costumbre
customary, habitual, usual
customer, cliente (comprador)
cut, cortar; **cut its way through,** labrar su camino por

dam, represa
dance, baile; bailar
dancer, bailador(a), bailarín, bailarina
dangerous, peligroso
dare, atreverse
dark, obscuridad; obscuro
date, cita; **make a date with,** concertar una cita con
daughter, hija
daughter-in-law, nuera
day, día; **day after tomorrow,** pasado mañana; **day before yesterday,** anteayer
daytime: in the daytime, de día
dead, muerto
deal: a great deal (of), mucho
dear, querido; **oh dear!** ¡Dios mío!
death, muerte
December, diciembre
decide, decidir

deck, piso
declaration, declaración
dedicate, dedicar
deep, profundo; **five feet deep,** cinco pies de profundidad
deer, venado
defective, defectivo
definite, definido
definitely, definitivamente
definition, definición
degree, grado; título académico
delicious (*of food*), delicioso
demand, demandar, exigir
democracy, democracia
democratic, democrático
demonstrative, demostrativo
dentist, dentista
dentistry, dentistería
department store, gran almacén
depend, depender; **depend on,** depender de
deposit, depósito
derive, derivar
descendant, descendiente
describe, describir
description, descripción
desert, desierto
desk, escritorio
dessert, postre
destroy, destruir
determination, determinación
develop, desarrollar
development, desarrollo
diagram, diagrama
dial, cuadrante; marcar el número
diamond, diamante
diary, diario
dictation, dictado
dictionary, diccionario
die, morir
diet, dieta, régimen; **go on a light diet,** ponerse a una dieta ligera
differ, diferir; **differ from,** diferir de

difference, diferencia; **it makes no difference to me,** no me importa
different, diferente; **different from,** diferente de
difficult, difícil
difficulty, dificultad
diminutive, diminutivo
dining room, comedor
dinner, comida
diphthong, diptongo
diplomat, diplomático
direct, directo; **direct object,** complemento directo
direction, dirección
directly, directamente
dirty, sucio
disadvantage, desventaja
disagree, no estar de acuerdo
disappear, desaparecer
discover, descubrir
dish, plato; **dishes,** vajilla; **do the dishes,** lavar la vajilla
disillusioned, desilusionado
distance, distancia
distinction, distinción
distinctive, distintivo
distinguish, distinguir
distribute, distribuir
distribution, distribución
district, distrito
divide, dividir
do, hacer; *como auxiliar no se traduce;* **have nothing to do with,** no tener nada que ver con; **they will do,** servirán
doctor, médico
dog, perro
dollar, dólar
dominant, dominante
dominate, dominar
Dominican Republic, República Dominicana
donkey, burro
door, puerta
doorbell, timbre
double, doble
double-deck (*adj.*), de dos pisos
doubtful, dudoso
down, abajo; **down the river,** río abajo
downstairs, abajo
downtown, centro de una ciudad
dozen, docena
drawer, cajón, gaveta
dream, sueño; soñar; **dream about,** soñar con
dress, vestido; vestir(se); **evening dress,** vestido de noche
drink, beber, tomar
drive, manejar (*un automóvil*)
driver, chófer
drug, droga
druggist, farmacéutico, boticario
drugstore, droguería, farmacia
dry, seco
dune: sand dune, duna de arena
duration, duración
during, durante
Dutch, holandés
dynamite, dinamita

each, cada; **each other,** se, el uno al otro
ear, oreja, oído
earache, dolor de oídos
early, temprano; **early days,** primeros días; **early history,** primeros años
earn, ganar; **earn a (one's) living,** ganarse la vida
east, este; al este; **to the east,** hacia el este
eastern, del este de los Estados Unidos
Easterner, habitante del este de los Estados Unidos
easily, fácilmente
easy, fácil

eat, comer
economics, economía
education, educación
educational, educacional
educator, educador
Edward, Eduardo
effort, esfuerzo
egg, huevo; **boiled eggs,** huevos cocidos al agua (con cáscara); **fried eggs,** huevos fritos; **scrambled eggs,** huevos revueltos
eight, ocho
eighth, octavo; **the eighth of July,** el ocho de julio
eighty, ochenta
either, el uno o el otro; **either... or,** o... o; **I am not either,** ni yo tampoco
elaborate, elaborado, elegante, esmerado
elect, elegir
election, elección
electric, eléctrico
electricity, electricidad
elegant, elegante
elementary, elemental
elevator, ascensor
eleven, once
embrace, abrazar
emphasis, énfasis
emphasize, dar énfasis a
emphatic, enfático
Empire, imperio
end, fin, cabo; terminar
ending, terminación
endless, interminable
engage in, dedicarse a
engagement, compromiso
engineer, ingeniero
engineering, ingeniería
England, Inglaterra; **New England,** Nueva Inglaterra
English, inglés, ingleses

Englishman, inglés
enjoy, gozar de; **enjoy oneself,** divertirse
enjoyment, goce
enormous, enorme
enough, suficiente, bastante
enrich, enriquecer
enter, entrar (en)
entertain, divertir
entertaining, divertido
entrance, entrada, admisión; ingreso
environs, alrededores
equality, igualdad
equally, igualmente
equator, ecuador
equivalent, equivalente
errand, diligencia, mandado
erroneous, erróneo
escape, escapar
especially, especialmente
establish, establecer
estimate, calcular
Europe, Europa
evaporate, evaporarse
evaporation, evaporación
even, aún
evening, tarde, tardecita, (el) anochecer; **in the evening,** por la tardecita
event, acontecimiento
ever, alguna vez, jamás; **not ever,** nunca
every, todo(s); **every day,** todos los días
everybody, todos
everyday (*adj.*), cotidiano, ordinario
everyone, todos
everything, todo
evident, evidente
exact, exacto
exactly, exactamente
exaggerate, exagerar
examination, examen; **take an examination,** sufrir examen

examine, examinar
example, ejemplo; **for example,** por ejemplo
excellent, excelente
except, excepto
exception, excepción
exceptional, excepcional
exchange, cambio; **in exchange for,** en cambio de
exciting, emocionante
exclusive, exclusivo, de primera
excuse, excusar, disculpar
exercise, ejercicio
exhibit, exhibición, exposición
exist, existir
existence, existencia
expanse, extensión
expect, esperar
expedition, expedición
expense, gasto
expensive, caro
experience, experiencia
explain, explicar
explanation, explicación
exploration, exploración
explore, explorar
explorer, explorador
export, exportación; exportar
express, expresar
expression, expresión
extend, tender, extender
extensive, extenso
extent: to such an extent, hasta tal punto
eye, ojo

fabulous, fabuloso
facility, facilidad, oportunidad
fact, hecho; **as a matter of fact,** en efecto; **in fact,** en efecto; **the fact is that,** es que
factory, fábrica
fail, fracasar; **fail an examination,** salir suspenso en un examen
faint, desmayarse
fair, regular, así así
fairyland, país de hadas
fall, otoño; caer(se); **fall in love,** enamorarse
falls, salto, catarata(s)
fame, fama
familiar, de confianza
family, familia
famous, famoso
far, lejos; **as far as,** hasta; **by far,** sin duda; en mucho; **far from,** lejos de; **Far West,** Lejano Oeste; **how far?** ¿a qué distancia?
fare, tarifa, valor del pasaje
farm, hacienda, finca
farming, agricultura
fascinated, fascinado, encantado
fast, rápido; rápidamente
fat, grueso
father, padre
father-in-law, suegro
fathom, braza
favorite, favorito, predilecto
February, febrero
fee, honorarios, derechos
feel, sentir(se)
feeling, sentimiento
female, hembra; feminino
feminine, feminino
fence, cerca
ferry, barco de transporte a corta distancia
fertile, fértil
fertilizer, abono
festival, fiesta
fever, fiebre
few, pocos, algunos; **a few,** unos pocos, algunos
field, campo; ramo (*de estudios*)
fifteen, quince
Fifteenth Street, Calle quince
fifth, quinto

Fiftieth Street, Calle cincuenta
fifty, cincuenta
fight, combatir, luchar
fill, llenar; **fill a prescription,** preparar una receta; **fill out,** llenar
filled with, lleno de
film, película
finally, al fin, finalmente
financial, financiero
find, encontrar, hallar; **find out,** averiguar, descubrir
fine, bueno, bello, agradable; muy bien; **Fine Arts,** Bellas Artes; **just fine,** muy bien
finger, dedo (de la mano)
finish, terminar, acabar
fire, incendio, fuego; **fire insurance,** seguro contra incendios
firearm, arma de fuego
fireplace, chimenea, hogar
first, primero; **first name,** nombre de pila
fish, pez, peces; pescado
fishing, pesca; de pesca; **go fishing,** ir de pesca
five, cinco
five-thirty, las cinco y media
fix, reparar, arreglar
flag, bandera
flat, plano
fleet, flota
float, flotar
flood, inundación; inundar
floor, piso; suelo; **eightieth floor,** piso ochenta; **floor lamp,** lámpara de pie; **fortieth floor,** piso cuarenta; **main floor,** luneta; **sixtieth floor,** piso sesenta
florist: at the florist's, en la tienda de flores
flour, harina
flow, fluir, correr
flower, flor

flunk (*colloquial*), fracasar
fly, mosca; volar
fog, niebla
follow, seguir; **as follows,** como sigue
following, siguiente
fond of, aficionado a
food, alimento
foot, pie; **on foot,** a pie
football, fútbol
for, para, por; porque, pues
foreign, extranjero
foreigner, extranjero
forested, con bosques
forget, olvidar(se)
forgive, perdonar
form, forma; formar
formal, respetuoso; con ceremonia
formation, formación
fortunately, afortunadamente
fortune: tell fortunes, decir la buenaventura
forty, cuarenta
Forty-second Street, Calle cuarenta y dos
found, fundar
foundation, fundación
founder, fundador
four, cuatro
fourteen, catorce
Fourteenth Street, Calle catorce
fourth, cuarto; **the Fourth of July,** el cuatro de julio
fox, zorro
France, Francia
Franciscan, franciscano
frankly, francamente
free, libre, desocupado; gratuito; libertar
freedom, libertad
freeze, congelar
freight, carga; **freight boat,** buque de carga
freighter, buque de carga

French, francés; **French Quarter,** barrio francés
frequency, frecuencia
frequent, frecuente
frequently, frecuentemente, con frecuencia
fresh, fresco; **fresh water,** agua dulce
freshman, estudiante del primer año de colegio o de universidad
Friday, viernes
friend, amigo
friendly, simpático, amistoso
friendship, amistad
from, de
front (*adj.*), de enfrente; **in front of,** delante de
fruit, fruta
full, lleno; **full name,** nombre completo; **full of,** lleno de
funny, chistoso, cómico
fur trader, comerciante en pieles
furnish, suministrar
furniture, muebles
furs, pieles
futile, inútil
future, futuro

gallery, galería
gallon, galón
game, juego
garden, jardín
gasoline, gasolina
gateway, puerta de entrada
gay, alegre
gaze (at), contemplar
gear: in low gear, en primera marcha
gender, género
generally, generalmente
generate, generar
George, Jorge
German, alemán
gerund, gerundio

get, conseguir, obtener; recoger, buscar; **get a letter,** recibir una carta; **get a letter off,** despachar una carta; **get a meal,** preparar una comida; **get ahead,** avanzar; **get along,** marchar; **get along with,** simpatizar con; **get back,** volver; **get better,** mejorarse; **get in(to),** subir (a) (*un automóvil*); **get married,** casarse; **get off,** bajarse (de) (*un vehículo público*); **get on,** subir (a) (*un vehículo público*); **get out of,** bajarse (de) (*un automóvil*); **get over** (*disease*), ponerse bien; **get ready,** alistarse; **get rid of,** deshacerse de; **get thin,** adelgazar; **get through,** terminar; **get tired,** cansarse; **get to,** llegar a; **get together,** reunirse; **get up,** levantarse; **get used to,** acostumbrarse a; **get warm,** calentarse; **get well,** ponerse bien; **get wet,** mojarse
geyser, geiser
giant, gigantesco
gigantic, gigantesco
Ginny, Ginny (*diminutivo de Virginia*)
girl, muchacha
give, dar; **give back,** devolver; **give in,** asentir; **give up,** darse por vencido; renunciar a
glacier, ventisquero
glad: be glad, alegrarse
glass, vaso; vidrio, cristal
glasses, anteojos
glory, gloria
glove, guante
glue, cola
glycerin, glicerina
go, ir; **go away,** irse; **go back,** volver; **go back on** (*one's*

word), faltar a; **go climbing,** hacer el alpinismo; **go down,** bajar, descender; **go fishing,** ir de pesca; **go for a walk,** ir a pasear(se) (a pie); **go on (with),** seguir (con), continuar; **go out,** salir; **go over,** tener éxito; examinar; **go sailing,** hacer una excursión en buque de vela; **go skiing,** ir a esquiar; **go swimming,** ir a bañarse; **go to bed,** acostarse; **go up,** subir
God, Dios
godchild, ahijado
godfather, padrino
godmother, madrina
gold, oro; **Gold Rush,** fiebre del oro
Golden Gate, Puerta Dorada
good, bueno; **good afternoon,** buenas tardes; **good evening,** buenas noches; **good morning,** buenos días; **Good Neighbor Policy,** Política del Buen Vecino; **good night,** buenas noches
good-bye, adiós; hasta luego
goose, ganso
gorge, cañón, abra
government, gobierno
governor, gobernador
graceful, gracioso
grade, año escolar; calificación
graduate, graduado; graduarse
grammar, gramática
grandchildren, nietos
granddaughter, nieta
grandeur, grandeza
grandfather, abuelo
grandmother, abuela
grandparents, abuelos
grandson, nieto
grapefruit, toronja
gray, gris

great, gran, grande, importante; **a great deal (of),** mucho
great-grandfather, bisabuelo
Greek, griego
green, verde
greet, saludar
greeting, saludo
groceries, víveres, abarrotes
grocery store, almacén de víveres
ground, tierra
group, grupo
grow, crecer
growth, crecimiento
guard, guardia
Guatemalan, guatemalteco
guava, guayaba
guess, adivinar
guest, invitado
gulf, golfo

habit, hábito, costumbre
hair, pelo, cabello
half, medio, mitad; **half an hour,** media hora; **half past five,** las cinco y media
halfway between, a mitad del camino entre
hand, mano; **by hand,** a mano; **on the other hand,** de otra parte
handkerchief, pañuelo
hang (up), colgar
happen, ocurrir, suceder, pasar
happy, feliz
harbor, puerto
hard, difícil, duro; mucho (*adv.*)
hardy, fuerte
harvester, segadora
hat, sombrero
Havana, la Habana
have, tener, haber; **have a good time,** divertirse; **have a sore throat,** dolerle la garganta; **have breakfast,** desayunarse; **have dinner,** comer; **have**

lunch, almorzar; **have to,** tener que
headache, dolor de cabeza
headquarters, cuartel general; sede
health, salud
hear, oír; **hear about,** oír hablar de; **hear from someone,** recibir noticias de alguien; **hear of,** oír hablar de
heart, corazón; **by heart,** de memoria
heat, calor
heavy, pesado; **heavy traffic,** mucho tráfico
help, ayuda; ayudar
here, aquí, acá
hero, héroe
hide, cuero
high, alto; **high school,** institución de educación secundaria; **high spots,** puntos importantes
highway, carretera
hill, colina
hilly, montañoso
historical, histórico
historically, históricamente
history, historia
hither, acá
hog, cerdo
hold, tener, sostener, contener; **hold on,** agarrarse
hole, hueco, hoyo
holiday, día de fiesta
Hollywood Bowl, Hollywood Bowl (*nombre de un anfiteatro*)
home, hogar, casa propia; **at home,** en casa; **go home,** ir a casa; **home town,** ciudad natal o en donde ha crecido uno
homework, tarea
honest, honrado, honesto
honeymoon, luna de miel
hope, esperar
horizontally, horizontalmente

horse, caballo
horseback: on horseback, a caballo
horseshoe, herradura
host, anfitrión
hostess, anfitriona
hot, caliente; **hot springs,** aguas termales
hour, hora
house, casa
how, ¿cómo?; **how about?** ¿qué le parece?; **How are you?** ¿Cómo está Vd.?; **How do you like it?** ¿Qué tal le parece?; **how do you say?** ¿cómo se dice?; **how long?** ¿cuánto tiempo?; **how many?** ¿cuántos?; **how much?** ¿cuánto?; **How old are you?** ¿Cuántos años tiene Vd.?; **How tall is he?** ¿Cómo es de alto?; **How's everything (with you)?** ¿Cómo le va?
however, sin embargo
huge, enorme
hundred, cien(to)
hungry, hambriento; **be hungry,** tener hambre
hurry, apresurarse; **be in a hurry,** tener prisa
hurt, lastimar, hacer daño, herir
husband, esposo

ice cream, helado
identification, identificación
idiom, modismo
idiomatic, idiomático
ill, enfermo
illness, enfermedad
illustrious, ilustre, célebre
imaginary, imaginario
imagine, imaginar(se)
imitation (*adj.*), de fantasía
immediately, inmediatamente
immense, inmenso

337

immigration, inmigración
imperative, imperativo
implication, implicación
imply, denotar, significar
import, importación; importar
importance, importancia
important, importante
imposing, imponente
impossible, imposible
impression, impresión
impressive, impresionante
in, en, de, por; **be in,** estar aquí; **in addition,** además
incident, incidente
incidentally, incidentalmente
include, incluir
inconvenience, inconveniencia
incorrectly, incorrectamente
incredible, increíble
indefinite, indefinido
indefinitely, indefinidamente
independent, independiente
Indian, indio
indicate, indicar
indirect, indirecto
industry, industria
inequality, desigualdad
infinitive, infinitivo
influence, influencia
informal, familiar; **informal writing,** estilo familiar
information, informes; información
inhabitant, habitante
injection, inyección
ink, tinta
inland, del interior
inner, interior
insert, insertar
inside, adentro; dentro de
insist, insistir; **insist on,** insistir en
inspect, inspeccionar
instance: for instance, por ejemplo
instead of, en vez de
institute, instituto

institution, institución
insurance, seguro; **fire insurance,** seguro contra incendio
intellectual, intelectual
intend, pensar, tener la intención de
intention, intención
interest, interés
interested, interesado
interesting, interesante
international, internacional
interpret, interpretar
interrogation, interrogación
interrupt, interrumpir
into, en
intransitive, intransitivo
intransitively, de un modo intransitivo
introduce, introducir, presentar
introduction, presentación
invert, invertir
invitation, invitación
invite, invitar
Irish, irlandés
iron, hierro; **iron-grilled,** con reja de hierro
ironworks, fundición de hierro
irrigation, irrigación
island, isla
isle, isla
Italian, italiano
italics, letra bastardilla

James, Jaime
January, enero
Japan, el Japón
Japanese, japonés
jazz, música popular sincopada
Jesus Christ, Jesucristo
Jew, judío
jewelry, joyas
Jim, Jim (*diminutivo de James*)
job, empleo, puesto, posición
John, Juan
Johnny, Juanito

joke, broma, chiste
journey, viaje largo
judge, juez
July, julio
jump, saltar
June, junio
junior, estudiante del tercer año de colegio o de universidad; **Junior,** hijo
just, solamente, exactamente; **have just,** acabar de; **just a moment,** un momento (nada más)

keep, guardar, quedarse con
key, llave
kill, matar
kind, clase; amable; **that is very kind of you,** Vd. es muy amable
kindergarten, escuela infantil
king, rey
kitchen, cocina
knife, cuchillo
knock, llamar a una puerta; golpear
know, saber, conocer; **know how to,** saber

laboratory, laboratorio
lack, faltar, carecer de
lady, dama
lake, lago; **lake front,** orilla del lago
lamp, lámpara; **floor lamp,** lámpara de pie; **table lamp,** lámpara de mesa
land, tierra, terreno; aterrizar
lane, vía
language, idioma, lengua
lard, manteca
large, grande
last, último, pasado; finalmente, **last but not least,** lo último pero no lo menos importante; **last name,** apellido; **last night,** anoche; **last week,** la semana pasada

late, tarde; **later,** más tarde
Latin American, latinoamericano
latitude, latitud
latter, éste, éstos
laugh, reír; **laugh at,** reírse de
law, ley, derecho
lawn, prado
lawyer, abogado
lay, poner, colocar
lazy, perezoso
leadership, dirección
leading, principal
leaf, hoja
learn, aprender
learning, estudio, educación
least, (el) menos (*superlativo*)
leather, cuero
leave, dejar; salir, marcharse
leave-taking, despedida
lecture, conferencia
left, izquierda; **there is one left,** queda uno
leisurely, pausado
lemon, limón
lend, prestar
Lent, Cuaresma
less, menos (*comparativo*)
lesson, lección
let, permitir, dejar; **let one know,** avisarle a uno
letter, carta; letra
lettuce, lechuga
levee, dique
level, nivel; piso; **sea level,** nivel del mar
levy, imponer, fijar (*impuesto*)
liberal arts college, institución de estudios generales superiores
liberty, libertad
library, biblioteca
lie, mentira; yacer, estar situado
life, vida
light, luz; claro, ligero
lightning rod, pararrayos

339

like, como; gustar; **How do you like it?** ¿Qué (tal) le parece?; **I should like,** me gustaría
likewise, asimismo
limit, límite; limitar
limited, limitado
line, línea; compañía (*de autobuses*)
lined with, bordeado de
link, eslabón
lip, labio
list, lista; hacer una lista
listen (to), escuchar
literally, literalmente
little, pequeño; poco; **a little,** un poco; **little by little,** poco a poco
live, vivir
living room, sala
load, cargar; **loaded with,** cargado de
loading, cargue
loaf (of bread), pan
lobster, langosta
located, situado
location, situación
lock, cerrar con llave
locomotive, locomotora
locust, langosta
lofty, muy alto
long, largo; **a long time,** mucho tiempo; **as long as,** mientras que; **how long?** ¿cuánto tiempo?; **not any longer,** no más; **ten miles long,** diez millas de largo; **wait long,** esperar mucho tiempo
look, mirar; parecer; **look after,** cuidar; **look at,** mirar; **look for,** buscar; **look like,** parecerse a; **look out for,** cuidado con; **look over,** examinar; **look up,** buscar
lose, perder

lot: a lot of, mucho; **lots of,** mucho(s)
Louisiana, Luisiana
love, amor; amar
lovely, hermoso
low, bajo; **low gear,** primera marcha; **lower,** más bajo, inferior
Lowells, los Lowell (*familia linajuda*)
luck, suerte
lucky: be lucky, tener suerte
lumber, madera para construcción
lumbering, industria de maderas
lunch, almuerzo

machine, máquina
machinery, maquinaria
made of, hecho de
magazine, revista
magnificent, magnífico
maid, criada, sirvienta; **old maid,** solterona
mail, correo; echar al correo; **air mail,** correo aéreo
mailman, cartero
main, principal; **main feature,** película principal; **main floor,** luneta
mainland, continente
mainly, principalmente
major, mayor; especializarse
majority, mayoría
make, hacer; **make a date,** concertar una cita; **make a difference,** importar; **make a mistake,** equivocarse; **make a speech,** pronunciar un discurso; **make an effort,** hacer un esfuerzo; **make friends,** hacer amigos; **make money,** hacer dinero; **make one's living,** ganarse la vida; **make oneself understood,** hacerse entender;

make over, reformar; **make the bed,** hacer la cama
male, varón
man, hombre; **man of letters,** literato
manner, manera
manufacture, manufactura; fabricar
manufacturing, manufacturero
many, muchos (-as)
map, mapa
marble, mármol
March, marzo
Mardi Gras, Martes de Carnaval
marked, marcado
market, mercado
marriage, matrimonio
marry, casarse con; **married,** casado
Mary, María
masculine, masculino
masked, de máscaras
match, fósforo
matter: as a matter of fact, en efecto; **What is the matter with you?** ¿Qué tiene Vd.?
May, mayo
meal, comida
mean, significar, querer decir
meaning, significado; **what is the meaning?** ¿cuál es el significado?
means, medio(s)
measure, medida
meat, carne; **meat packing,** empacadora de carne
medicine, medicina
medium, medio cocido
meet, reunirse; encontrar, encontrarse (con); conocer (*por primera vez*)
melt, derretirse
member, miembro
memorial, monumento
memorize, aprender de memoria

memory, memoria
mention, mencionar
message, recado, razón
metropolis, metrópoli
Mexican, mexicano
middle, mitad, centro; **medio;**
   middle name, segundo nombre;
   Middle West, Medio Oeste
midnight, medianoche
mild, suave
mile, milla
milk, leche
mill: textile mill, fábrica de tejidos
million, millón
mind, mente; importar, molestar;
   I don't mind, no me importa;
   I don't mind waiting, no me molesta esperar
mine, mina; el mío: minar, extraer
miner, minero
mining, minería
minus, menos
minute, minuto
mirror, espejo
miss: miss a person, echar de menos a una persona; hacerle falta a uno una persona; **miss the train,** perder el tren: **you can't miss it,** no puede equivocarse
mission, misión
missionary, misionero
mistake, falta, error: **by mistake,** por equivocación; **make a mistake,** equivocarse
mister (Mr.), señor
mix, mezclar
mixture, mezcla
modern, moderno
modifier, cualquier palabra o expresión que limite o califique
modify, modificar, calificar
moment, momento
Monday, lunes

money, dinero
monk, monje
monotonous, monótono
month, mes
monument, monumento
mood, disposición de ánimo
more, más; **not any more,** no más
Mormon, mormón (*miembro de una secta religiosa*)
morning, mañana; **in the morning,** por la mañana; **tomorrow morning,** mañana por la mañana; **yesterday morning,** ayer por la mañana
most, la mayor parte de, la mayoría de; (el) más (*superlativo*)
mother, madre; **mother country,** patria
mother-in-law, suegra
motion, movimiento; **motion picture,** cine, película
motorist, motorista
mountain, montaña
mouse, ratón
mouth, boca; desembocadura
move, mudarse, mover(se)
movie, película; **movies,** cine
moving picture, cine, película
much, mucho; **as much as,** tanto como; **too much,** demasiado; **very much,** mucho
mud, barro, lodo
munitions, municiones
museum, museo
mushroom, hongo
music, música
must, deber, tener que

name, nombre, apellido; nombrar; **full name,** nombre completo; **given name,** nombre de pila; **maiden name,** apellido de una mujer antes de su matrimonio; **middle name,** segundo nombre;

342

my name is..., me llamo...; **What is your name?** ¿Cómo se llama Vd.?
narrow, angosto, estrecho
nation, nación
national, nacional
nationality, nacionalidad
native, natural
naturally, naturalmente
nature, naturaleza
navigation, navegación
near, cerca de; cercano; **near by,** cerca
necessary, necesario
necessity, necesidad
need, necesitar
negative, negativo
neighbor, vecino
neighboring, cercano, adjacente
neither, ni; tampoco; **neither... nor,** ni... ni; **neither am I,** ni yo tampoco
nephew, sobrino
Netherlands (the), los Países Bajos
neuter, neutro
never, nunca, jamás
nevertheless, sin embargo
new, nuevo; **New England,** Nueva Inglaterra; **New Mexico,** Nuevo México; **New Orleans,** Nueva Orleáns; **New Year's Day,** el día de año nuevo; **New York,** Nueva York
news, noticias; **the news is,** las noticias son
newspaper, periódico
newsreel, noticiero
next, próximo, que viene; luego; **next to,** junto a; **next year,** el año próximo
nice, bonito, atractivo, simpático; agradable de cualquier modo
nickname, diminutivo, apodo
niece, sobrina

night, noche; **at night,** por la noche; de noche; **night club,** cabaret
nine, nueve
Nineteenth Street, Calle diez y nueve
ninth, noveno
no, no; ninguno; **no longer,** no más; **no one,** nadie
nobody, nadie
noise, ruido
noisy, ruidoso
none, ninguno
noon, mediodía
North, norte; al norte; **North American,** norteamericano; **North Carolina,** la Carolina del Norte; **to the north,** hacia el norte
northeastern, del noreste de los Estados Unidos
northwest (*adj.*), noroeste; **Northwest** (*n.*), noroeste de los Estados Unidos
northwestern, noroeste
nose, nariz
not, no; **not at all,** nada, de ninguna manera; **not only ... but also,** no solo ... sino también
note, nota; notar, apuntar; **take notes,** apuntar
notebook, cuaderno
noted, célebre
nothing, nada; **have nothing to do with,** no tener nada que ver con; **nothing in particular,** nada de particular
notice, notar; fijarse en
noun, sustantivo
novel, novela
November, noviembre
now, ahora
number, número; **a number of,** cierto (gran) número de
numerous, numerosos

nun, monja
nurse, enfermera
nylon, nilón

oats, avena
object, objeto, complemento; **direct object,** complemento directo
objective complement, complemento atributivo
obligation, obligación
obtain, obtener
obvious, obvio, claro
occasion, ocasión
occasionally, ocasionalmente
occupation, ocupación
occupy, ocupar
occur, ocurrir, suceder
ocean, océano; **ocean liner,** vapor grande
o'clock, la hora según el reloj; **six o'clock,** las seis
October, octubre
of, de
off, de; **take off,** quitar(se)
offer, ofrecer
office, oficina, consultorio
often, a menudo; muchas veces
oil, petróleo; aceite
old, viejo, antiguo
old-fashioned, a la antigua, anticuado
omit, omitir
on, en, sobre; **on arriving,** al llegar
once, una vez; **at once,** en seguida
one, uno, único; **one by one,** uno a uno
only, único; solamente; **not only ... but also,** no solamente ... sino también
open, abierto; abrir
open-air, al aire libre
operator, telefonista, operador
opportunity, oportunidad, ocasión

343

opposite, opuesto, contrario; frente a, al otro lado de la calle; **opposite sex,** el otro sexo
optimistic, optimista
or, o
orange, naranja
orchestra, orquesta
order, orden, pedido; ordenar, mandar; **in order to,** para; **out of order,** dañado
ordinary, ordinario
organ, órgano
Orient, Oriente
origin, origen
originally, al principio
originate, originar
other, otro
ought to, debería
out, afuera; **out of,** fuera de; **out of order,** dañado
outdoor, al aire libre
outdoors, fuera de casa; al aire libre
outlet, salida
outline, esquema, bosquejo
outnumber, exceder en número
outside, afuera; fuera de
outstanding, destacado
over, directamente encima de
overflow, desbordar
overlook, dominar
owe, deber
own, poseer; ser dueño de
ox, buey
oyster, ostra

Pacific, Pacífico
pack, empacar
package, paquete
packing: meat packing, empacadora de carne
page, página
paint, pintar
pair, par
palm, palma

344

Panamanian, panameño
parade, desfile
paragraph, párrafo
parent, padre o madre
parentheses, paréntesis
Parisian, parisiense
park, parque
Parliament, Parlamento
part, parte
participle, participio
partly, en parte
party, fiesta
pass, pasar
passenger, pasajero
passive, pasivo
past, pasado
path, sendero
patience, paciencia
patriot, patriota
Paul, Pablo
paved, pavimentado
pay (for), pagar
pea, guisante
peace, paz
peak, pico
pedestrian, peatón
pen, pluma, plumafuente
pencil, lápiz
penetrate, penetrar
Pennsylvania, Pensilvania
people, gente, personas
per cent, por ciento
percentage, porcentaje
perfect, perfecto
perfectly, perfectamente
perform, ejecutar, hacer
perhaps, tal vez, quizá(s)
period, período
permanent, permanente
permission, permiso
permit, permitir
persecute, perseguir
persecution, persecución
persist (in), persistir (en)

person, persona
Peruvian, peruano
pet, animal domesticado y acariciado, consentido
petroleum, petróleo
phenomenon, fenómeno
Philippine Islands (the), las Islas Filipinas
philosopher, filósofo
philosophy, filosofía
phone (*colloquial*), teléfono; telefonear
phonetic, fonético
photograph, fotografía
phrase, locución
physical, físico
pick, coger; **pick out,** escoger; **pick up,** recoger, descolgar (*un receptor*)
picnic, merienda al aire libre
picture, cuadro, película, fotografía, representación; **take pictures,** sacar fotografías
picturesque, pintoresco
piece, pedazo
Pilgrim, peregrino
pill, píldora
pineapple, piña
pioneer, colonizador, explorador
pioneeress, colonizadora, exploradora
place, lugar; colocar; **take place,** tener lugar
plain, llanura; llano
plan, proyectar, planear
plane, avión
plantation, plantación
plateau, altiplanicie
play, pieza teatral; jugar, divertirse, tocar
pleasant, agradable
please, sírvase, haga el favor de
pleased, contento
pleasure, placer, gusto

plenty of, mucho(s), bastante
pocket, bolsillo
poetry, poesía
point, punto
Pole, polonés
policy: Good Neighbor Policy, Política del Buen Vecino
polish, pulir
polite, cortés
political, político
pond, estanque
poor, pobre
population, población
porch, pórtico
port, puerto
position, posición
possess, poseer
possession, posesión
possessive, posesivo
possessor, poseedor
possibility, posibilidad
possible, posible
possibly, posiblemente
post office, casa de correos
postman, cartero
potato, papa
pottery, alfarería
pound, libra
power, energía (eléctrica)
powerhouse, planta de la energía
practical, práctico
practically, prácticamente
practice, práctica
precede, preceder
predicate, predicado
predominate, predominar
prefer, preferir
preference, preferencia
prefix, prefijo
preliminary, preliminario
prepare, preparar
preposition, preposición
prescription, fórmula, receta
presence, presencia

present, regalo; presente; presentar
preserve, conservar
president, presidente
pretty, bonito, lindo
prevailing, predominante
prevent, impedir
preview, trailer, escenas de un estreno exhibidas anticipadamente
price, precio
primary, primario
principally, principalmente
printer, impresor
prisoner, prisionero
private, particular
prize, premio
probability, probabilidad
probably, probablemente
proceed, proseguir
produce, producir
product, producto
profession, profesión
profound, profundo
program, programa
progress, progreso
progressive, progresista
project, proyecto
promise, promesa; prometer
promptly, puntualmente
pronoun, pronombre
pronounce, pronunciar
pronounceable, pronunciable
pronunciation, pronunciación
proof, prueba
proper, propio
propose, proponer
prosperity, prosperidad
prosperous, próspero
protect, proteger
proud, orgulloso
provide, proveer
province, provincia
public, público

publishing house, casa editorial
Puget Sound, Puget Sound (*nombre de un estrecho grande*)
Pullman, coche dormitorio
pulse, pulso
pump, bombear
Puritan, puritano
purpose, propósito
put, poner, colocar; **put away,** colocar en su lugar; **put off,** aplazar; **put on,** ponerse (*ropa*); **put out,** apagar, extinguir; **put up with,** tolerar, aguantar

Quaker, cuáquero
quality, calidad
quantity, cantidad
quart, cuarto de galón, poco menos de un litro
quarter, cuarto; moneda de veinticinco centavos; barrio, sección de una ciudad; **French Quarter,** barrio francés
queen, reina
question, pregunta; **question mark,** signo de interrogación
quick, rápido
quickly, rápidamente
quiet, tranquilo
quietly, tranquilamente, en silencio
quite, bastante

radish, rábano
railing, barandilla
railroad, ferrocarril
rain, lluvia; llover
raincoat, impermeable
raise, levantar; criar
ranch, hacienda, hato de ganado
range, cordillera
rapidly, rápidamente
rare, raro; poco cocido
rarely, raramente, rara vez
rather, bastante; más bien; **would rather** (*aux.*), preferiría

ratio, proporción
reach, llegar a
read, leer
reading, lectura
ready, listo
real-estate, de bienes raíces
realize, darse cuenta de
really, verdaderamente
reason, razón
reasonable, razonable
receive, recibir
receiver, receptor, auricular
recent, reciente
recently, recientemente
recognize, reconocer
recommend, recomendar
record, disco; **record player,** fonógrafo, tocadiscos
red, rojo
refer, referirse
refinery, refinería
reflexive, reflejo, reflexivo
refuse, no querer, rehusar
regards, recuerdos
regularly, regularmente
related to, relacionado con
religious, religioso
remain, quedarse
remember, recordar, acordarse de
remind, recordarle a uno
reminder, recuerdo
rent, renta; alquilar, arrendar
repeat, repetir
replace, reemplazar
reply, contestar, replicar
represent, representar
representative, representante; representativo
reproduce, reproducir
republic, república
require, requerir, exigir
resemble, parecerse a
reservation, reservación; territorio reservado para los indios
residence, residencia
resident, residente
residential, residencial
resort, lugar para pasar temporadas
respect, respeto
responsible, responsable
rest, resto, descanso; descansar
restaurant, restaurante
result, resultado; **as a result,** como resultado
return, volver; devolver
reverse, contrario
review, repaso; repasar
revolution, revolución
ribbon, cinta
rice, arroz
rich, rico; fértil
ride, paseo; montar, pasear en vehículo; **ride along,** seguir viajando en cualquier vehículo; **ride horseback,** montar a caballo
right, derecha, derecho; correcto: **all right,** está bien; **right now,** ahora mismo, en este momento
ring, sonar
ripe, maduro
rise, levantarse
rivalry, rivalidad
river, río; **down the river,** río abajo
road, camino, carretera; **take a road,** seguir un camino
Robert, Roberto
rock, roca
rocky, rocoso
roll, rodar
roof, techo, tejada
room, cuarto, alojamiento
rose, rosa
rough, rudo
round, redondo; **the year round,** durante todo el año
route, ruta, camino
routine, rutina

347

rug, alfombra
rule, regla
run, correr; **run into,** dar con
run-down: be run-down, estar agotado
Russian, ruso
rye, centeno

sacred, sagrado
safe, seguro
sail, navegar
sailor, marinero
Saint Louis (St. Louis), San Luis
salad, ensalada
salesman, vendedor
salt, sal
salty, salado
same, mismo
sand dune, duna de arena
sandwich, emparedado
satisfy, satisfacer
Saturday, sábado
save, salvar; ahorrar
say, decir; **that is to say,** es decir
scenery, paisaje
scenic, pintoresco, escénico
scholarship, beca
school, escuela, facultad; **in school,** en la escuela; **school year,** año escolar; **to school,** a la escuela
scientist, hombre de ciencia
sea, mar; **sea food,** mariscos y pescado
seaport, puerto de mar
search, búsqueda; **in search of,** en busca de
season, estación (*del año*)
seat, asiento
second, segundo
secretary, secretario (-a)
sect, secta
section, sección
see, ver; **see about,** ocuparse de; **see through,** calar

seem, parecer
seize, tomar, agarrar, asir
seldom, rara vez
select, escoger
self, mismo
sell, vender
senator, senador
send, enviar, mandar; **send out,** exportar
senior, estudiante del cuarto año de colegio o de universidad
sense, sentido
sentence, frase
separate, separado; separar
separation, separación
September, septiembre
serenade, serenata
serious, serio, formal
seriously, seriamente; **take seriously,** tomar en serio
serve, servir; **serve as,** servir de
set aside, apartar
settle, colonizar, establecerse
settlement, colonia
settler, colono
seven, siete
seventh, séptimo; **the seventh of December,** el siete de diciembre
seventy, setenta
several, varios
shadow, sombra
shake, sacudir; **shake hands,** darse la mano
shallow, poco profundo
shape, forma; formar
share, compartir
shave, afeitarse
sheep, oveja(s)
shine, brillar; pulir, lustrar
ship, nave, buque, vapor
shipbuilding, construcción de barcos
shipping, embarque
shoe, zapato
shop, tienda

shore, orilla
short, corto
shorten, acortar
shot, inyección
show, espectáculo; mostrar
shower, aguacero, baño de ducha
shrimp, camarón, camarones
shrine, lugar sagrado
sick, enfermo
side, lado; **side by side,** uno al lado del otro
sight, vista; **by sight,** de vista
sign, letrero, señal; firmar
signal, señal
signature, firma
significant, significante
silent, silencioso, mudo
silk, seda
silver, plata
similar, semejante, parecido
simply, solamente, sencillamente
simultaneous, simultáneo
since, desde; desde que, puesto que
sing, cantar
singing, canto
single, solo; soltero
single-span, de un tramo o un solo arco
sink, hundir(se)
sir, señor
sister, hermana
sister-in-law, cuñada
sit (down), sentarse; **be sitting,** estar sentado
site, sitio
situated, situado
six, seis
sixteen, diez y seis
sixth, sexto
sixty, sesenta
size, tamaño
skilled, hábil
skirt, falda
sky, cielo

skyscraper, rascacielo
slave, esclavo
sleep, dormir
sleepy: be sleepy, tener sueño
slight, ligero
slope, pendiente
slow, lento
slowly, lentamente, despacio
small, pequeño
smile, sonreír(se)
smoke, fumar
snow, nieve; nevar
snow-capped, nevado
so, tan; así es que; **and so on,** etcétera; **say so,** decir que sí; **so am I,** yo también; **so long,** hasta luego; **so many,** tantos; **so much,** tanto; **so that,** para que, de modo que; **so ... that,** tan ... que
soap, jabón
soft, blando
soil, terreno
soldier, soldado
solid, sólido
some, unos, alguno(s)
somebody, alguien
someone, alguien
something, algo
sometimes, algunas veces
somewhat (*adv.*), algo
son, hijo
song, canción
son-in-law, yerno
soon, pronto; **as soon as,** en cuanto; tan pronto como
sophomore, estudiante del segundo año de colegio o de universidad
sorry: be sorry for, sentirlo (por)
so-so, así así, regular
sound, sonido; **sound equipment,** aparato de sonido
south, sur; al sur; **South America,** la América del Sur; **South**

349

American, sudamericano; **South Carolina,** la Carolina del Sur; **to the south,** hacia el sur **southeastern,** del sudeste de los Estados Unidos
southern, del sur de los Estados Unidos
Southwest, sudoeste de los Estados Unidos
souvenir, recuerdo
Soviet Union (the), la Unión Soviética
Spain, España
Spaniard, español
Spanish, español
speak, hablar
speaker, el que habla; interlocutor, orador
special, especial
specialty, especialidad
spectacle, espectáculo
spectacular, espectacular
speech, discurso, habla
speed, velocidad
spelling, deletreo, ortografía
spend, gastar, pasar
spice, especia
spider, araña
spirit, espíritu
spite: in spite of, a pesar de
splendid, espléndido
sport, deporte
spot, mancha, sitio; **high spots,** puntos importantes
spread, extender
spring, primavera
square, plaza; cuadrado
stairs, escalera
stamp, estampilla, sello
stand, estar de pie, ponerse de pie; **stand in line,** hacer cola; **stand (up),** ponerse de pie, estar de pie
star, estrella

start, empezar, comenzar; **start to school,** empezar la escuela; **start out,** ponerse en marcha
state, estado
stately, majestuoso
statement, frase declarativa
statesman, estadista
station, estación (*radio o ferrocarril*)
statue, estatua
stay, quedarse, alojarse; **stay long,** demorar; **stay overnight,** pasar la noche, pernoctar
steak, biftec
steal, robar
steam, vapor
steel, acero; **steel mill,** fábrica de acero
steep, muy inclinado
steeple, campanario
step, peldaño
stepchild, hijastro
stepfather, padrastro
stepmother, madrastra
stethoscope, estetoscopio
still, todavía
stocking, media
stockyard, corral de ganado, matadero
stomach-ache, dolor de estómago
stone, piedra
stop, escala, parada; parar(se), detenerse, demorarse; dejar de (*hacer algo*)
store, almacén, tienda; **department store,** gran almacén; **grocery store,** almacén de víveres, **shoe store,** zapatería
story, cuento, historia; piso
straight, derecho; **straight ahead,** todo derecho
strait, estrecho
strange, extraño
stranger, extranjero, forastero
stream, río, corriente

street, calle
streetcar, tranvía
stress, énfasis; dar énfasis a
stretch, extenderse
strong, fuerte
structure, construcción
student, estudiante
study, estudio; estudiar
style, estilo
subject, sujeto
subjunctive, subjuntivo
subordinate, subordinado
substitute, substituto; substituir
suburb, suburbio, pueblo contiguo a la ciudad
subway, ferrocarril subterráneo
succeed (in), lograr, tener éxito (en)
successful: be successful (in), lograr, tener éxito (en)
such, tal; **such a,** tal; **such as,** tal(es) como
suffix, sufijo
sugar, azúcar
suggest, sugerir
suggestion, sugestión
suit, traje, vestido sastre
sum, suma
summer, verano
sun, sol; **sun oneself,** tomar el sol
Sunday, domingo
sunset, puesta del sol
sunshine, luz del sol, solana
superlative, superlativo
supper, cena
supply, suministrar
suppose, suponer
supreme, supremo
sure, seguro
surely, seguramente
surface, superficie
surname, apellido
surprise, sorpresa; sorprender; **by surprise,** de sorpresa; **surprised at,** sorprendido de

surround, rodear, circundar; **surrounded by,** rodeado de; **surrounding,** que rodea
survive, sobrevivir
suspend, suspender
suspension (*adj.*), colgante
Sweden, Suecia
swim, nadar; **swim across,** atravesar nadando
swimming, natación; **go swimming,** ir a bañarse
swing, balancear(se), mecer(se)
switch, interruptor
Switzerland, Suiza
syllabication, silabeo
symbol, símbolo
symbolize, simbolizar
symphony, sinfonía
synonymous, sinónimo
system, sistema

tabernacle, tabernáculo
table, mesa; **table lamp,** lámpara de mesa
tailor, sastre
take, tomar, llevar; **it takes a day,** se necesita un día; **take a course,** seguir un curso; **take a long way,** seguir un camino indirecto; **take a ride,** dar un paseo (en auto); **take a road,** seguir un camino; **take a trip,** hacer un viaje; **take a walk,** dar un paseo (a pie); **take after,** parecerse a; **take an examination,** sufrir examen; **take back,** devolver; **take care of,** cuidar; **take charge of,** encargarse de; **take lessons,** recibir lecciones; **take life easy,** llevar una vida despaciosa; **take off,** quitar(se) (*ropa*); **take out,** sacar; **take pictures,** sacar fotografías; **take place,**

351

tener lugar; **take seriously**, tomar en serio; **taken,** ocupado
talk, hablar
tall, alto; **how tall?** ¿ (de) qué estatura?
tame, manso
tannery, tenería, curtiduría
tax, impuesto
taxation, imposición de tributos
tea, té
teach, enseñar
teacher, profesor, maestro
tear, romper, rasgar
technology, tecnología
telegram, telegrama
telephone, teléfono; telefonear; **telephone book,** lista de teléfonos; guía telefónica
tell, decir, contar; **tell about,** contar; **tell fortunes,** decir la buenaventura
temperature, temperatura
temple, templo
ten, diez; **ten minutes to two,** las dos menos diez
tenaciously, tenazmente
tendency, tendencia
tennis, tenís
tense, tiempo (*de un verbo*)
tenth, décimo
term, término, vocablo
terrace, terraza
Texan, tejano
Texas, Tejas
textile mill, fábrica de tejidos
than, que (*en comparaciones*)
thank, agradecer; **thank goodness,** ¡ gracias a Dios !; **thank you (very much),** (muchas) gracias; **thanks,** gracias; **thanks a million,** un millón de gracias
that, ese, aquel; eso; que; **that is to say,** es decir; **that one,** ése, aquél

the, el, la, los, las
theater, teatro
then, entonces; pues
there, allí, allá; **there is, there are,** hay
therefore, por eso
thermometer, termómetro
these, estos, estas; éstos, éstas
thick, espeso, grueso
thief, ladrón
thin, delgado
thing, cosa
think, pensar; **think about (of),** pensar en; **think of** (*opinion*), pensar de; **think of going,** pensar ir
third, tercero
thirteen, trece
thirty, treinta
Thirty-fourth Street, Calle treinta y cuatro
this, este, esta; esto; **this one,** éste, ésta
those, esos, esas, aquellos, aquellas; ésos, ésas, aquéllos, aquéllas
though, aunque
thousand, mil
three, tres
thriving, próspero
throat, garganta; **have a sore throat,** dolerle a uno la garganta
through, por, a través de
throw, echar, lanzar
thunder, trueno
Thursday, jueves
thus, así
ticket, billete, boleto
timber, bosques, madera
time, tiempo, hora, vez; **have a good time,** divertirse; **have a wonderful time,** divertirse de lo lindo; **in time (for),** a tiempo (para); **on time,** a

tiempo; **what time?** ¿ (a) qué hora?
tip, propina; dar una propina
tired, cansado
title, título, grado
to, a, hasta, para
tobacco, tabaco
today, hoy
toe, dedo del pie
together, juntos
tomb, tumba
tomorrow, mañana; **tomorrow morning,** mañana por la mañana
ton, tonelada
tone, tono
tongue, lengua
tonic, tónico, medicamento
tonight, esta noche
too, también, demasiado; **too many,** demasiados; **too much,** demasiado
tool, herramienta
tooth, diente
toothache, dolor de muelas
top, parte superior
touch, tocar
tourist, turista
toward, hacia
tower, elevarse
town, ciudad, pueblo; **home town,** ciudad natal o en donde ha crecido uno
toy, juguete
tradition, tradición
traffic, tráfico
train, tren; **train the ear,** educar el oído
transfer, billete de transbordo; transbordar
transitive, transitivo
transitively, transitivamente
translate, traducir
translation, traducción

transportation, transporte
travel, viajar
traveler, viajero
treatment, explicación
tree, árbol
tremendous, tremendo
tribal, de la tribu
tribe, tribu
tributary, afluente, tributario
trip, viaje; **take a trip,** hacer un viaje
tropics, trópico
truck, camión
true, verdad; verdadero
trunk, baúl
truth, verdad
try, tratar de; **try on,** probarse
Tuesday, martes
tuition, precio de la enseñanza
tunnel, túnel
turn, turno; dar vuelta, doblar; **be one's turn,** tocarle a uno; **turn off,** apagar; **turn on,** encender
twelve, doce
twenty, veinte
Twenty-first Street, Calle veinte y una
Twenty-second Street, Calle veinte y dos
twice, dos veces
twin, gemelo, mellizo
two, dos
type, tipo; escribir a máquina
typical, típico

ugliness, fealdad
ugly, feo
umbrella, paraguas
unbelievable, increíble
unbreakable, irrompible
uncle, tío
under, directamente debajo de
understand, comprender, entender

353

unfinished, incompleto, no acabado
unforgettable, inolvidable
unfriendly, poco amistoso
unique, distinto, singular, único en su género
unit, unidad
United States, Estados Unidos
university, universidad
unknown, desconocido
unless, a menos que
unlike, diferente de
unloading, descargue
unnecessary, innecesario
unstressed, atono
until, hasta; hasta que
up, arriba, hacia arriba; **up the river,** río arriba
upon, en, sobre
upper, superior
upstairs, arriba en una casa o edificio
urge, urgir, persuadir
usage, uso
use, uso; usar
used to, acostumbrado a; solía (*auxiliar del tiempo imperfecto*); **be used to,** estar acostumbrado a; **get used to,** acostumbrarse a
useful, útil
usually, usualmente, generalmente

vacation, vacaciones
valley, valle
variation, variación
varied, variado
variety, variedad
various, vario, de varias clases
vegetable, legumbre, verdura
vegetation, vegetación
Venezuelan, venezolano
verb, verbo
vertically, verticalmente
very, muy
vibration, vibración

vicinity, vecindad
victory, victoria
view, vista
village, aldea, población pequeña
visit, visitar
visitor, visitante
vitamin, vitamina
vocabulary, vocabulario
vocal cords, cuerdas vocales
voice, voz
voiced, con voz
voiceless, sin voz, mudo
volcano, volcán
volition, voluntad
volume, volumen
vote, votar
vowel, vocal

wagon, carreta de tracción animal
wait (for), esperar; **wait on,** atender (*a uno*)
waiter, camarero
waiting room, sala de espera
wake, despertarse; **wake up,** despertarse
walk, paseo; pasear, andar; **go for a walk,** ir a pasear(se) (a pie); **take a walk,** dar un paseo (a pie); **walk up,** subir a pie, trepar
wall, pared, tapia, muralla
want, querer
war, guerra
warm, caluroso, caliente; **be warm,** hacer calor, tener calor
warn, prevenir, advertir
wash, lavar(se); **wash one's hands,** lavarse las manos
washable, lavable
wastebasket, cesto para papeles
watch, reloj; observar
water, agua; **fresh water,** agua dulce; **water front,** tierra

ribereña; **water power,** energía hidráulica
waterway, vía fluvial
way, manera, modo; **all the way to,** (toda la distancia) hasta; **by the way,** a propósito; **by way of,** por la vía de; **come a long way,** recorrer una distancia larga; **in this way,** de esta manera; **on the way to,** en camino de; rumbo a; **take a long way,** seguir un camino indirecto; **that way,** así
wealth, riqueza
wealthy, rico
wear, llevar, usar (*ropa*)
weary, muy cansado
weather, tiempo
Wednesday, miércoles
week, semana; **week end,** fin de semana
weigh, pesar
weight, peso
welcome: you're welcome, no hay de que
well, bien, pues; **as well as,** así como; **well done,** bien cocida (*carne*)
west, oeste; al oeste; **Far West,** Lejano Oeste; **to the west,** hacia el oeste
western, del oeste de los Estados Unidos
westward, hacia el oeste
wet: get wet, mojarse
wharf (*pl.* **wharves**), muelle
what, lo que; ¿qué? ¿cuál?; **what a long time!** ¡qué tiempo tan largo!; **What can I do for you?** ¿Qué se le ofrece?; **what...for?** ¿por qué? ¿para qué?; **What's new?** ¿Qué hay de nuevo?
wheat, trigo
when, cuando; ¿cuándo?

where, dónde; ¿dónde? dónde? ¿en dónde
whereas, mientras que
whether, si
which, que, el cual; ¿cuál?
while, rato; mientras
white, blanco
who, quien(es); ¿quién(es)?
whole, entero
whom, a quien, que; ¿a quién?; **from (of) whom,** de quien; ¿de quién?; **to whom,** a quien; ¿a quién?
whose, de quien, cuyo; ¿de quién?
why, ¿por qué?
wide, ancho; **five miles wide,** cinco millas de ancho
width, anchura
wife, esposa
wilderness, tierra silvestre
willing, dispuesto; **be willing to,** querer, consentir en
willingness, buena voluntad
win, ganar
wind, viento
window, ventana
windy, ventoso
wine, vino
winter, invierno
wisdom, sabiduría
wish, deseo; desear; **I wish that ...,** Ojalá (que) ...
with, con
within, dentro (de)
without, sin; sin que
woman, mujer
wonder, maravilla; preguntarse
wonderful, maravilloso; **have a wonderful time,** divertirse de lo lindo
wood, madera
woods, bosque(s)
wool, lana
word, palabra

355

work, trabajo; trabajar
world, mundo
worried, preocupado
worse, peor (*comparativo*)
worship, adorar, venerar
worst, (el) peor (*superlativo*)
worth: **be worth,** valer
worthless, sin valor
worthy, digno
write, escribir
writing, escritura, letra; **informal writing,** estilo familiar
wrong, equivocado, errado

yard, patio; espacio alrededor de una casa
year, año
yellow, amarillo
yes, sí
yesterday, ayer; **yesterday morning,** ayer por la mañana
yet, todavía; sin embargo
yield, producir
young, joven; **young people,** los jóvenes

zone, zona

SPANISH–ENGLISH

a, to, at, in
abrigo, coat
abrir, to open
aceptar, to accept
acercarse (a), to approach
acostumbraba, (I, *etc.*) used to
además de, besides
adivinar, to guess
agotado, run-down
agua, water
ahora, now
algo, something
alguien, someone, somebody; anyone, anybody
almacén, store
alto, high, tall
allí, there
americano, American
amigo (-a), friend
anoche, last night
anteojos, glasses
antes de, before
antes de que, before
anticipación: con anticipación, in advance
año, year
apellido, surname, last name
aprender, to learn
aquel (-lla), that; *pl.*, those
aquél (-lla), that one; *pl.*, those
aquí, here
arrendar, to rent
asistir (a), to attend
atravesar, to go through
automóvil, automobile, car
avisar, to let know
azul, blue

bailar, to dance
bajarse (de), to get off (*the bus*)
billete, bill, ticket
biografía, biography
bonito, pretty
borrador, eraser
buque, boat; **buque de carga,** freight boat, freighter

café, coffee
calle, street
cama, bed; **en la cama,** in bed
cambiar, to change
campo, country
carta, letter
cartero, postman, mailman
casa, house, home
casado (-a), married
catarata, waterfall; **las cataratas del Niágara,** Niagara Falls
centavo, cent
cerca de, near
cerrar, to close, shut
cerveza, beer
cinco, five
cincuenta, fifty
cine, movies
cita, appointment
ciudad, city
claro, light
clase, class
comprar, to buy
compromiso, engagement
con, with
conferencia, lecture
conocer, to know, meet
conseguir, to get

contestar, to answer
corral de ganado, stockyard
cortar, to cut
cosa, thing; **cosas que hacer,** things to do
costa, coast
costar, to cost
costumbre, custom
creer, to believe, think; **creo que sí,** I believe so, I think so
cuaderno, notebook
¿cuál(es)? what? which? which one(s)?
cualquiera, anyone, anybody
cuando, when
¿cuándo? when?
¿cuánto? how much?; *pl.*, how many?; **¿cuánto tiempo?** how long?
cuñado, brother-in-law

cheque, check
chófer, driver

dañado, out of order (*telephone*)
dar, to give; **darse por vencido,** to give up
de, of, from, off
debajo de, under, below
deber, must; **(yo) debería,** (I) should, ought to
decir, to say, tell
delante de, in front of
depender (de), to depend (on)
dependiente, clerk
desayuno, breakfast
descansar, to rest
desde (que), since
después de (que), after
diez, ten
diferente (de), different (from)
difícil, difficult, hard
dinero, money

Dios, God
dirección, address
divertirse, to have a good time
dólar, dollar
doler, to ache; **me duele una muela,** my tooth aches, I have a toothache
domingo, Sunday
¿dónde? where?
dos, two
durante, during

echar de menos, to miss
edificio, building
el (la, lo, los, las), the
él, he, it; (*after prep.*) him, it
ella, she, it; (*after prep.*) her, it
ellos (-as), they; (*after prep.*) them
emparedado, sandwich; **hacer emparedados,** to make sandwiches
empezar, to begin, start
en, in, at; **en casa,** at home; **en cuanto,** as soon as
encima de, over, above
encontrar, to meet, find
enfermo, ill, sick
enfurecer, to make angry
ensalada, salad
enseñar, to teach
entrar (en), to enter, go in(to)
entre, between, among
escribir, to write
ese (-a), that; *pl.*, those
ése (-a), that one; *pl.*, those
esfuerzo, effort; **hacer un esfuerzo,** to make an effort
eso, that
esperar, to wait, hope, expect; **espero que sí,** I hope so
esposa, wife
esposo, husband
esquina, corner
estación, station
estampilla, stamp

estar, to be
este (-a), this; *pl.,* these
éste (-a), this one; *pl.,* these
esto, this
estudiante, student
estudiar, to study

fácil, easy
falta, mistake, error; **hacer faltas,** to make mistakes *or* errors
familia, family
feliz, happy
fiesta, party
fin, end; **al fin,** finally, at last
firma, signature
frase, sentence
frente a, opposite
fundar, to found

gracias, thanks, thank you
grande, large, big; great
guante, glove
guerra, war
gustar, to like, please; **¿ le gustaría ... ?** would you like ... ?
gusto, pleasure; **mucho gusto en haberlo visto,** (I am) very glad to have seen you

haber, to have
habitante, inhabitant
hacer, to do, make; to be (*weather*); to have (*causal*); **hace calor, frío,** *etc.,* it is warm, cold, *etc.;* **hace un año,** a year ago; **hace un año que** (*presente del verbo*), for a year; **hacer un favor,** to do a favor; **hacerse entender,** to make oneself understood; **hacía un año que** (*copretérito del verbo*), for a year; **hágame el favor de ... ,** please; **hizo llevarlo a su hija,** she had *or* made her daughter wear it
hacia, toward

hasta, until, as far as; **hasta luego,** good-bye; **hasta que,** until
hay, there is, there are
hermana, sister
hermano, brother
hija, daughter
historia, history
hora, hour, time; **¿ Qué hora es?** What time is it?
hoy, today

industria, industry
inglés, English
interesante, interesting
invierno, winter
invitación, invitation
ir, to go

Jaime, James
Juan, John
jugo, juice
junto a, next to

lado, side; **al lado de,** beside, at the side of
lago, lake; **los Grandes Lagos,** the Great Lakes
lámpara, lamp
lana, wool
largo, long; **¡ Qué tiempo tan largo !** What a long time!
lección, lesson
leer, to read
lejos de, far from
libro, book
limpiar, to clean
lista, list; **lista de teléfonos,** telephone directory
lo (*dir. obj.*), it; him, you (*S.A.*): **lo que,** what
lustrar, to shine (*shoes*)

llamar, to call
llave, key
llegar, to arrive

llevar, to carry, wear
llover, to rain

madre, mother
mañana, morning; tomorrow
más, more, most; **no ... más,** any more, any longer
médico, doctor
mes, month; **al mes, por mes,** a month
mesa, table
mi(s), my
minuto, minute
mío (-a, -os, -as), mine; **el mío,** *etc.*, mine
montaña, mountain
muchacho, boy
mucho, much (*pl.*, many), a great deal (of), a lot (of); hard
mundo, world
muy, very

nacionalidad, nationality
nada, nothing, anything
nadie, no one, nobody
naranja, orange
necesitar, to need
niño, child; *pl.*, children
no, no, not
nombre, name
noticiero, newsreel
novela, novel
nuestro (-a, -os, -as), our; ours; **el nuestro,** *etc.*, ours
nuevo, new

obscuro, dark
ofrecer, to offer; **¿ Qué se le ofrece?** What can I do for you?
olvidar(se), to forget
orden, order
otro, other, another

padre, father
país, country

palabra, word
par, pair, couple; **un par de días,** a couple of days
para, for (*with noun*); in order to, to (*with verb*)
parar, to stop
pardo, brown
parecer, to appear, seem; **¿ Qué (tal) le parece?** How do you like it?
parque, park
parte, part
pasar, to pass, spend (*time*); to happen
pedir, to ask (for)
película, movie, picture
pelo, hair; **hacerse cortar el pelo,** to have one's hair cut
pequeño, small, little
perfectamente, perfectly
pero, but
perro, dog
persona, person
plata, silver
plato, plate
pluma, pen
poco, little; *pl.*, few; **poco a poco,** little by little
poder, to be able, can
ponerse, to put on
por, for, by, through; **por semana,** a week
¿ por qué? why?
porque, because
precio, price
preferir, to prefer
pregunta, question; **hacer una pregunta,** to ask a question
preparar, to prepare
presidente, president
prestar, to lend
primo (-a), cousin
profesor (-a), teacher, professor
programa, program

pronto, soon
pronunciación, pronunciation
pronunciar, to pronounce
puerta, door

¿ qué? what?
quedarse, to stay, remain
querer, to want, wish; **¿ Quiere Vd. que yo ... ?** Shall I ... ?
¿ quién? who? whom?; **¿ de quién?** of whom? whose?

recibir, to receive, get
repetir, to repeat
resfriado, cold
respirar, to breathe; **respirar profundo,** to take a deep breath
río, river

sábado, Saturday
saber, to know
sacar (de), to take out (of)
salir (de), to leave, go out (of)
saltar (por), to jump (out of)
seda, silk
seguro, sure, certain
semana, week; **la semana pasada,** last week; **por, a la semana,** a week
sentarse, to sit (down); **sentarse en luneta,** to sit on the main floor
sentir, to be sorry
señor, gentleman, man, Mr.; **los señores Miller,** the Millers, Mr. and Mrs. Miller
señora, Mrs.
ser, to be
servir, to serve; **creo que servirán,** I think they will do
siempre, always
significar, to mean
simpático, friendly
sirvienta, servant, maid
sofá, sofa, couch

solo, alone, by himself
sombrero, hat
su(s), his, her, its, your, their
sufrir, to suffer; **sufrir examen,** to take an examination
suponer, to suppose
suyo (-a, -os, -as), his, hers, yours, theirs; **el suyo,** *etc.*, his, hers, yours, theirs

también, also, too, so
tampoco, (not) ... either; **ni ... tampoco,** neither, not either
tan ... como, as ... as, so ... as
tanto (-a), as much, so much; *pl.*, as many, so many
tarde, afternoon; late; **no más tarde que,** by, no later than
tarea, homework; **hacer la tarea,** to do the homework
tarjeta, card; **tarjeta de visita,** calling card
taza, cup
teatro, theater
teléfono, telephone
temprano, early
tener, to have; **¿ Qué tiene Vd.?** What's the matter with you?; **tener cuidado,** to be careful; **tener que,** to have to, must; **tener planes para,** to plan to
terminar, to finish, end
tiempo, time; **a tiempo,** on time; **a tiempo para,** in time for; **mucho tiempo,** a long time
todavía, yet, still
todo (*pron.*), everything, all
todos (-as), all, every; **everyone,** everybody
tomar, to take; eat, drink, have; **tomar en serio,** to take seriously
tomate, tomato
trabajo, work; **hacer el trabajo,** to do the work

traducir, to translate
tráfico, traffic
traje, suit
tranvía, streetcar
tratar (de), to try
través: a través de, through
tres, three

un(o), una, a, one; *pl.*, some
usado, common
usar, to use

varios, several
vaso, glass
veinte, twenty
venir, to come

ver, to see; **ir a ver quién llamaba a la puerta,** to answer the door
verano, summer
verde, green
vestido, dress
vez, time; **a veces,** at times
viaje, trip
vidrio, glass
viejo, old
vista, view
vivir, to live
volver, to return
vuelta: a la vuelta de, around

ya, already

zapato, shoe

INDEX

References are to page numbers.

a great deal of, 77–78
a lot of, 77–78
about, 257–258
above, 79–80
adjective clauses, 229–232
adjectives: comparison of, 132–137; demonstrative, 53–54; form of, 9; past participles used as, 177; position of, 9; possessive, 50–2
adverbial clauses, 242–248
adverbs: comparison of, 132–137; formed from adjectives, 76; of frequency, 42–43; position of, 76–77
after: as conjunction, 242–243; as preposition, 62–63
ago, 156–157
alike, 134–135
already, 196–197
among, 90
any, 120–122
any longer, 196
anybody, 235–237
anyone, 235–237
anything, 235–237
arrive: with preposition **in** or **at,** 18–19
articles: forms of, definite and indefinite, 7–8; omission of definite, 27–29; uses of indefinite, 13–14, 29–30
as . . . as, 133–134
as far as, 62–63
at, 18–19, 62–63, 80, 256–258
auxiliary verbs: **can,** 167–169; **could,** 167–169; **did,** 59–61; **do, does,** 25–26, 38, 40; **had better,** 192–194; in shortened sentences, 202–207; in translations of ¿no es verdad? 95–97; **may,** 168–170; **might,** 168–170; of obligation, 177–180; **shall,** 157–159; **should,** 159–161, 179–180; **will,** 94–95, 157–159; **would,** 159–161; **would rather,** 192–4

be: be used to, 194–195; in negations, 39–40, 48–49; in passive voice, 174–177; in questions, 19, 48–49; in shortened sentences, 202–207; past tense, 48–49; present tense, 9; with past participle used as adjective, 177
before: as conjunction, 242–243; as preposition, 62–63
behind, 30
below, 79–80
beside, 30
besides, 30
between, 90
by, 114–116; *see* 257

can, 167–169
capitalization, 321
cardinal numerals, 316–317
cause: adverbial clauses of, 245–246; use of **have** and **get** with meaning of, 287–289
clauses: adjective, 229–230; adverbial, 242–248, 253–256; definition of, 212–213; noun, 213–217
comparison of adjectives and adverbs, 132–137
concession, adverbial clauses of, 244–245
conditional: perfect tense, 160; sentences, 253–256; tense, 159–161
conjugation of regular verbs, 309–314

363

contractions: **be,** 9, 39–40, 48; **can,** 167–168; **could,** 167–168; **do,** 38, 40, 59–60; **had better,** 192–193; **have,** 151–152, 166; **must,** 178; **shall,** 158; **should,** 160; **will,** 158; **would,** 160; **would rather,** 192–193
could, 168–170

days of the week, 318; used with preposition **on,** 17–18
dead, 153
demonstrative adjectives and pronouns, 53–54
died, 153
different (from), 134–135, 258
do: as auxiliary verb, 38, 40, 59–61; as principal verb, 284

either: in shortened sentences, 207
ever, 42–43
everybody, 234–235
everyone, 234–235

far from, 30
few, 136–137
for, 97–99, 155–156, 258
from, 44, 257–258
future indicative, 49–50, 94–95, 157–159; perfect tense, 159

gender of adjectives, pronouns, nouns, 6
gerund, 274–276; after prepositions, 97, 115, 256–258
get, 152, 288–290
going to: used with **be** to express future time, 49

had better: as auxiliary verb, 192–193
hanged, 153
have: as auxiliary verb, 286–288;
364

as principal verb, 287–288; **have to,** 177–178; in shortened sentences, 202–207; interrogative, 25–26; negative, 38; present tense, 9
how: used with adjectives and adverbs, 89–90
hung, 153

imperative forms, 85–86
in, 17–19, 80, 257; after superlative, 135
in front of, 30
in order to, 97
infinitive: after **make, let, help,** and verbs of the senses, 217–218; as substitute for Spanish subjunctive, 122–123
into, 80
irregular verbs: lists of, 72–75, 152–153, 314–316
it: as object pronoun, 16–17; as subject pronoun, 7, 109–111

less, 132–133, 136
like: as preposition in comparisons, 134–135; as verb, 26–27
little, 136
lots of, 77–78

make, 152, 284–286
many, 77–78
may, 168–170; **may have,** 169
measure: indefinite article in expressions of, 13–14, 29
might, 169–170; **might have,** 169
months: names of, 318; with preposition **in,** 17–19; with preposition **on** in dates, 17–19
more: in comparisons, 132–133, 136
most: in comparisons, 132–133, 136
much, 77–78, 136
must, 178–179; **must have,** 179

near, 30
neither: in shortened sentences, 207
news: with singular verb, 16
no, 40–41
¿ no es verdad? 95–97, 203–204
no one, 235
nobody, 235–237
not, 38–39, 41–42
nothing, 235–237
nouns: gender of, 6; plural forms of, 8, 15–16; used as adjectives, 61–62

objects: direct and indirect, order of, 86–88; direct, followed by a noun, adjective, or past participle, 218–219; pronoun, 16–17
of, 43–44, 257–258
off, 90
ojalá, 273–274
on, 17–19, 257
one: as indefinite pronoun, 234; used after an adjective, 112
opposite, 30
order of words: adjectives, 61–62; adverbs of frequency, 42–43; adverbs of place, manner, and time, 76–77; direct and indirect objects, 86–88; in affirmative questions, 19, 25–26, 59–61; in affirmative statements, 5–6; in negative questions, 40, 59–61; in negative statements, 38–39, 59–61
ordinal numerals, 317; order of, used with cardinal numerals, 61–62
ought to, 180
out of, 80–81

past participle: as adjective after **be,** 177; in passive voice, 175–177; of irregular verbs, 152–153; of regular verbs, 151

past perfect tense: indicative, 165–167; subjunctive, 274
past tense: indicative, 18, 58–59, 72–75; subjunctive, 273–274; with **ing,** 48–49, 124
people: with plural verb, 16
possessive nouns, adjectives, and pronouns, 50–52
prepositions: **at, from, in, of, on,** etc.; after certain verbs, adjectives, and past participles, 256–258; at end of adjective clauses, 231–232; at end of questions, 233; with gerund, 97–115, 256–258
present participle: after verbs of the senses, 217; with **be,** 10–11, 48–49, 155–157, 167
present perfect tense, 151–157
present tense: indicative, 9–11; subjunctive, 270–272
principal parts of irregular verbs, 152–153, 314–316
pronouns: demonstrative, 53–54; gender of, 6; indefinite, 234–236; **it** as subject pronoun, 109–110; object, 16–17; possessive, 51–52; reflexive, 112–113; subject, 7
purpose: adverbial clauses of, 246–247; expressed by **in order to, to, for,** 97

quantity: expressions of, 43, 77–78
questions, 19, 25, 40, 42–43, 48, 53, 59–60, 75; indirect, 214–217; **¿ no es verdad?** 95–97; with **how,** 89–90; with preposition at end, 233; with **what ... for,** 99; with **which** or **what,** 111–112

reflexive pronouns, 112–113
result: adverbial clauses of, 247–248

365

same: the same as, 133-134
say, 87-88
seasons: names of, 318; with preposition **in**, 17-18
shall, 157-159
shined, 154
shone, 154
shortened sentences with **be, have,** auxiliaries, and certain other verbs, 202-207
should, 159-161, 179-180; **should have**, 180
similar (to), 134-135
since: as conjunction, 245-246; as preposition with present perfect tense, 155
so: in shortened sentences, 205-206, 213-214
so ... as: in comparisons, 133
some, 120-122
somebody, 235-237
someone, 235-237
spelling: some rules for, 319-320
states of the United States of America with abbreviations, 318-319
still: position of, 195
subjunctive tenses: past, 273-274; past perfect, 274; present, 270-2
superlative, 135-137
syllabication, 321

take, 290-291
tell, 87-88
tenses, *see* present, past, etc.; *see also* Appendix
that: as demonstrative adjective and pronoun, 53-54; in adjective clauses, 229-232; omission of, 213, 230-232
there is (are), 19
these: as demonstrative adjective and pronoun, 53-54
this: as demonstrative adjective and pronoun, 53-54

366

those: as demonstrative adjective and pronoun, 53-54
through, 80
time: adverbial clauses of, 242-243; adverbs of, position, 76-77; measure of, with indefinite article, 13-14, 29; prepositions used in expressions of, 17-19
to, 62-63, 80; with certain verbs in shortened sentences, 207; with infinitive to express purpose, 97
too: in shortened sentences, 205-206
toward, 80

under, 79-80
until: as conjunction, 242-243; as preposition, 62-63
upon, 90
used to, 75, 194

verbs: multiple uses of **do, make, have, get, take**, 283-291; conjugation of regular verbs and principal parts of irregular verbs, *see* Appendix; two-word verbs, 296-299; *see also* present tense, past tense, etc.
voice: active, 309-312; passive, 174-177, 312-314

what: interrogative, 111-112
what ... for, 99
which: in adjective clauses, 229-232; interrogative, 111-112
whose, 53-54, 229-232
will, 94-95, 157-159
with, 257-258
word order, *see* order
would, 159-161
would rather, 193

yet: position of, 196